Environment and Development:
An Economic Approach

Economy & Environment

VOLUME 6

The titles published in this series are listed at the end of this volume.

Environment and Development: An Economic Approach

by

Jan Bojö
The World Bank,
Washington D.C., U.S.A.

Karl-Göran Mäler
The Beijer Institute,
Stockholm School of Economics,
Stockholm, Sweden

and

Lena Unemo
Swedish International Development Authority (SIDA),
Stockholm, Sweden

Springer-Science+Business Media, B.V.

Library of Congress Cataloging-in-Publication Data

Bojö, Jan.
Environment and development : an economic approach / by Jan Bojö, Karl-Göran Mäler, Lena Unemo.
p. cm. -- (Economy & environment ; 6)
Includes bibliographical references and index.
ISBN 978-90-481-4181-4
1. Economic development--Environmental aspects. I. Mäler, Karl-Göran. II. Unemo, Lena. III. Title. IV. Series.
HD75.6.B65 1992
333.7'2--dc20 92-21700

ISBN 978-90-481-4181-4 ISBN 978-94-015-8008-3 (eBook)
DOI 10.1007/978-94-015-8008-3

Printed on acid-free paper

Foreword

This book is the second edition of a text based on a report commissioned by the Swedish International Development Authority (SIDA). The financial grant from SIDA which made the work possible is hereby gratefully acknowledged.

There are already many books on the market about environmental economics, some of them very good. What is special about this one? We do not claim to have obtained new results, but we have our own way of presenting the subject matter. In particular, we are of the opinion that *policy failures* are often overlooked as an obstacle to efficient environmental management. Although the main emphasis in this book is on project level analysis, it is essential that such analyses be linked to an understanding of the (dis)incentives for environmental improvements that general economic and particular environmental policies provide.

Another essential feature of the book, although this is not unique, is the links provided between theory and empirical illustrations. We hope that this will illustrate to our readers the practical usefulness, but also the difficulties, of applying economics to environmental problems. In particular we hope that the text can be of interest to decision-makers, development programme personnel, teachers and the general public interested in how economics can contribute to better environmental decision-making. In principle, this book can be read by anyone interested in the subject matter, without any formal education in economics. However, some background in microeconomic theory makes the reading easier.

The second edition of the book has been extended to include a chapter on management of environmental resources and environmental policy instruments. The chapter also includes a discussion on common property resources, a subject which was only briefly dealt with in the first edition of the book. Two case studies concerning policy failures have been added to the last chapter of the book. Finally, several corrections of misprintings found in the first edition have been made. Undoubtedly some misprintings remain, and some new may have appeared. They are the responsibility of the authors.

The authors share a collective responsibility for the book. The group has been chaired by Mäler. The main responsibility for drafting specific chapters has been divided as follows: Bojö; chapters 1, 2, 3 and 5, Mäler; chapters 4 and 6, and Unemo; chapter 7. Unemo has also compiled a substantial portion of the literature surveyed in this book.

The authors have basically typed their own chapters, but we want to thank Kerstin Niklasson and Britt Rosen for editing assistance. We also thank Lucy Loerzer, Tamara Carlin-Söderlind and Bill Harris from the PCS Unit at the Stockholm School of

Economics for improving our English. Ossian Ekdahl and Daniel Barr were helpful in dealing with malfunctioning computers.

Stockholm School of Economics

May 1992

Jan Bojö Karl-Göran Mäler Lena Unemo

ENVIRONMENT AND DEVELOPMENT - AN ECONOMIC APPROACH

Table of Contents

1. Summary

1.1 Introduction

All over the world, aid agencies and NGOs are reviewing their development approach in the light of increasingly intensified debate about environmental issues. This book is intended as a contribution to the efforts to incorporate environmental concerns into development work. The main purposes of this book are:

(1) to discuss, from an economic perspective, the causes of environmental degradation;

(2) to provide a conceptual framework for the organization of information in order to enhance environmental decision-making;

(3) to provide an overview of economic methods that can assist in the valuation of environmental costs and benefits;

(4) to give examples of applications of the theoretical methods described.

The economic analysis of environmental effects should not be confined to the scope of projects. Attention is therefore also given to the links between economic policy in general and natural resource degradation.

Referencing is used generously, in response to the demand for at least a partial overview of the rapidly growing literature on environmental economics.

This book is concerned with consequences pertaining to the physical environment: land, air, water and vegetation. The functions of the environment that we are concerned with can be specified as:

(1) a source of natural resources (raw material, energy);

(2) a source of environmental services (life-support, recreation, beauty);

(3) an assimilator of waste.

Chapter 2 further elaborates the background and purposes of this book.

1.2 Distortions in the Economic System and the Need for Economic Analysis

As discussed further in chapter 3, environmental problems can be analysed in economic terms on three major levels:

(1) The general policy level, where the links to environmental damage may not be particularly obvious, but nevertheless at times quite strong;

(2) The environmental policy level, where conscious decisions are made to limit environmental degradation through regulation, taxation, subsidies, etc.;

(3) The project level, where adjustments can be made to optimize environmental damage;

The three approaches should be seen as complements; one without the others may not do much good.

Much of the environmental degradation is the result of large numbers of individuals engaging in destructive (but privately rational) actions. We cannot hope to reach them all by area-based projects. These must be complemented and supported by sound general economic policies.

Our point of departure is the neoclassical model of a perfectly competitive market. This is not because we believe this model to be a good description of the real world, but because it is an analytically clear bench-mark. Deviations from this model are grouped in two categories: *market failures* and *policy failures*.

Attention is restricted to the market failures that contribute particularly to environmental degradation: externalities, public goods/bads, lack of risk and future markets. A key problem underlying market failures is the lack of completely defined property rights. This is partially explained by the impossibility of achieving them in all cases - this is discussed further below. However, there are also cases where property rights are not defined for political or cultural reasons, even when this would be technically possible. An additional concern with market solutions is the resulting distribution of income.

Market failures (as well as other social forces) give rise to government interventions. However, these are not without cost and result in another set of problems: policy failures affecting, for example, international trade, population growth, price regulation, taxation, bureaucratic sub-optimization, misdirected public investments and suppression of environmental information.

The environmental damage caused by market and policy failures can be analysed by a combination of economic and other means to:

(1) alter general economic policy so as to achieve beneficial environmental effects;

(2) institute specific environmental policies in the service of sustainable development;

(3) design development projects so that environmental damage is optimized;

(4) design specific projects to counteract environmental damage.

1.3 General Equilibrium Analysis and Environmental Accounting

Chapter 4 is devoted to the subject of general equilibrium analysis and economic environmental accounting on the national level.

A change in one sector of the economy may have repercussions throughout the economy by changing relative prices and thereby changing incentives to produce and to consume various goods and services. This is of relevance for economic analysis of environmental resources for several reasons. Firstly, a particular project may have important repercussions on the rest of the economy. Secondly, quite often, national and regional policies (fiscal, agricultural, trade policies, etc.) that are not directly aimed at environmental issues, will have substantial impact on the environment and income distribution through repercussions on the economy.

Finally, the economic analysis of a set of environmental problems is quite often directed toward optimization, for example minimizing the necessary costs for achieving an environmental improvement. General equilibrium models give one set of tools that can be used to implement such optimization. They are also suitable for the study of interdependencies within the economy.

The current system of national accounts used in most countries does not provide a complete picture of the environmental status of a nation. In particular, the degradation of an environmental stock (forests, fish, iron ore and so on) is not reflected, whereas the income from the flow of exploited resources is. Different ways of adjusting the system of national accounts are discussed in chapter 4.

1.4 Economic Analysis of Environmental Consequences on the Project Level

Project level analysis is dealt with in more detail in chapter 5. Environmental impacts can be analysed through many approaches. Some of them can be labelled specification techniques. They organize information about environmental impacts in a consistent but multi-dimensional framework through e.g. Environmental Impact Assessment (EIA). This is often a good starting point for economic analysis.

The techniques discussed in chapter 5 can be labelled evaluation techniques. They aim at summarizing different dimensions of an environmental problem into a common unit. For practical reasons, this unit is generally money, although any other widely known and accepted yardsticks (gold, shells, camels ...) can also be used.

1.4.1 CBA and its Major Steps

The core method for environmental economic evaluation is cost-benefit analysis (CBA). This is defined here as a process containing the following components:

(1) Identification and quantification of social advantages (benefits) and disadvantages (costs) in terms of a common monetary unit;

(2) Benefits and costs are primarily valued on the basis of individuals' willingness to pay for goods and services, marketed or not, as viewed through a social welfare order representing the preferences of the relevant decision-maker;

(3) The flow of monetary units over time is brought together to a net present value;

(4) Unvalued effects (intangibles) are described qualitatively or quantitatively and put against valued items.

CBA is a normative exercise aimed at providing policy relevant conclusions, aiding, but not dictating, environmental decision-making. CBA ultimately rests on ethical values. The belief that results emanating from CBA are somehow "objective" is not supported here.

There are several possible perspectives for a CBA of a project. The general cases could be classified in three groups:

(1) looking at a planned project (or projects) in advance (ex-ante appraisal);

(2) looking at an operational but not completed project (on-going evaluation);

(3) looking at a completed project (ex-post evaluation).

Given this initial perspective, most CBAs contain a sequence of analytical steps such as those outlined below. These are discussed further in chapter 5.

Evaluation Criteria: The gathering of data should be done in the context of what we need to know, in order to make good decisions. This is simplified if we can bring together the streams of future costs and benefits to one point in time, and express them in a common unit, as far as possible. The basic concept in CBA in this respect is the Net Present Value (NPV).

Assessing distributional consequences is a part - implicitly or explicitly - of the use of decision criteria, since the NPV contains a weighted sum of individual costs and benefits. The fact that all weights are usually set to the same value for all individuals does not relieve us from the responsibility of considering this aspect. This appears particularly relevant in a developing country context. This book suggests that:

(1) The search for any significant distributive effects should be mandatory in CBAs;

(2) That any significant effects should be presented to the decision-makers;

(3) That such effects should not be weighed implicitly, but that explicit values that would affect the decision (switching values) should be illustrated.

Identification of Costs and Benefits: A common mistake in the appraisal situation is to limit unnecessarily the number of alternatives considered. Often, only one single project idea is presented. A thorough CBA critically looks at the available alternatives and may therefore result in a much more interesting conclusion than simply "accept" or "reject".

Quantification of Costs and Benefits: This usually presents problems since our knowledge of the underlying natural scientific relationships is quite incomplete. However, decisions still have to be made, and CBA can be a useful aid in organizing available information.

Valuation of Costs and Benefits: This entails applying "social price tags" on the effects we have quantified. The extent to which we can actually capture environmental effects in monetary terms will differ depending on their nature and their relationship with existing markets. In some cases, we will have to look for indirect market relationships, or even construct artificial markets to reveal people's valuation of environmental consequences. Valuation approaches are discussed in further detail in chapter 5.

Discounting: This is done using a real social rate of discount. Inflation is a separate issue and need not concern us here. A general, uniform rise in the value of all costs and benefits will not affect the result in terms of our evaluation criteria.

Most people find it natural to regard the value of a dollar today as greater than the value of a dollar in ten years. This applies even if the future dollar can be received with absolute certainty and with compensation for inflation. Several reasons for this position can be advanced:

(a) A dollar now could be invested and could therefore be worth more in ten years (there is an opportunity cost in terms of return on capital foregone);

(b) If I am richer in ten years than I am now, an extra dollar will mean less to me then (the marginal utility of income will diminish);

(c) I am impatient to use the dollar now rather than later (the pure rate of time preference).

These perceptions have been formalized by economists and have led to three major, but not distinctly separable, approaches in the determination of actual rates:

(1) The social opportunity cost of capital (SOC) approach which looks for empirical evidence of (before tax) profits on alternative investment opportunities. The main argument here is that public development investments displace other investment with this return;

(2) The consumption rate of interest (CRI) approach which is based on market data revealing consumer preferences for consumption today versus tomorrow. Empirically, this entails looking at (after tax) returns to the investor on risk-free bonds, etc.;

(3) The social time preference rate (STPR) approach. This takes the rate to be mainly a political parameter set on the basis of decision-makers' views on (a) the per capita income growth perspective, (b) the rate at which utility of increases in marginal income diminishes and, sometimes, (c) an assumption of the pure rate of time preference among consumers.

If they are to be comparable, CBAs should apply certain standards, one of them being a consistent social rate of discount. Arguments have been made for adjusting the rate of discount both upwards and downwards to account for peculiarities in *environmental* analysis. We reject these arguments in favour of a consistent application of a social rate of discount.

Setting an Appropriate Time Horizon: In principle, an infinite length of time should be considered. In practice, CBAs often limit the horizon to 20, 30 or 50 years, because effects of a project tend to decline after some time. The choice of time horizon is also related to the choice of discount rate. The higher the discount rate, the lower the weight attached to long-term effects.

Uncertainties and Risks: This point is problematic for all environmental evaluation, economic and non-economic, CBA or non-CBA. While economics does not contain any magic solution to the lack of perfect information, it offers sensitivity analysis as a tool in systematically assessing the importance of specific assumptions.

This text argues that adjustments for risk are best done by using the probability distribution for costs and benefits when illustrating the impact on project worth, rather than through adjustments in the rate of discount. This also goes for irreversible effects.

Policy Conclusions: Conclusions should be drawn in terms of the criteria set up, and considering the setting of planning goals that the decision-maker (government, aid agency etc.) has defined. Interesting comparisons can be made between the economic result and the financial result - the latter reflecting the incentives that markets will provide to individuals. Policy interventions need to be designed with a clear view of the contrasting results and based on additional cost-benefit considerations as to the interventions themselves.

1.4.2 Valuation Approaches

The valuation we are concerned with here is one which is seen from the perspective of society: the economic perspective. The economic valuation techniques discussed in detail in chapter 5, section 2, are grouped in three sections discussing valuation using:

(1) conventional markets;
(2) implicit markets;
(3) artificial markets.

Each of these has several sub-categories.

1.4.2.1 Valuation Using Conventional Markets

Four types of analysis are exemplified under this heading:

(1) changes in production;
(2) replacement cost;
(3) preventive expenditure;
(4) the human capital approach.

The fact that conventional markets are used does not necessarily mean that market prices are adopted without alterations. When significant distortions are present, appropriate shadow prices have to be estimated.

Many environmental impacts have a direct bearing on production values. Pollution may directly damage the production of fish, drinking water or irrigation water, soil erosion diminishes the value of crops grown in an area, etc. The analysis of these effects is a straightforward extension of traditional CBA.

The replacement cost method analyses the cost of repairing environmental damage through erosion, flooding, corrosion, etc. The preventive expenditure method analyses what costs individuals have incurred in order to mitigate environmental hazards. The human capital approach is not satisfactory, but may give lower bound estimates for environmental health damage.

1.4.2.2 Valuation Using Implicit Markets

The basic idea behind this set of techniques is that there are links between the consumption of ordinary goods sold on markets and the consumption of non-marketed goods, including environmental values. Thus, changes in environmental quality will also be reflected in prices of ordinary goods, such as land and houses.

The same basic idea has also inspired the study of travel cost in relation to recreation as a means to delimit willingness-to-pay for implicit environmental values.

There are major problems of application of these techniques in a Third World context. Lack of market transactions and market data is a considerable obstacle. More market oriented policies in LDCs may open a future for these approaches.

1.4.2.3 Valuation Using Artificial Markets

When researching the values of individuals it is not always possible to make inferences from actual behaviour as we have in the approaches presented above. Instead, we may have to measure consumer preferences in hypothetical situations by creating artificial markets.

The strength of these methods is that they can be applied to a variety of situations where no other data is available. Artificial markets have been used to test individual valuation regarding water and air quality, aesthetic beauty, recreational values, preservation of open farmland, existence values of natural environments, disposal of hazardous waste, risk in relation to air travel, car travel, cigarette smoking, nuclear energy, and so on.

There are many difficulties pertaining to the use of artificial markets. However, these can to some extent be statistically controlled and to some extent minimized through careful survey design. The appropriateness of these techniques will vary, depending on the purpose of the study. They should at least be considered and carefully assessed in cases where individuals' willingness-to-pay cannot be read from an existing market. In countries with poorly developed monetary markets, appropriate adjustments may have to be made. Willingness to donate labour hours, bags of maize and so on, may of course be substituted for the traditional monetary measurement.

1.4.3 Complementary and Other Methods

The appropriateness of a particular method of economic evaluation depends on the task at hand. The framework presented in this book is very flexible and can easily accommodate methods that are sometimes presented as "alternatives". This is discussed further in chapter 5, section 3.

An *environmental impact assessment* (EIA) can be seen as a complement, even as a necessary foundation for a proper CBA. The EIA specifies the impacts for the CBA to evaluate.

Cost-effectiveness analysis is a useful approach when benefit estimation is found to be impossible or not demanded. Certain goals may be given by the decision-makers without any explicit benefit estimation.

The *opportunity-cost approach* measures what has to be given up in order to preserve an unpriced asset, say a recreational area or the habitat of a species threatened by extinction. By comparing the costs of development at different sites, a trade-off could be made between cost differences and anticipated environmental effects.

Planning balance sheets offer a method of more decomposed, but complex presentation of CBA results. The costs and benefits for particular interest groups are given special attention. This matter is fully compatible with CBA, and indeed, builds on its foundation.

Goal achievement matrices have been suggested as alternative planning tools. But the contribution to other goals than economic growth, such as income distribution, employment creation, regional balance, etc., can also easily be included in the CBA framework as weights or restrictions.

Rather than entering into a detailed separation of CBA versus other approaches we think that one should test available alternatives according to a number of criteria for a "good" method. It is suggested that such criteria could include:

(1) Analytical cost - should not be greater than the value of the information produced;

(2) Comprehensiveness - the degree to which the approach takes relevant impacts into account;

(3) Comprehensibility - the degree to which the method and its results could be usefully interpreted by the users of the information;

(4) Democratic basis - the degree to which individuals' own preferences are reflected;

(5) Relevance for decision-making - the degree to which the information makes a difference to policy makers.

1.4.4 Critique against CBA

There are critics who reject the foundations of CBA on philosophical grounds. Other are critical to its practical usefulness in dealing with environmental matters.

This book argues that criticism of the fundamental method of cost-benefit comparisons is often based on misunderstandings of what CBA aims at doing.

Criticisms of the limited usefulness of CBA in environmental matters have some merit with regard to informational constraints . However, criticism of the limited information availability strikes equally hard at all methods of evaluation, CBA or non-CBA. This is why we quote with sympathy the pragmatic attitude of Maurice Chevalier, who responded to the question of how he perceived old age, with the following remark: "Well there is quite a lot wrong with it, but it isn't so bad when you consider the alternative."

1.5 Management of Environmental Resources and Evironmental Policy

As discussed in previous chapters it may be argued that the basic problem in managing environmental resources is the problem of incentives. The basic objective of environmental policy is therefore to create an economic environment in which the incentives are correct, that is, to create a system in which the best interest of individuals, households, companies, etc. coincides with the collective or public interest. The design of mechanisms to improve the incentive structure will depend not only on the characteristics of the resource, but also on the general economic and legal background.

In designing policies, it is, for example, vitally important to know whether the resource concerned is a common property resource and whether it is currently managed by a functioning set of social norms. Failing to consider such aspects, any policy intervention may be counter productive and possibly result in deterioration of the resource.

The particular way of changing the incentive structure is often referred to as a policy instrument. Examples of environmental policy instruments are emission standards, taxes, subsidies, and transferable pollution permits. Five criteria are of importance in choosing such instruments:

- *Static efficiency*. This criterion concerns the cost of achieving a desired environmental improvement by applying a certain instrument. The lower the cost, the more attractive is the instrument.

- *Dynamic efficiency*. This criterion concerns the ability of the instrument to cope with (unanticipated) changes and with the incentives to develop new and better technical solutions to environmental problems.

- *Information requirements*. In order to exploit different environmental policy instruments, the policymaker needs in general different kind and amount of information in order to implement them. The more available the information is, the more attractive is the instrument.

- *Measurement and monitoring costs*. Different instruments require different monitoring and , since monitoring is costly, and sometimes impossible, this is an important aspect in choosing between different instruments.

- *Political and ethical feasibility*. For example, different instruments can have (but will in general not have) different impacts on income distribution.

Which instrument, or what combination of instruments, that are actually the best to implement in a particular situation, depends very much on the nature of the pollution, as well as on other factors. This is a very extensive subject, and an important part of applied environmental economics. We focus in this text mainly on the theoretical reasoning behind some different policy instruments, and evaluate them with respect to the criteria cited above.

1.6 Case Studies

It would be futile to try to summarize the case studies, since the presentation contained in chapter 7 of this book is already a condensed version of very substantial material. It should only be mentioned that the case studies represent some of the most burning environmental issues in the Third World and elsewhere: soil erosion, range degradation, deforestation and air and water pollution.

The empirical studies given have an emphasis on measuring direct changes in production values. This is the most straightforward and promising application of economic analysis as regards the valuation of developing countries' environmental problems.

Apart from the case studies where the approach is to assess the environmental impact of various kinds of projects, a few studies are presented where the aim is to illustrate how the overall prevailing economic incentives may contribute to an improper use of environmental resources. These studies highlight the importance of removing misdirected economic incentives first, if development projects and environmental action plans are to succeed.

2. Introduction

2.1 Background

Internationally, the "Brundtland Report"[1] has been the focus of much debate on the meaning of "sustainable development" and the role of environmental issues in development. While the operational implications often remain unclear, it is certainly true that environmental matters have emerged as an issue at the top of the international agenda of development concerns.

Several events and actions exist, all pointing to the increased awareness concerning the vital importance of environmental elements of development. For example, donor agencies all over the world are in the process of (re)defining their environmental policies. UNEP initiated some pioneer work on cost-benefit analysis of environmental impact already in the late 1970s and has shown a continued interest. The World Bank has undergone a reorganization implying a higher profile in environmental matters. USAID has recently published a new policy paper on "Environment and Natural Resources", and similar efforts are underway within the British Overseas Development Administration. In 1988, the Swedish Parliament adopted an additional goal for Swedish foreign aid; "sustainable use of natural resources and environmental protection".

This book is written as a contribution to the efforts to adequately address environmental concerns in development efforts. The main purposes of this book are:

(1) to discuss, from an economic perspective, the causes of environmental degradation,

(2) to provide a conceptual framework for the organization of information in order to enhance environmental decision-making,

(3) to provide an overview of economic methods that can assist in the valuation of environmental costs and benefits,

(4) to give examples of applications of the theoretical methods described.

The economic analysis of environmental effects should not be confined to the project scope, but placed in its proper policy perspective. Therefore, considerable attention is also given to the links between economic policy in general and natural resource

---

1. "Our Common Future", formally the work of The World Commission on Environment and Development (WCED), but often named after its chairperson.

degradation. Through generous referencing, we also want to respond to the demand for links to more profound discussions of this complex topic.

2.2 Sustainable Development

Definitions of Sustainable Development

The concept of sustainable development was introduced in the World Conservation Strategy (IUCN 1980) and adopted by the World Commission on Environment and Development (WCED) in 1987 as a key concept. However, the exact meaning of sustainable development has not been defined. In *Our Common Future* by WCED there are at least six different definitions, all not consistent with each other. However, all definitions and discussions around sustainable development have in common their focus on the long run performance of the economy, and in particular the possibilities for future generations to achieve a satisfactory life. WCED gives a workable description;

> "Sustainable development is development that meets the needs of present generations without compromising the ability of future generations to meet their own needs"

This statement can be interpreted in many different ways. Some would interpret the sustainability requirement as a requirement that all options are preserved, which would imply the preservation of all kinds of resources. As such a requirement leads to ridiculous conclusions (we would never use iron, oil or other exhaustible resources) most people would drop the requirement that exhaustible resources are left completely unused for future generations. The use of exhaustible resources would therefore be permitted along this revised version of sustainable development. However, the exhaustion of the non-renewable resources must be compensated by an increase in some other resource. This compensation means that substituting one resource for another would be possible and one should ask why this should not be true for all productive assets. This leads us to suggest the following definition of sustainable development:

> The economic development in a specified area (region, nation, the globe) is sustainable if the total stock of resources - human capital, physical reproducible capital, environmental resources, exhaustible resources - does not decrease over time.

The basic idea behind this definition is the notion of substitutability between resources. If physical or human capital can be substituted for an environmental resource, then the environmental resource can be exploited in such a way that it is severely reduced if, and only if the investments in the stock of human and physical capital are such that the total resource base is not reduced. The exploitation of oil reserves may therefore be part of a sustainable development, but only if investments in alternative energy sources and in energy conservation are made in such a way that the welfare of future generations is not threatened by the exhaustion of the reserves. For example, the cutting down of forests in order to increase export earnings is consistent with sustainable development only if the whole or parts of the proceeds are invested in other export earning or import reducing activities in order to maintain the welfare of future generations.

Issues

This definition of sustainable development raises several questions that must be addressed:

(1) Is sustainable development feasible?

(2) How should resources be valued in order to decide the necessary compensating investments?

(3) How should incentives be designed to promote sustainable development?

(4) What are the implications for the choice of an interest rate?

(5) How can accounting systems be developed that monitor the economic development from a "sustainable development" point of view?

Feasibility

The first question cannot be answered today because of lack of sufficient empirical information. If exhaustible resources are difficult to replace with other resources[2] sustainable development is not feasible. As exhaustible resources are bound to disappear, the low substitution possibilities between these and physical and human capital will ultimately lead to reductions in future production possibilities and to reductions in the welfare of future generations.

However, there are no firm empirical evidence on the degree of substitutability. Barnett and Morse (1963) made the first serious empirical study of the role of natural resources in economic growth processes and found no economic signs of increased resource scarcity. Their conclusions are shared by most economists. However, there are scholars that are of the opposing point of view. N. Georgescu-Roegen (1971) and H. Daly (1980) are the best known proponents of a more pessimistic view. Both use the second law of thermodynamics - the ever increasing entropy - to argue that a closed system cannot go on expanding forever. However, they would agree that if solar energy could be captured

2. Technically speaking, if the elasticity of substitution between an exhaustible resource and physical- and human capital is less than one.

more efficiently than today, it would be possible to reach a stationary situation with constant production.

One particular aspect that is worth discussing in this connection is population growth. A constant and positive growth in the population will ultimately destroy the possibilities for sustainable development. Thus, one important issue is how to design incentives for families to reduce their family size and thereby reduce population growth. It may be that the only ways to do that is by stimulating non-sustainable economic growth for a while in order reduce the value of many offsprings as insurance against security during old age and sickness. This is further discussed in chapter 3.

For our purpose, it is not necessary to decide on the feasibility of sustainable development. Even if sustainable development were infeasible in the very long run, that would not change the conclusions to follow. In fact, the rules for valuing environmental resources would not change at all. These rules imply that resources should be valued and priced in such a way that the values reflect the improvement on present and future welfare from a marginal increase in the resource. These values should thus reflect both the direct impact on welfare from a change in the resource such as from water and air pollution but also the value of the resource as an input in production.

Valuation

Obviously, we do not know the preferences of future generations or their production possibilities, that is, we do not know the impact on their welfare from current resource use. We must therefore forecast both the preferences and the technology[3]. Usually, we assume that the preferences of future generations are identical to those of the present and that the technology can be forecasted by trend extrapolations. This means that the value of resources can in general be based on observations on the value of these resources to the present generations. This introduces, of course, substantial uncertainty in assessments of resource values and we will in a later part come back to an analysis of this uncertainty. The bulk of this book deals with techniques that can be used to estimate resource values to the present generation. Given the assumptions made, these values therefore also reflect the values to the future generations and can therefore be used for estimating the sustainable resource values.

---

3. Note the difference between forecasting preferences and forecasting choices. Choices are made on the basis of prices, income and other similar "environment" variables in such a way to be "best" from the point of view of the preferences. Thus, by forecasting preferences and income and prices we would also be able to forecast choices. On the other hand, there is a deep theorem in consumption theory that says that knowing the choices for all conceivable prices and incomes is sufficient to enable one to predict the preferences.

Incentives

Due to poorly defined property rights - either because of policy failures or because of the intrinsic difficulties of defining property rights - individuals and firms have in general not the correct incentives to economize with environmental resources. The lack of individual property rights to land in Madagascar has, for example, created severe problems with soil erosion and threatened a sustainable development of agriculture. One major objective of not only environmental policies but all economic policies should be to define property rights whenever it can be done and to design other incentive schemes in the remaining cases. This will be touched upon in chapter 3. For an excellent discussion of the role of property rights, the reader is also referred to Tietenberg (1988).

Interest rate

Sustainable development has to do with intertemporal resource allocation. It is therefore very natural to expect a close connection between the choice of a social discount rate and sustainability. The interest rate r (or rather the discount factor $1/(1+r)$) is the current price of one dollar available one year from now. As the interest rate is in general positive, the value of a dollar one year ahead is less than the value of one dollar now. Why is this? There are fundamentally three reasons for this[4]:

(1) by investing one dollar now, a value of more than one dollar can be produced next year,

(2) as individuals expect increases in their wealth, one dollar more next year will mean less than one dollar now,

(3) individuals are in general shortsighted, that is, they will value future gains less than corresponding current gains.

As we are interested in sustainable development, the first reason can be excluded immediately. However, the two remaining reasons are of relevance. They point to the fact that the market interest rate will approximately, at least in the long run and in the average, reflect the growth rate of the economy. If the growth rate is the correct growth rate, that is including all variables that directly or indirectly affect human welfare, then a positive interest rate means a positive growth in human welfare[5]. This simple point is overlooked in most discussions of discounting. Most critics of the discounting procedure take the interest rate from a black box, without relating it to the general performance of the economy. However, the fact is that the interest rate is related to the performance and

4. Reasons formulated in 1884 by the Austrian economist Böhm-Bawerk.

5. There is a problem in this argument resulting from population growth, for more details see Mäler 1990.

in particular to the long run growth of the economy.[6]

In order to make this clear, let us consider a case in which resources are exploited today, an exploitation that will affect future welfare negatively. If the real rate of interest is 4%, this means (in the absence of distorting taxes and other interventions on the capital market) that the return on investments in physical capital is 4% and that the long run growth rate is about 4 % p.a. Assume that the proceeds from the exploitation are $1 million. If the whole amount is invested, the economy would earn $40,000 annually. If the annual damage to the future generations is less than $40,000, the exploitation of the resource together with the investment in physical capital is obviously part of a sustainable programme. But this comparison is nothing but the calculation of the present value of the future damage (at 4 % interest rate) and the comparison of this present value with the present benefits from the exploitation.

Thus, if the chosen interest rate reflects both the long run return on capital investment and the long run average growth rate of the economy, the use of a discounting procedure is wholly consistent with the notion of sustainable development. In fact, it is a necessary requirement for the calculation of whether a particular resource use is consistent with sustainable development or not.

However, in real life, the market rate of interest may not reflect the long run economic growth rate perfectly. The main reasons for this are:

- short run financial and macro economic fluctuations
- taxes and other interventions in the capital markets
- poorly designed and implemented property rights
- uncertainty about future technology, ecological mechanisms, etc.

Because of the first problem above, it is necessary to look at long run series in order to estimate the long run real rate of interest. The day to day fluctuations may result in very high real rates which do not reflect any long run tendencies in the economy.

In many countries, taxes on capital income create a wedge between the social rate of return on capital and the market rate of interest. The taxation of the capital income only implies that the social return is divided between the government budget and the owners of the capital. From the point of view of sustainability, it is of course the social rate of return that is of interest and not the net dividend to the owners of capital. Whenever the capital market is regulated, one can expect other differences between the market rate of interest and the social return on capital. Still, the general principal is that it is the social

6. This was first explored by John von Neumann (1937) who showed the equivalence between the growth rate and interest rate in a general equilibrium model. The modern formulation is in terms of the Golden Rule - in a growth process that maximizes consumption the rate of growth equal the interest rate. For an introduction to this literature, see Burmeister and Dobell (1970) and Dasgupta and Heal (1979).

return that should be used for discounting future costs and benefits. However, regulations of the capital market very often imply that the marginal rate of return on capital will differ between different sectors of the economy. Thus there is not one return on capital, but many. If one does not know which alternative investment will be displaced or made in connection with a project on environmental resources, the best way out is to use an average return on capital in the economy.

But even if we could neglect short run fluctuations and if the capital markets were perfect, the lack of property rights to many resources may distort the market rate of interest rate. If investment opportunities in environmental resources are neglected because of the lack of property rights, the market interest rate may be quite different from what it should have been, had the opportunities been exploited. As an example, if due to the release of greenhouse gases, the future global climate changes, and if this is foreseen, the expected return on capital investments made today will evidently be affected negatively. Together with the lack of perfect foresight, the present interest rate would be too high. Thus the combination of imperfect information and lack of well defined property rights, may cause the present interest rate to be higher that would correspond to the long run growth rate. In chapter 5 we will come back to these issues on uncertainty and interest rates.

Finally, in chapter 4 we will come back to the question how the national accounting systems can be extended in order to provide means for monitoring sustainable development.

2.3 Disposition and Delimitations

The word "environment" literally means "... the entire range of external influences acting on an organism ..." (Encyclopaedia Britannica). However, in this context we will concern ourselves with a sub-group of consequences pertaining to the physical environment - land, air, water and vegetation. The functions of the environment that we are concerned with can be specified as:

(1) a source of natural resources (raw material, energy)
(2) a source of environmental services (life-support, recreation, beauty)
(3) an assimilator of residuals

Freeman (1979) has made a useful summary of how environmental changes (in the widest sense of the word) affect human beings (Table 2.3.1 on next page)

Table 2.3.1 Channels through which Environmental Changes Affect Human Beings

A. Through living systems

1. Human health

2. Economic productivity:
   agriculture
   forestry
   fisheries
   recreation (production)

3. Other ecosystem impacts:
   recreation (amenities)
   ecological diversity,
   stability

B. Through non-living systems

1. Material damage:
   soiling
   production costs

2. Weather, climate

3. Other:
   odor
   visibility
   visual aesthetics

Source: Adapted from Freeman (1979) p. 20

Given the context of developing countries, our main concern will be with economic productivity of ecological systems. Examples of economic analysis of soil and water conservation, range management, agroforestry, forestry and fisheries will be discussed in chapters 5 and 7.

Questions of human health pose considerable problems from the point of economic valuation. Some approaches are presented in chapter 5 and examples dealing with air pollution effects on health are summarized in chapter 7.

Recreational analyses have attracted widespread attention in the industrialized world. Its relevance may seem more limited at present in the developing world. However, recreational services in developing countries may provide a rich source of foreign exchange earnings, and need to be carefully assessed before sacrificed for other investments options. The theoretical basis for such studies is discussed in chapter 5, and an example of a recreational cost-benefit study is presented in the following chapter.

In principle, the least problematic of the channels operating through nonliving systems deals with materials damage and increased production costs. An example of this kind of study is given in chapter 7, based on a replacement cost approach presented in chapter 5.

Climatic effects (greenhouse effects and damage to the ozone layer etc.) will not be considered. They are certainly relevant also to the Third World, but entail a discussion of global modelling of effects that we consider to be outside the scope of this book.

The channels listed under "other" (odor, visibility, aesthetics) may be dealt with through artificial market methods. These are presented in chapter 5 and examples are given in chapter 7.

Leaving table 2.3.1 aside, it is important to point out that this text does not form a complete "hand-book" of economic analysis applied to environmental problems. It is rather an introduction to modes of thinking and ways of approaching the analysis. The references provided here will have to be pursued to find the details of practical analysis.

The remainder of the book is organized as follows. Chapter 3 discusses the rationale for economic analyses. It does so from the perspective of looking at mechanisms in the market system and the political system that adversely affect the environment.

Chapter 4 deals with general equilibrium modelling, concerned with the overall perspective of linking the economic system with the ecosystem. Such models may be useful for macro-economic analyses and for dealing with projects having substantial repercussions on other social sectors. The chapter also discusses national income accounting. After a brief look at existing conventions, it goes on to discuss possible modifications in order to properly reflect changes in environmental values.

Chapter 5 is concerned with the project level analyses of environmental costs and benefits. Cost-benefit analysis is presented in some detail and considerable attention is given to a variety of valuation approaches.

In chapter 6 criteria for the choice of policy instruments to combat environmental problems are discussed. Different policies like regulations, taxes and transferable pollution permits are evaluated with respect to these criteria. The chapter also includes a discussion on common property resources.

Finally, chapter 7 provides numerous illustrations of applied economic analysis. The case studies being surveyed are, with a few exceptions, all based on the different methods of analysing environmental impacts outlined in chapter 5. The case studies deal with some of the most burning environmental issues in the Third World: soil erosion, deforestation, range degradation and pollution of air and water.

3. Distortions in the Economic System and the Need for Economic Analysis

Environmental problems can be analysed in economic terms on three major levels:

(1) The general policy level, where the links to environmental damage may not be particularly obvious, but nevertheless at times quite strong. This chapter and the following will be concerned with this level;

(2) The environmental policy level, where conscious decisions are made to limit environmental degradation through taxation, subsidies, etc. As mentioned previously, we will not discuss the appropriate design of such policy in this book;

(3) The project level, where adjustments can be made to optimize[1] environmental damage. The main emphasis in this text lies on this level, and we return to this theme in chapters 5 and 7.

The three approaches should be seen as complements; one without the other may not be very useful. Since much of the environmental degradation is the result of large numbers of individuals engaging in destructive (but privately rational) actions, we cannot hope to reach them all by area-based projects. These must be complemented and supported by sound general economic policies.

3.1 The "Bench-mark" Economy

Our point of departure is the neoclassical[2] model of a perfectly competitive market. This is not because we believe this model to be a good description of the real world, but because it is an analytically clear bench-mark. With this as a starting point, we can clearly see why the need for economic interventions from society arises.

The "bench-mark" economy is characterized by the fact that the resource allocation is

---

1. We use the word "optimize" rather than "minimize". The minimum level of environmental damage is zero. If "environmental damage" is taken to mean any negative impact on an existing ecosystem, reaching the zero level would be incompatible with most forms of human activity, such as agriculture and industry.

2."Neoclassical" refers to a school of thought within economics that has its roots in late 19th century theory and was developed by economists such as Jevons, Marshall Menger and Walras. The prefix "neo" serves to distinguish this school from earlier "classical" economics with Smith, Ricardo and Malthus as the leading theorists. For details, see Landreth and Colander (1989).

efficient, i.e. no one can achieve an increase in welfare without diminishing someone else's. This condition is achieved automatically in an equilibrium in a market economy, but only under certain quite restrictive conditions.[3] Where these conditions are not satisfied, we speak about *distortions*. These can be grouped in two broad categories: *market failures* and *policy failures*.

Market failures are an extensive subject and concern both the results existing markets achieve, and the fact that markets have not developed enough. Broadly speaking, one category concerns cases where production technology tends to give rise to monopolies and therefore a lack of competition. The other category concerns cases where markets are incomplete in different ways. Therefore all goods and services will not be sold on competitive markets. We will deal with the second category in this book.

In addition, the fact that markets - even if competitive and complete - may produce an income distribution that is politically unacceptable is particularly relevant for Third World circumstances. We shall return to these points below.

Policy failures have traditionally been given less attention, but as the World Bank (1988, p. 1) remarks:

> "... the perception of government has shifted during the past decade; where government was once commonly seen as a catalyst of development, many now think it an obstacle."

Although all governments definitely cannot be treated as a homogeneous group, some failures are common enough[4] to warrant our attention in this context. Policy failures regarding international trade, property rights definition and enforcement, population growth, prices and taxes as well as bureaucratic sub-optimization, misdirected public investments and suppression of environmental information seem to be the major points of relevance to our book.

3.2 Market Failures

In this book we will restrict our attention to the distortions that contribute particularly to environmental degradation. From this perspective, externalities, public goods/"bads", lack of risk and future markets appear particularly relevant.

---

3. See e.g. Bohm (1973) for an introduction to the stringent conditions that have to be fulfilled.
4. As one long-time observer of Africa has rather sweepingly put it:"... there is very little difference between African countries. The trend for the state to lose its role as instrument of development is evident throughout sub-Saharan Africa. Instead of becoming more effective, the post-colonial state is in danger of becoming good for little except provision of boundless employment." (Hydén, 1983, p. xii).

3.2.1 Externalities

A useful definition of externality has been suggested by Baumol and Oates (1975, p. 17):

> "An externality is present whenever some individual's (say A's) utility or production relationships include real (that is, nonmonetary) variables, whose values are chosen by others (persons, corporations, governments) without particular attention to the effects on A's welfare."

Externalities can be both positive and negative, and originate from and affect both consumers and producers. Some relevant examples of possible cases are:

- Spraying with pesticides upstream decreases fish catches and therefore production and consumption of fish downstream;
- Increased off-take among my neighbours' cattle in a communal grazing area increases availability of fodder for my cattle, which increases their yield of milk;
- The neighbours' trees provide wind shelter and shade for my crops.

Many more examples could be thought of, but these should suffice to suggest that everyday life is full of externalities, many of them significantly affecting the level of welfare of people. The main point in these examples is that the effects are *not recorded in the market system.* There is no monetary transaction to compensate for losses or gains in welfare.

Externalities become increasingly important when property rights are poorly defined. This is often the case when resources have been abundant and/or when communal management traditionally has been practiced. The correlation between the two is less than perfect. Farmland may not always be individually owned although it may be quite scarce (cf. China) and trees may not be privately controlled although near extinction (cf. Lesotho).

Externalities are at the heart of cases when privately rational individuals may well produce disastrous social results. The debate about common property resource management has given rise to the "tragedy of the commons school", following Garrett Hardin's celebrated article in Science:

> "Ruin is the destination toward which all men rush, each pursuing his own best interest in a society that believes in the freedom of the commons. Freedom in the commons brings ruin to all." (Hardin, 1968).

The famous passage quoted above - implying the need to define rights that can provide the basis for market transactions - has also met strong challenges. Pearce (1988) offers a more balanced view, and points to the distinction between "open-access resources" and "common property resources". It is only the former that has no control structure for its management.

Dasgupta (1982) strongly criticizes Hardin's pessimism and argues that freedom in the commons may bring ruin to none: the price of output may be insufficient to induce over-stocking e.g. Moreover, the policy prescription sometimes advanced on the basis of Hardin's vision -privatization - could bring impoverishment to the former land-users, Dasgupta argues.

We lack the space to pursue the argument in detail here, and take note of the need to analyse the common property resources from a comparative financial and economic view, taking into account indigenous resource management norms, and to suggest remedies that are both socially efficient and that have acceptable income distribution effects.

Public Goods and "Bads"

Under the more general heading of externalities, we can identify a particular category with peculiar characteristics which make them problematic from a market perspective: public goods (and "bads"). We can define a "public good/bad" X as a good (or a service) where consumption by individual A does not diminish the quantity of X available to B.

Common examples of public goods include clean air, defence, the judicial system, radio broadcasts, the control of pests etc. Public "bads" are the mirror image of these goods: polluted air, threats to national safety, pests etc.

Prices should reflect the marginal cost of consumption to society. Since my consumption of public goods is of no direct cost to anyone else, it follows that these should have a zero price. However, the provision of the goods, such as the ones mentioned above, is clearly not costless. This contradiction is neatly summarized by the following quote:

> "... private firms will either be unable to charge for the public good in which case they will not produce it; or if they are able to charge (by excluding its free consumption by all and sundry), there will be too little consumption of it." (Cooper, 1981, p. 16).

Whereas the willingness to pay for ordinary (private) goods can be read from the markets, it is more complicated to estimate people's appreciation of public goods. This is particularly relevant here, because of the public bad character of environmental quality items like polluted air and water, loss of genetic diversity, noise, smells, aesthetics etc. where one person's consumption does not rival another's.

Where there are no existing markets, people's valuation will have to be derived from "hidden" or implicit markets by looking at the consumption of related private goods, or by constructing artificial markets where people are invited to reveal their preferences. We will return to this in chapters 5 and 7.

3.2.2 Risk Markets

Few people would willingly bet all they own on roulette. Yet this is sometimes what an investment in improved inputs amounts to for the poor peasant living in a climatically erratic area. Clearly, the perspective on risk differs from the point of view of the individual and from the point of view of *all* individuals in society taken as a group.

Society can refer to both *risk-spreading* (many people will share the burden of failure, each one risking little) and *risk-pooling* (many different projects - some work, some fail). Arrow & Lind (1970) argue that if the risks are borne by the government, risk-spreading and non-correlation with the general state of the economy implies that society should be risk-neutral when discounting future costs and benefits. In other words, no adjustment to the usual discount rate needs to be made.

It is commonly assumed that private individuals may have a quite high rate of discount when considering investment options. This may render long-term investments, such as tree planting, financially unattractive. Given the precarious situation of most smallholder farmers, this tendency to weight immediate impacts much higher than long-term effects is natural. The individual's discount rate can be assumed to be based on considerations of risk/uncertainty as well as present income level and future income prospects in general.[5]

The point we wish to make is that if the farmer could insure himself against crop failures in bad years and pay a small premium as a fraction of the long run increased surplus, he would be willing to take the risks of investing in better technology, which may include soil conservation measures. Higher yields per hectare may also alleviate some of the pressure to clear marginal land for additional cultivation. However, such risk markets are usually not available as a result of spontaneous market forces.

One reason is that *transaction costs* may be high. In other words, making up contracts with a large number of perhaps illiterate peasants in sometimes quite inaccessible areas and collecting their insurance premiums may be a considerable obstacle.

There may also be an element of *moral hazard*, i.e. the insurance may affect the individual's behaviour in an adverse way. E.g., the peasant may sell some of the seeds and fertilizer, skip the weeding and then claim full compensation for the resulting loss in crops.

---

5. See e.g. Hoekstra (1985) for a discussion. We will return to this theme in chapter 5.

There could also be a problem of *adverse selection* in insurance markets. Assume that we have two villages both seeking insurance of a village woodlot, to safeguard against forest fires and theft. In the absence of detailed information, the insurance company will offer them both the standard contract. However, one village borders a major town and theft of wood for fuel is widespread. The other village is remote and expects little thefts. When faced with the average insurance fee, the remote village declines to participate, but the other village pays.

In the next round, the insurance company finds itself making a loss, because the fee was calculated on the average risk of theft. It may go out of business or raise its fees. The point is that only those who expect to gain from insuring themselves, given the fee level, will take out an insurance. Thus, there will be an automatic, adverse selection of individuals or groups who will be attracted by the availability of insurance.

Interestingly enough, the problem with moral hazard and adverse selection is not the risk itself due to imperfect information about the future. Rather, it is the asymmetric distribution of information among agents (Arrow, 1969). If everyone had access to the same information, insurance companies would see through moral hazards and design differentiated insurance schemes to tackle adverse selection.

3.2.3 Future Markets

A related problem is the insufficiency of markets relating future goods and services to values today. The lack of such markets will affect people's time horizon. This is often quoted as an obstacle in tree planting campaigns. If the individual farmer had an unambiguous right to the trees he plants and could sell this right to anyone (including the right of re-planting for future harvests), he could at any point in time realize the present value of even a very distant future benefit of the trees. The time horizon would then not be a perspective that differed in private and public decision-making - it would be infinite.

As we know, this is not how markets usually work. One reason could be the lack of defined *property rights* or lack of respect for such when defined. Trees planted on communal grounds may be subject to decisions by the chief, and trees under private ownership may be subject to theft of fruit and wood. This makes future benefits uncertain and discourages investment. Another reason is, again, the *transaction costs* of making such contracts including the cost of making forecasts about the future demand and prices for fuel, tree growth, survival rates, etc.

Chambers (1988) argues that the problem of short time horizons among poor people is exaggerated. Apart from the very poor, who are on the brink of starvation, poor people actually invest for the long run. More children means an immediate burden, but a net income some years ahead and long term social security. Even poor people invest in their children's education and sometimes substantially reduce consumption in order to pay off loans in order to retain long-term rights to land holdings.

3.2.4 Income Distribution

Finally, the concern for improved income distribution is one that has to be dealt with on the macro level. Individual agents cannot be expected to consider this in their own private decisions - private charity being the exception. The outcome of market forces at work may be politically unacceptable. Although we can argue about the extent to which the distribution is brought about by "free markets" or because of policy interventions, the result is usually to call for some form of government measures to correct this "injustice". However, such intervention is not trivial or without cost, which brings us to the next topic.

3.3 Policy Failures

The scope of this theme is potentially quite wide. If we agree with the Brundtland report that "Poverty is a major cause and effect of global environmental problems" (WCED, 1987, p. 3) the entire area of economic policy becomes relevant. If the general economic policy creates growth and employment opportunities in urban areas, the pressure on marginal land and forests may decrease. Higher income promotes conversion to electricity and petroleum products which reduce deforestation. However, the links between economic development and environmental degradation are not uni-directional: higher incomes may also breed demand for new products (such as beef) which may promote deforestation for cattle ranching, and new consumer habits may result in waste damaging the environment.

The discussion under the heading of policy failures affecting the environment will deal with policies concerning international trade, population, prices, taxes, political elites, public investment and environmental information.

3.3.1 International Trade Policy

Opinions differ as to what weight should be given to international policy failures versus national ones. This has been subject to an extensive debate between the "dependency school" (Blomström & Hettne, 1984) and neo-classical and other economists. We cannot pursue this debate here, but merely note some points of principle.

WCED (1987) blames both the workings of the international system and national policy failures for the environmental crisis, with some emphasis on the former. The emphasis is reversed in World Bank (1981, 1987). Trade restrictions that limit access to agricultural markets in the industrialized world discourage investments in agriculture in the developing world. However, this is not likely to be a major factor behind environmental degradation in the Third World.

Firstly, the effect of a liberalization would be limited for the countries most affected by the environmental crisis, namely sub-Saharan Africa (World Bank, 1981).[6] Secondly, to the extent that there is a connection between trade liberalization and agricultural investments in the Third World, its impact on environment is ambiguous - examples are given below.

3.3.2 Property Rights Definition and Enforcement

Moving down to the national level of policy making, we want to highlight a fundamental issue on the basis of which other incentives will act. This concerns the way in which property rights are defined and enforced. As noted under the discussion on market failures, the public goods/bads nature of environmental impacts sometimes prevent a definition of property rights which would make market transactions possible in the conventional way; consider e.g. the problem of defining property rights to clean air.

However, there are many cases where property rights are technically quite possible to define, but this is not done for political or cultural reasons. These reasons may be more or less strongly related to high transaction costs. Consider e.g. the problems of defining, enclosing and enforcing private patches of grazing land on a village's communally owned property. While there is no strict borderline between political and cultural reasons, one could exemplify by contrasting the (now changing) politically determined East European systems of state property with the historically evolving African forms of communal ownership of land. A system of common grazing property may be intended to fulfill an equitable social function, but increasing human and livestock populations have changed the scenery:

> "The most widespread and evident environmental problems of Lesotho are directly or indirectly related to overstocking. Estimates of overstocking of rangeland vary

---

6. "... a 60 percent cut in agricultural tariff and nontariff barriers by the developed countries would have increased African exports by only $292 million in 1974. This was only 7 percent of the estimated increase for all developing countries, or 1.8% of African nonfuel exports in that year.... Second, the restrictions do not affect Africa as much as they do other developing regions because the Sub-Saharan nations receive preferential access to the EEC ... , protectionism by developed countries had little effect on African growth in the last decade." (World Bank, 1981, p.20).

> from 150 to 300% of estimated carrying capacities. Continuous and uncontrolled grazing has resulted in progressive deterioration in the condition of the rangeland ..." (Kingdom of Lesotho, 1988, p. 19).

One should not underestimate the difficulties in transforming common property rights to crop and grazing land, trees, houses, industries and so on into private property. However, it is clear that the existence of private accountability for environmental degradation is a key factor for sound environmental management. If the tree I am planting is definitely mine, the incentive for tree planting is obviously greater than if the chief and his council will decide over its use - perhaps to their own benefit rather than mine.

Paradoxically, the introduction of inappropriately designed property rights may actively promote environmental degradation. When property rights are automatically conferred on those who "develop" the land by clearing it from forest vegetation, this accelerates deforestation (Binswanger, 1989; Mahar, 1988; Southgate, 1988).

Obviously, it is not enough to define property rights on paper; a legal system must also be created for the active protection of such rights:

> "In Mexico there is an excellent set of legislation to deal with pesticides. There is strong legislative control dealing with pesticide production and importation and a framework for the implementation of a nationwide monitoring system. There is a large bureaucratic apparatus, but, however, little effective control." (Meister, 1989, p. 22).

Some countries have provisions for penalties when land is abused and erosion proceeds unchecked, but they may never be enforced. Similarly, regulations on emissions and effluent discharges from industries may amount to a piece of paper and no field control. Even if such control is carried out, individuals who are negatively affected are sometimes barred from suing the polluter, effectively denying them the property right of clean air or water.

This is not to say that defined property rights are the ultimate and complete solution to all environmental problems, but we are suggesting that such rights, when properly enforced in the company of environmental laws, are a powerful contributing factor for successful environmental protection. Many governments fail on this account.

3.3.3 Population Policy

Population policies may refer to population *distribution* as well as to population *growth*. Uneven distribution of land holdings may e.g. contribute to marginal land degradation, where the poorer peasants have to carve out a meager living from steep slopes and thin soils, often clearing forests in the process. Governments may have to undertake land reforms in order to alleviate some of the environmental pressure.

Turning to the issue of population growth and public policy, we are faced with three challenging questions before any statement about population policy failure can be made:

(1) What is the relationship between population growth and environmental quality?

(2) If there is a negative relationship between population growth and environmental quality, why should the government intervene? After all, people may prefer to have more children even when this has an environmental cost;

(3) If there is a case for government intervention in order to reduce population growth, is there any effective way of achieving it?

Firstly, in the long run, even with a sound distribution of the population on the land, rapid population growth will aggravate environmental pressure. Failure to tackle rapidly increasing populations is often cited as a strong determinant of environmental degradation:

> "No single factor contributes more to environmental degradation in developing countries than rapid population growth (World Bank, 1989, p. 6).

This view is controversial. Boserup (1981) emphasizes the adaptability of agricultural systems under pressure of an increasing population. Growing populations could be a blessing or a problem depending on the situation. The fate of the country is likely to depend on the ability of the ruling elite to organize society, what Boserup calls the "administrative technology." Simon (1981) argues that people are "the ultimate resource" that will find new and ingenious ways to overcome short run scarcities.

While we acknowledge that the general issue of population growth and economic growth remains a bone of contention (Birdsall, 1984), it appears evident that rapid population growth presents a severe challenge for institutional change, if environmental degradation is to be avoided. Especially, when property rights are poorly defined, as in much of Africa, the effect is often increasing deterioration due to deforestation, overgrazing and overcultivation.

Moving on to the second question posed above, a case for government intervention has to be made before any charge of negligence can be made. What are the main arguments in favour of public population policies?

Firstly, the social cost of population growth exceeds the private - there is a negative externality in the jargon established above. Some of the cost of raising additional children is carried by others through the overutilizaton of common property, school subsidies, and so on. Secondly, the private markets undersupply family planning services. (Birdsall, 1988; World Bank, 1984). This argument appears more convincing when it relates to research and public information rather than supply of contraceptive devices, where, in principle, private agents should be able to furnish necessary services. However, given other market imperfections, public intervention may be necessary also in this case.

Turning to the third question: even if one accepts the proposition that rapid population growth in general presents an environmental problem, and that there is a need for government intervention, one may still be unconvinced that this is a matter that the government can effectively deal with.

Government policy in relation to population growth is not simply a matter of handing out contraceptives. Policies regarding the status of women, especially their education, children's schooling, health care, marriage ages, children quotas, family taxation, family allowances, and so on may affect decision about having children as much as specific family planning programmes.

It is extremely difficult to isolate the impact that active government measures can have on population growth. However, existing evidence from both cross-country studies and in-country studies gives the impression that "... public support for family planning programs ... can lower fertility quickly (World Bank, 1984, p. 107). Examples are quoted from Colombia, Costa Rica, India, Indonesia, Mexico and Thailand. Such programmes will of course be most powerful when they coincide with other socio-economic factors contributing to the desire for smaller families.

In summary, population growth matters for environmental degradation, governments have a role to play in shaping population policy, and there are - although in a qualified sense - effective means of achieving a decline in population growth. Yet, many governments rank low in terms of commitment and public spending for family planning (World Bank, 1984).

3.3.4 Price Policy

A case of obvious relevance to environmental effects in Third World countries is the often heavy state intervention in pricing. This affects directly both the use of inputs and production of agricultural outputs. Some examples are:[7]

7. See Barbier (1987, 1989), Repetto (1987), Repetto & Gillis (1988), Southgate (1988), Veloz et al (1985), Warford (1987) and World Bank (1988).

- too low royalties on harvesting of mature timber has set off "timber-booms" with devastating impact on natural forests in many countries;
- subsidies of pesticides which pollute streams and threaten fisheries and drinking water;
- fertilizer subsidies that promote nitrogen leakage and eutrophication;
- price control of firewood and charcoal discourage the adoption of agroforestry schemes and firewood plantations;
- irrigation subsidies promoting low-return investments that have caused or aggravated flooding and salinization, increased human exposure to water-borne diseases and caused losses to fisheries.

There are also indirect environmental effects of pricing of foreign currencies and other commodities: the overvaluation of the Dominican Republic currency has discouraged the environmentally relatively beneficial production of coffee and citrus fruit for export (Veloz et al, 1985). Overvaluation of the domestic currency is a common feature of Third World economies.

However, the effects are complex and can go in various directions:

- fertilizer subsidies increase environmental pollution but also increase plant cover, thus reducing erosion;
- a devaluation provides incentive to cultivate an export crop but this may be favorable (as coffee vs corn in Haiti) or unfavorable (as groundnut cultivation vs livestock rearing on grazing land in the Sahel).[8]
- a rise in prices on agricultural production may encourage investments in erosion control measures, but may also give an incentive to cropping of marginal land, thus causing deforestation and increasing erosion (Southgate & Pearce, 1988).

Macro-economic policy of developing countries has often had an "urban bias" with a low share of investments directed to agriculture and adverse intersectoral terms of trade (Lipton, 1981). This has discouraged sound agricultural development.[9] Whatever the direction of the environmental micro-level effects are, they may be substantial and should be carefully assessed.

---

8. These examples are based on a given crop management regime. Repetto (1987) argues that most export crops are less erosion inducing than food crops. However, crop management is much more important than the type of crop grown (Hudson, 1981).

9. There is common agreement that low agricultural prices can be a disincentive to production. To what extent supply responds to higher prices is more controversial, and the data base for Africa is so poor that nothing reliable can be said about agricultural production trends (Fones-Sundell, 1987).

3.3.5 Tax Policy

Another economic policy instrument that influences individuals' behaviour is taxation. There are many examples of how tax policies encourage (or fail to discourage) inefficient use of environmental resources. Like the other policy failures presented in this chapter, this type of consequences has often been neglected. Some examples are given below.

Investment tax credits have encouraged exploitation of environmentally weak areas in Brazil. A case study by Mahar (1989) presented in chapter 7 discusses this in some detail.

Differential rates of taxation among commodities may strongly influence cropping patterns and land-use. Within the agricultural sector, many countries discriminate against export crops. In the case of Haiti, a raised export tax on coffee caused coffee trees to be replaced with staple crops such as corn. This increased erosion of steep lands (Lundahl, 1979). Lowering the export tax for certain commodities, such as tropical timber, may also have environmentally detrimental impacts. Thus, the environmental impact will have to be assessed case by case.

Income tax exemptions impact environmental management. In some countries, virtually all agricultural income is exempt from income tax. This tends to increase demand for land and contribute to a rapid increase in the conversion of forest to agricultural uses. A case study with an illustration from Brazil by Binswanger (1989) is presented in chapter 7.

3.3.6 Political Elites and Bureaucratic Sub-optimization

The "lack of political will" is often cited as a factor behind failure to stop environmental degradation. The implicit assumption seems to be that government well represents the interest of the masses. Obviously, there are many countries where this is not true and where the following observation would be appropriate:

> "Desertification is a low priority for politicians because the people who live in arid zones have little political power. Government want aid spent in cities, where the results benefit the nations's élite." (Grainger, 1982, p. 4)

A reason for the relative lack of interest in conservation programmes may be that they rarely bring opportunities for personal advancement for bureaucrats, in comparison with the issuing of import-export licenses, the handling of foreign business, and the control of state-controlled markets (Blaikie, 1985). Therefore, environmental protection will not attract the more thrusting bureaucrats, Blaikie argues. On the contrary, favouring exploitative interests may carry substantial rewards:

> "The existence of large resource rents from harvesting mature timber has attracted politicians as well as businessmen to the opportunities of immediate gain."
> (Repetto & Gillis 1988, p. 388).

Furthermore, environmental programmes bring out conflicts of interests with e.g. large cattle-owners, land-owners and forest contractors. These people may also be a part of, or associated with, the political élite and its bureaucracy, which makes the task even more delicate. Job security and risk-minimization are most important considerations for many government employees. The lack of government implementation of carefully worded resolutions and laws may have quite logical explanations.

Politically, this is a delicate issue. There are strong vested interests in status quo. The political élites have a direct interest in maintaining current positions, or lack the incentives to alienate other powerful groups. The difficulties continue all the way to the village level, where local élites benefiting from current "communal management" will tend to block changes.

3.3.7 Public Investment

The misuse of public funds for unwise investment, such as military spending, prestige projects and other unprofitable undertakings is a theme that is not unique to Third World countries. But the effects in terms of retarded economic growth and lack of resources to combat environmental damage is one that is felt even more strongly by poor people with limited options.

Public investment is very closely connected to environmental degradation in the case of deforestation (Repetto & Gillis, 1988). Such investments - often with the support of an external donor agency (Shane, 1986) - have led to substantial intrusions in natural forest to make room for estate crops such as rubber, palm oil and cocoa. Large-scale infrastructural investments in mining, dams and roads have also resulted in large-scale destruction of forests.

The theme of misdirected public investments is elaborated by the "Palme Commission's" report on Common Security (1982). The report argues that military spending not only crowds out alternative investment, but also retards growth in general. Our reflection is that the impact on growth may or may not have negative environmental effects depending on the nature of alternative investments. It remains clear that military spending in developing countries amount to almost as much as expenditure on education and health combined (World Bank, 1984, p. 150). There are good alternative uses for these resources in terms of environmental protection.

3.3.8 Environmental Information

This type of policy failure takes many forms. The denial of freedom to publicize and criticize freely will also put a lid on the vital debate about environmental management. Societies without free elections will prevent competing movements from capitalizing on the need for public intervention in the interest of environmental improvements. Environmental mismanagement and neglect may not be reported for fear of reprisals. The recent avalanche of environmental scandals in Eastern Europe bears testimony of the importance of this point. Suddenly, following the political reforms embodied in the concept of "glasnost", the problems have been brought out into the open, and responsible solutions can be demanded.

The Brundtland report (WCED) addresses this theme and notes that progress will be facilitated by recognition of:

- the right of individuals to have access to current information on the state of the environment;
- the right to participate in decision-making on activities with a significant effect on the environment;
- the right to legal remedies for those whose health or environment has been or may be seriously affected.[10]

Therefore, democratic reform is an issue of importance also from an environmental perspective.

3.4 Summary

Taking the theoretical model of a perfectly competitive economy with complete markets as our bench-mark, we have argued that several distortions are sources of environmental damage. We label the first category of these distortions *market failures*: such as externalities, public goods/"bads", lack of risk and future markets.

Market failures (as well as other social forces) give rise to government interventions. However, these are not without cost and problems, and result in another set of problems: *policy failures* in the area of international trade, property rights definition and

10. WCED, 1987, pp. 326-332 develops this theme further.

enforcement, population growth, price regulation, taxes, bureaucratic sub-optimization, misdirected public investments and suppression of environmental information.

The environmental damage caused by market and policy failures can be analysed by a combination of economic and other means to:

(a) alter general economic policy so as to achieve beneficial environmental effects;

(b) institute specific environmental policies in the service of sustainable development;

(c) design development projects so that environmental damage is optimized;

(d) design specific projects to counteract environmental damage.

With this chapter, we wanted to sketch the overall economic and policy environment within which economic analysis will have to operate. The micro-level of project analysis will be the focus of chapters 5 and 7. However, the macro-level - best handled in a more general framework - is the subject of the chapter that now follows.

4. General Equilibrium Analysis and National Accounting

4.1 General Equilibrium Analysis

Introduction

The core theory of economics is the theory of general equilibrium. While the approaches discussed in previous chapters have been based on partial equilibrium analysis, we will in this chapter survey approaches based on general equilibrium analysis, i.e. approaches which try to include most of the interdependencies in the economy.

Behind the constructs to be presented in this chapter are the ideas of a general market equilibrium that were advanced by Leon Walras during the last part of the 19th century. A change or "disturbance" in one sector of the economy will have repercussions throughout the economy by changing relative prices and thereby changing incentives to produce and to consume various goods and services.

This is relevant to economic analysis of environmental resources for several reasons. Firstly, a particular project may have important repercussions in the economy and in order to incorporate them an approach based on general equilibrium theory may be necessary. One particular instance of this is exemplified by the cost of pollution control. The cost of reducing, for example, sulphur emissions in a country can be estimated in many different ways, differing according to how many adjustment mechanisms are included.

The usual "engineering" approach is based on the cost of operating pollution control equipment, i. e. the cost of reducing the emissions from an existing structure without changing neither the technology nor the output. By including fuel switching as one control option new (and lower) control costs can be estimated. By also including the possibility of switching from fuels to electricity from hydropower and nuclear power, the cost of controlling sulphur can be further reduced.

Further repercussions on the rest of the economy occur through changing relative prices. By changed relative prices, the economy will adjust its production structure as well as its trade with other countries in such a way as to minimize the cost of pollution control. It is quite possible that these last adjustments will mean a large reduction of the relevant cost for pollution control.[1]

Secondly, quite often, national and regional policies (fiscal, agricultural, trade policies, etc.), that are not directly aimed at environmental issues, will through the repercussions in the economy have a substantial impact on the environment. This may be particularly true in conjunction with the income distribution effects from the policies. In order to trace these repercussions, a general equilibrium modelling framework is needed.

Finally, quite often, the economic analysis of a set of environmental problems is directed toward optimization, for example minimizing the necessary costs for achieving an environmental improvement. General equilibrium models give one set of tools that can be used to implement such optimization.

Applied general equilibrium analysis is almost always based on the standard national accounts. As such accounts, if properly extended, can also be used as a database for judging environmental effects, we will in the next section survey these accounts.

4.2 National Income Accounting and Environmental Resources

Introduction

National income accounting can be traced back to the 17th century in England when William Petty estimated the national income in Britain.[2] However, it was not until the second world war that national accounts and national income concepts were used more frequently. The system of national accounts (SNA) that was developed within the United Nations in the late 1940's is still essentially the same as the one currently in use in most countries. The objective of these accounts is to provide a database for macroeconomic analysis and in particular such analyses that fall within the Keynesian theoretical framework. However, besides this use of the national accounts, they have to a large extent been used to provide aggregate measures of economic performance and economic welfare. Gross national product (GNP) has for a long time been used as the measure of the economic progress of a country. However, this use of the standard national accounts has during the last decade come under heavy criticism for neglecting important environmental resources. In this section, we will review this discussion and suggest ways by which better aggregated indicators of human well being can be constructed.

---

1. Carlsson (1988) has analysed the differences between different cost concepts for the Swedish energy system and found substantial differences between an engineering approach and a general equilibrium approach.
2. See Sir Richard Stone's Nobel prize lecture 1984 "The accounts of Society" for a fascinating discussion of the history of national accounts.

The Standard National Accounts

In order to establish an understanding of the meaning of national accounts, let us look at the main accounts. In SNA, the economy is divided into four main accounts and for each account the income and expenses. The accounts are production, consumption, accumulation and the rest of the world. Let us take a closer look at the production account.

Table 4.2.1 The Production Account

Outgoings			Incomings	
Value added	GDP		Sales of consumption goods	C
Imports	M		Sales of capital goods	GI
			Exports	X
Total outgoings		=	Total incomings	

Value added is a measure of the total production in the economy. Value added for a company is defined as the value of sales minus the value of purchases of intermediary products. This means that the value added is equal to the wage bill plus the return on capital plus direct and indirect taxes (except for indirect taxes paid on purchases of intermediary goods). We will disregard taxes in the sequel. The return on capital or the operating surplus is commonly estimated as the difference between revenues and expenditures for intermediary products and labour. For goods produced in the public sector, there are no records of sales. Thus the operating surplus cannot be estimated as for private companies. Instead, the value added is defined simply as the wage bill. Thus, gross national product - GNP - is equal to the sum over all firms - private or public - of their value added. Implicit in this definition is the requirement that the value added gives rise to factor payment to the national factor owners. Thus, value added produced abroad is included in GNP, as net factor payments from abroad. If only domestically produced value added is included, we have Gross domestic product - GDP. For most countries, the difference between GNP and GDP is quite small. However, for many countries with workers migrating across national borders such as Botswana or Lesotho, the difference may be substantial.

The reason for the prefix "gross" is that we have not deducted the decrease in the value of assets following depreciation of the capital stock. If depreciation of the capital stock is deducted, we will have the net national product - NNP - concept. We will return to this later.

Note that sales of consumption goods and capital goods to the public sector are included in the account above.

It follows from the account above that

$$GNP + M = C + GI + X,$$

i.e. the total supply of goods and services (the left hand side) is equal to the total use (the right hand side). Thus, gross national product can be calculated in three ways. The first two relate to this balance between supply and demand: as the sum of value added over the economy or as the value of final demand

$$C + GI + X - M,$$

i.e. as expenditures on consumption plus expenditures on gross investment plus the surplus in the trade balance (including net factor payments across the national borders). As the value added is equal to the remuneration of capital and labour, it also follows that GNP can be calculated as the sum of capital and labour income, that is equal to the national income. However, because of the difficulties of obtaining reliable independent estimates of capital income, this third method is very rarely used.

The income and outlay account is shown in table 4.2.2.

Table 4.2.2 The Income and Outlay Account

Outgoings			Incomings	
Purchases of Consumption Goods	C		Gross income	GDP
Savings	S		Capital depreciation	-D
Net current transfers	NT		Net factor payment	NP
Total outlays		=	Total income	

The accumulation or capital transaction account can be found in table 4.2.3.

Table 4.2.3 The Capital Account

Outgoings			Incomings	
Purchases of capital goods	GI		Savings	S
less depreciation	-D			
Net borrowing abroad	-L			
Total investment		=	Total savings	

Finally, the rest of the world account (balance of payment account) is given in table 4.2.4

Table 4.2.4 The Balance of Payment Account

Outgoings			Incomings	
Purchases of export	X		Sales of import	M
Net factor payment	NP		Net current.transfer	NT
			Net borrowing	-L
Total outlays		=	Total receipts	

Social accounting matrices and computable general equilibrium models

These accounts can be consolidated in a social accounting matrix - SAM.[3] With these four main accounts, the matrix would look like the one in table 4.2.5. In order to simplify, we have disregarded net factor payment from abroad as well as net transfers to other countries and the depreciation of the capital stock.

Row and column 1) represent institutions' accounting. In the simplest case, institutions are households and the public sector, but it is quite possible to break down institutions into different classes of households, different levels of governments, different types of private enterprises etc. We will come back to such disaggregation later. The row corresponds to the incomings of the institutions. The income of the institutions is in this table the factor rewards. The column corresponds to the outgoings, that is the uses of the income - consumption and saving. Note that the row sum equals the column sum. The row sum of the production account corresponds to the incomings in table 4.2.1 and the column sum to the outgoings in the same table.

3. For an introduction to the use of social accounting matrices, see Pyatt and Round (1985).

Table 4.2.5 A Social Accounting Matrix

	1)	2)	3)	4)	5)
1) Institutions		GNP			
2) Factors			GNP		
3) Production	C			GI	X
4) Capital Accounts	S				
5) Balance of Payments			M	- L	

In the same way, the row sum of the capital account corresponds to the incomings in the capital account and the column sum to the outgoings, and the row sum of the balance of payment or Rest of the World - RoW - corresponds to the incomings of the balance of payment and the column sum to the outgoings.

Thus the total system of national accounts can be represented in a very compact form by presenting the data in a social accounting matrix. It has already been indicated that in general, the different accounts can be disaggregated in order to give information on different institutions, different industrial sectors, different commodity groups etc. However, the general principle remains the same: the rows correspond to payments to the account, while the columns correspond to outlays. There are three different disaggregations that are interesting in this connection. First, value added can be disaggregated into one labour income account and one capital income account; second the disaggregation of institutions and in particular households into special groups of households like skilled and non-skilled workers, rural and urban households, high income and low income households. By that kind of disaggregation, it is possible to study income distributional effects from policy changes. We will come back to this later.

The third disaggregation of interest is the disaggregation of the production account into different production sectors. Such a disaggregation means that there would be one row and one column for each sector, the rows showing the sales of the output from the sector and the column showing the purchases of intermediary products, imports, the wage bill, taxes and the operating surplus (i.e. capital income). This disaggregation means that the conventional input-output tables can be integrated in a very natural way in the accounting framework. Thus a SAM enables the analyst not only to carry out conventional input-output analysis but even more advanced general equilibrium studies.[4]

We will illustrate this by assuming that the production sector has been disaggregated into two sectors - agriculture and manufacturing. We have also introduced some arbitrary numbers for a hypothetical economy. We have also disaggregated factors into capital and labour and institutions into households and government.

Table 4.2.6 A Hypothetical SAM (in US$)

	1)	2)	3)	4)	5)	6)	7)	8)	Tot
1) Household			150	40					190
2) Government	30						5		35
3) Labour					50	100			150
4) Capital					20	20			40
5) Agriculture	70	20			10	15			115
6) Manufacturing	70	15			20	30		30	165
7) Capital Account	20								20
8) R.o.W.					15		15		30
Total	190	35	150	40	115	165	20	30	

At the risk of being repetitious, let us once again look at the meaning of the various items in this social accounting matrix. Each column and row correspond to an account in the economy. In this particular SAM, we can distinguish between the following types of accounts:

4. Input-output analysis is presented in most elementary and intermediate textbooks on microeconomics. Dersvis et al (1982) gives a complete introduction to input-output analysis.

- Factors of production: labour and capital
- Institutional accounts: households and the government
- Production accounts: agriculture and manufacturing
- Capital account or savings and investment
- Rest of the world or the balance of paymeant (RoW)

Each column shows the expenditures in the account, and the corresponding row the revenues. The column 5, i.e. the agriculture column, gives the purchases in agriculture from other accounts., i.e. wages to labour ($50), return on capital ($20), purchases of intermediate goods from agriculture ($10), manufacturing ($20) and imports ($15). The corresponding row shows that the agricultural sector received $70 from sales to the households, $20 from sales to the government, $10 from sales within the agriculture and $15 from sales to the industry.

The third and fourth rows show the incomes that accrue to the owners of the factors of production, labour ($150) and capital ($40). The sum of these gives the total value added, i.e. the gross national product in this country. The first row shows that it is the households that own the factors of production and therefore receives the whole product, that is, the national income. The first column shows that the income was spent on taxes ($30), purchases of agricultural goods ($70), purchases of industrial goods ($70), and savings ($20). The second row shows that in addition to the tax receipts ($30), the government also borrowed ($5).

Finally, the eigth column shows that the industry exported for $30 and the eigth row shows that agriculture imported for $15, giving a surplus of $15. The household savings were thus partly lent to the government ($5) and partly invested abroad.

Real SAMs have been constructed for a large number of developing countries, mainly by the World Bank[5]. These are, of course much more disaggregated than the illustration we have used here. One particular interesting disaggregation is the identification of different types of households - skilled and non-skilled workers, rural vs. urban households, low income households. Such disaggregation allows the analysis of the income distributional effects of policy changes.

A SAM gives a picture of the main payments in an economy in a given year. By modelling these payments, i.e. introducing behavioural assumptions and mechanisms by which these payments can be explained, it is possible to study how the economy would react to a change in the economic environment, such as policy changes, changes in terms of trade, productivity etc. The modelling efforts are based on rather sophisticated economic analysis and it is impossible to go into any detail here.[6]

5. See King (1981).
6. Dersvis et al (1982) gives a rather complete description of techniques of modelling.

The payments to the factors of production are most often modelled by using the standard neoclassical theory of cost minimization, the payments for purchases of intermediate goods are generally modelled by assuming fixed input-output coefficients. The household expenditures on different goods and services are explained by using econometrically estimated systems of demand functions. Foreign trade is usually explained in terms of the relative prices between domestically produced goods and the prices on the world market. Government expenditures are generally assumed to be exogenous, explained outside the model.

The weak points in constructing such CGE models (Computable General Equilibrium models) have been in relation to the explanations of savings, exports and imports and capital movements across the borders. These weaknesses do not, however, need to deter us from using CGE models, as it is in many cases absolutely essential to include the most important interdependencies in the economy in the analysis.

Besides catching the interdependencies in the economy, a CGE model can be very useful in finding the income distributional effects from various policies on the macrolevel. The way income distribution can be studied is by disaggregating different accounts in the SAM. By separating out different types of households - rural vs urban vs migrant workers and by wealth, and by separating out different types of labour - skilled vs non-skilled, and by separating out different forms of capital - land, real capital, financial capital etc, it is possible to catch many interesting income distributional consequences. For example, the SAM prepared for Botswana 1978/79 includes six different types of labour, nine different types of households, five different types of other institutional accounts and one type of capital.[7]

On the basis of a such disaggregated SAM, it is possible to calibrate a CGE model, which could be used to simulate the welfare impact of different macroeconomic policies on different types of households. This approach has been successfully employed by Adelman and Robinson in a study of Korea.[8] A similar modelling attempt can be found in "A Model of Distribution and Growth"[9]. As the physical environment to a very large extent is a "public good", policies that lead to changes in the environment will usually have very strong income distributional effects, and it becomes perhaps more important than otherwise to take these changes into account.

During the last ten years, there have been major advances in modelling CGE, mainly thanks to research carried out at the World Bank. Computer software has been

7. Central Statistical Office, Gaborone, Botswana.
8. Adelman and Robinson (1978).
9. Ahluwalia & Chenery (1981).

developed[10] which has simplified the construction and analysis of CGE-models substantially.

The main purposes of a system of national accounts are to provide an empirical and analytical framework for a discussion of macroeconomic policy options and to provide a database for empirical modelling. It should be recognized and stressed that for this purpose, the system has worked very satisfactorily. It is possible to extend them so as to make them more useful for the analysis of environmental resources, and we will discuss such extensions shortly. However, the accounts have also been used for other purposes. One such purpose is to measure the performance of the economy. Of course, the accounts are defined in such a way that they can be used for some measurements of performance. For example, if total demand is expanded through expansive fiscal policies, employment and national income should go up. To monitor this response to economic policy, the system is well suited. But GNP or national income has also been used as an aggregate measure of economic wellbeing. This is much more questionable.

4.3 Aggregate Welfare Measures

There are two obvious arguments that gross national product as it is currently defined is not a good measurement of wellbeing. First, it does not include income distributional considerations. However, it seems difficult to construct a single measure that would include both distributional considerations and production performance. Moreover, there are other ways of measuring the development of the income distribution. Second, gross national product is not the proper concept because it does not deduct the cost of capital depreciation.[11] Instead, the net national product is more appropriate.

However, there are also a number of criticisms that have been raised in connection with environmental resources.[12] These are

(1) "defensive expenditures" against environmental deterioration are presently included in final demand but should be excluded,

(2) damage to individuals and firms from environmental degradation is presently

10. GAMS and Hercules are names of softwares developed at the Bank and now available through commercial channels. GAMS is a general purpose modelling system and Hercules is designed to construct, calibrate and solve CGE-models.

11. There are many other kinds of relevant criticism that can be raised against the use of national product measures as welfare measures such the existence of non-competitive markets and the bad estimates of value added in the public sector. We will not go into a discussion of these here. However, there are also many misunderstandings in the discussion of the role of national product and most critical points against the use of NNP as a welfare measure are not valid.

12. See for example Ahmad, El Serafy and Lutz (1989) for a discussion.

not deducted from national income but should be,

(3) depreciation of stocks other than the stock of real capital is not included but should be.

We will argue in the following that 1) is wrong, that 2) is partly correct and that 3) is correct.

Defensive expenditures are defined as those expenditures by households and the public sector that are made in order to "defend" households from environmental degradation. The concept includes both "preventive expenditures" and "replacement cost" as defined in chapter 5. For example, when households have to clean their windows more often because of air pollution, the resulting increase in spending on cleaning equipment is one kind of defensive expenditures. When the local government decides to clean up a previous heavily polluted area, we have another example of defensive expenditures. When the public sector is installing extra water treatment equipment in order to avoid deterioration of tap water, it is still another example of defensive expenditures.

It has now been argued that these defensive expenditures should not be included in the net national product. The basic reason is that they do not correspond to an improvement in human wellbeing. Instead, they are only indications of environmental degradation. This argument is sometimes strengthened by saying that defensive expenditures in the private sector are treated as intermediary products, so that they are deducted from the sales in the calculation of value added.

This last argument is obviously nonsense. It is true that for each company buying products to defending itself against environmental degradation, the defensive expenditures corresponding to the purchases of intermediary products are not included in its value added. However, they are included in the value added of the selling companies, and are therefore included in NNP. There is thus no essential difference between the production account and the consumption account in the way defensive expenditures are included.

The counter argument against the main point (1) is more subtle. It is based on the observation that individuals, households and the public sector buy goods and services in order to achieve an improvement. The purchases of goods and services to protect oneself or others from a degrading environment are made to improve the wellbeing, at least for those who made the purchases. There is nothing that makes defensive expenditures different from other expenditures in this respect.

An example may clarify the situation. Assume that the public sector decides to clean up a beach so that it can be used for recreation. Assume further that there is a strong demand for more recreational areas so that the value of the improved beach means an improvement in human well being. Then conventional accounts would show no change in NNP (value added in the public sector will increase but will be offset by a decrease somewhere else in the economy that has to give up the resources used for the clean up). However, if defensive expenditures are deducted from final demand, NNP would actually fall - an absurd result. Because of the way public production is valued (i.e. only including the expenses for labour), conventional accounts will not be perfect - they may show a decrease in NNP, but they will perform much better than what would be the case if the criticism in point i) would have been taken into account.[13]

The criticism in point (2) that the environmental damage is not included in NNP as currently defined is partly correct and partly wrong. It is obvious that environmental damage to households is not included in NNP, although this damage may be of great importance to the wellbeing of the households. However, as far as the damage harmed companies, it is already included in the conventional accounts. This is so because environmental damage in this case implies a reduction in productivity and therefore in the value added. For example, if air pollution is damaging agriculture, the damage will show up in reduced sales and therefore in reduced value added. There is therefore no need to reform the accounts in order to explicitly include current damage to production from environmental damage.

On the other hand, damage to households (and the public sector) is not included in the present accounts and there is a need to develop a system to generate data on household damage. However, the main difficulty here is the valuation of environmental damage. One of the main purposes of this book is to show how environmental resources can be valued by using different techniques. However, it may be very difficult to use these techniques on a routine basis to provide annual national estimates of environmental damage. Therefore, approximations may be warranted.

Some authors have argued that damage to households and the public sector could be approximated by defensive expenditures. However, this will in general be a bad approximation, except for those few cases when such expenditures are perfect substitutes to environmental improvements. Moreover, some of the public defensive expenditures are made to protect production activities in firms. Including these expenditures would therefore mean double counting.

Another proposed approximation has been tried in several countries (foremost Japan and the Netherlands) and consists of the assumption that there are specified targets for environmental policies such as ambient air and water quality standards.[14] Environmental damage can then be approximated by the cost of achieving these targets. The

13. This is discussed in a rigorous theoretical framework by Mäler (1990b)

14. For Japan see K. Uno (1989) and for the Netherlands see Hueting in Ahmad, El Serafy and Lutz eds.(1989)

approximation is far from perfect and may imply double counting as some of the targets are determined on the basis of damage to production. Then, as we have already seen, this damage is already taken into account in the conventional accounts and the subtraction of the cost of achieving the target would thus imply double counting. Moreover, whenever environmental damage in one country is the result of activities in other countries, this approach will face serious difficulties because the cost of abatement in a foreign country is in general not known to the country in which the damage occurs. Unfortunately, the state of the art is currently such that we may have to rely on such approximations.

Finally, the criticism in point (3) is valid. When we go from GNP to NNP, we deduct the depreciation allowances for the stock of real capital. However, the stock of other assets also change over time. The stock of fish populations may go down because of overfishing, the stock of biomass in forests may go down because of to high timber production, the stock of ground water may go down because of too much pumping. All these stocks should be included in the national wealth, and what matters is the change in the national wealth. Therefore, changes in the national wealth (which may be positive for many countries) should be included in the accounts in order to provide of a real net national product - a concept which reflect the current wellbeing as well as the change in the future possibilities of producing wellbeing.

That such modifications are of importance is illuminated by a study by World Resources Institute on the accounting framework in Indonesia.[15] The study shows that if due account is taken of the changes in the stocks of top soil, forests and proven oil reserves, the annual growth rate changes from 7.1 % to 4 % during the period 1971 - 1984.

A "Green" Accounting System

The modifications of the accounting system suggested above can be illustrated in a social accounting matrix. In order to incorporate environmental resources, we need one new account - an environmental account. The matrix is shown in table 4.3.1.

NNP is here the net value added in production, net of the depreciation of real capital, that is, the conventional net national product. The total income consists of NNP plus rent on environmental resources. This income is equal to purchases of consumption goods C plus savings S minus the damage to households from a degraded environment ED. In the product account, it is assumed that there is an imputed value EnvU on the companies use of environmental resources, including the emission of pollutants to air and water. Savings S plus the depreciation D equals gross investment GI in real capital plus the foreign net investment X-M plus the value of the change in the stock of environmental resources ESt. In the environmental account, the total incomings are the imputed use of environmental resources EnvU plus the value of the change in the stock of resources ESt

15. See Repetto et.al. (1989)

less environmental damage ED to the households. These incomings are balanced by the environmental rent, which is assumed to be part of the income.

Table 4.3.1 A Hypothetical SAM

	Institutions	Factors	Production	S/I	RoW	Environment
Institutions		NNP				Rent
Factors			NNP			
Production	C			I	X-M	
S/I	S		D			
RoW				X-M		
Environment	-ED		EnvU	ESt		

Note that in this accounting framework, the sum in the first column C + S - ED gives the net "green" national product where environmental damage and changes in environmental stocks have been netted out. This is the aggregated measure of human wellbeing that we have been trying to find. In order to differentiate it from SNA, it should perhaps be denoted the net welfare measure - NWM. Note that it is equal to the conventional net national product NNP plus environmental rents.

Sustainable Development

It is interesting to note that in the accounting framework proposed above, the ideas of sustainable development in 2.2 fit in very well. In fact, it can be shown that the net green national product or NWM can be regarded as the sustainable income, that is the value of total consumption that can be maintained forever. This result follows from the fact that that NWM can be regarded as the return on the total stock of assets - the national wealth - including real capital, human capital, and the stock of environmental and natural resources. For details, see Mäler (1991) and Dasgupta-Mäler (1991).

Applications

So far, the empirical experiences from using modified accounts are very limited. The most ambitious attempt is probably the study by Repetto already referred to on the Indonesian development. However, in a couple of years, we will probably gain much more experience because of activities already decided upon. The World Bank and UNEP are planning to undertake country studies involving new designs of accounting systems in order to incorporate environmental concerns. Many countries such as West Germany and Sweden are planning to create satellite accounts that will include parts or all of the accounting framework described above. Therefore, we will shortly know the practicability of "green" accounts.

It is clear that the possibility of creating national accounts in the sense outlined above means that the sustainability of the current development can be monitored in an efficient way. Even if conventional GNP is increasing, the net national product as here defined or NWM, may be decreasing, indicating that the development path is non-sustainable. As politicians as well as the general public follow the development of GNP with great interest, a change in the interest from GNP to NWM may be of importance for the design of economic policies and in particular for the incentives to create policies that do take environmental consequences into account.

4.4 Natural Resource Accounting and Computable General Equilibrium Models

Natural Resource Accounting

The preceding discussion of national income accounting was based on accounts in monetary units. However, in some countries, attempts have been made to construct accounts on stocks and flows of natural resources in physical units. The most advanced attempts have been made in France and in Norway. The French Natural Patrnimony Accounts are presented in J. Theys (1989) and the Norwegian accounts in Alfsen et al (1987).

These systems try to keep account of the stocks of various natural assets such as fish populations, oil reserves, standing timber in the forests as well as flows such as discharges of sulphur dioxide, the production of electricity from hydropower stations. Thus, these systems are large databases on the state of and the change in the environment. They do not provide one measure of sustainability as the net national product could in principle (but perhaps not in practice) represent. Instead, they show for a number of different resources their development over time and the analyst has to make his own comparisons between growing and decreasing stocks in order to come up with a judgement on whether the overall development is sustainable or not.

Applications of CGE-models to Environmental Issues

The natural resource accounts are databases that could be used for constructing computable general equilibrium - CGE -models by which the interaction between economic development and environmental resource use can be studied. Up to now, the number of applications of fully developed CGE-models on problems of environmental resources are quite limited. However, there is a substantial number of applications that are built on parts of a full CGE.

That part of the SAM that is the intersection between the rows and columns representing the production accounts is usually called the input-output table. It describes the flow of goods and services between the different production sectors of the economy. By making assumptions on fixed input-output coefficients it is possible to use this part of the SAM to an analysis of production effects in connection with resource problems.[16] We will look somewhat more closely at this possibility in a short while.

This approach is based on the assumption that the activities in different production sectors have different effects on the environment and that these effects are proportional to the production in the sector. The effects can be the discharge of different harmful substances or the consumption of certain renewable or non-renewable resources. In order to exploit the approach fully, it would be desirable to expand the SAM so as to include an accounting system for environmental resources consistent with the accounts within the SAM.

By integrating natural resource accounts with a social accounting matrix, it would be possible to study some of the repercussions in the economy from say a limit on the discharge of sulphur or a reduction in the use of a fishery. Not only would the conventional economic effects be identified, but unexpected repercussions on the environment could also be discovered.

In order to get a better understanding of how natural resource accounts and standard national accounts can be integrated, let us expand the accounts given in table 4.2.6 by adding two rows corresponding to the physical use of an environmental resource such as crude oil and the emissions of sulphur dioxide to the atmosphere. The resulting SAM is given in table 4.4.1.

We can see from this table that the total use of oil in agriculture is 100 tons. On the other hand, the gross production in agriculture is 115 dollars, which means that the oil use in agriculture is 100/115 = 0.87 ton per dollar gross product. If one can make it reasonable to assume that this number remains fixed, we can find out the variations in oil use following from variations in the agricultural gross product. In the same way, the oil use per dollar gross product in manufacturing is 4.24. We can also see that an increase in the manufacturing gross product will necessarily mean an increase in the demand for agricultural products, as they are used as inputs in manufacturing. An increase in the

16. Försund (1985) gives a survey of the applications of input output analysis to pollution problems.

gross output in manufacturing with one dollar would increase the demand for agriculture products with 15/165 = 0.09 units. This increase in demand for agricultural products would necessitate an increase in agricultural production which would increase the use of oil still further.

Table 4.4.1 A Hypothetical SAM and Resource Use

	1)	2)	3)	4)	5)	6)	7)	8)	Tot
1) Households			150	40					190
2) Government	30						5		35
3) Labour					50	100			150
4) Capital					20	20			40
5) Agriculture	70	20			10	15			115
6) Manufacturing	70	15			20	30		30	165
7) Capital Accounts	20								20
8) RoW					15		15		30
Total	150	35	150	40	115	165	20	30	
Oil use					100	700			800
Emissions	5				20	100			125

In the same way it is seen that an increase in manufacturing of one unit will increase the emissions of sulphur dioxide directly of 100/165 = 0.61 tons. The increase in agricultural output that follows would increase the emissions with 0.09 x 20/115 tons or with 0.02 tons. As the increase in agriculture production requires a further increase in manufacturing and also in agriculture (agriculture products are used as input in agriculture) it follows that the emissions will increase further. The final increase in the emissions is given by input-output analysis, that is a way of mathematically analysing the final outcome of all these interdependencies.

The input-output analysis is, however, based on a rather narrow description of technology. It is based on the assumption that all these coefficients we have been calculating (0.87, 4.24, 0.09 etc) - the input-output coefficients - are constant. Alternative approaches have therefore been developed in which both the description of technologies and ecological relations is richer and more realistic. One extension is to CGE models with more realistic modelling of production and international trade. Bergman (1990) used such a model to study the cost to the Swedish economy from reducing the emissions of sulphur, nitrogen, and carbon dioxide. Hazilla and Kopp (1989) used CGE models to estimate the cost to the US economy of the environmental regulations. As could have been expected, the costs were in the short run lower that the official estimates because in a CGE model, the most important economic adjustments to the regulations are included, adjustments that tend to reduce the overall cost, while the official estimates were based on the direct engineering cost. In the long run, when the effects on investment and thereby economic growth were taken into account, the cost was significantly higher.

A different modelling approach to integrating ecology and economy is more oriented toward system analysis and operations research. Most of these approaches have been applied to regions which explains their name, REQM - Regional Environmental Quality Management models[17].

These models are in general optimizing models, i.e. they try to answer the question of how to meet environmental goals in a cost-effective fashion. Sometimes, they also include monetary measurements of environmental damage and optimize the total cost. However, most of these applications have so far been limited to pollution problems.

---

17. For a survey of REQM models see James (1985). A detailed description of the most ambitious effort to develop a REQM model can be found in Spofford (1976). A description of such models in connection with the application of CBA of natural resources is given by Bower in chapter 8 of Hufschmidt et al (1983).

5. Economic Analysis of Environmental Consequences

Many approaches can be used to analyse environmental impacts. Some of them can be labelled specification techniques, aiming at organizing information about environmental impacts in a consistent but multi-dimensional framework. This work, whether it is labelled environmental impact assessment or something else, is often a good starting point - but not an alternative - to the techniques dealt with here.

The techniques presented below can be labelled evaluation techniques in the sense that they aim at summarizing different dimensions of an environmental problem into a common unit. For practical reasons, this unit is generally money, although any other widely known and accepted yardstick would also do. Some cultures have used shells or cattle as a unit of account. This is a matter of convenience.

Evaluation in economic terms can be done in many different ways, as this chapter will show. However, there are some common elements that will allow us to utilize a cost-benefit analysis (CBA) framework for this discussion. We will use the brief term "CBA" to denote what some authors call "social cost-benefit analysis (SCBA). This is to differentiate the latter and "traditional" or "economic" CBA where allowance is not explicitly made for income distribution concerns. As will be explained later, we regard these concerns as inherent in CBA.[1]

This chapter will:

(1) define cost-benefit analysis;
(2) present the main steps in CBA and discuss some of them more in detail;
(3) present a menu of approaches to environmental valuation;
(4) briefly discuss some complementary and alternative approaches to CBA;
(5) briefly discuss some of the criticism levelled against CBA.

5.1 Major Steps in CBA

CBA in this context should be understood as:

> A coherent method to organize information about social advantages (benefits) and disadvantages (costs) in terms of a common monetary unit. Benefits and costs are primarily valued on the basis of individuals' willingness to pay for goods and

1. See e.g. Helmers (1979) and Irvin (1978) for a discussion of the typology.

> services, marketed or not, as viewed through a social welfare ordering representing the preferences of the relevant decision-maker. The flow of monetary units over time are brought together to a net present value. Unvalued effects (intangibles) are described qualitatively or quantitatively and put against valued items.

Ideally the willingness to pay measures (WTP) should represent the underlying individual welfare changes. These can theoretically be expressed as compensating variation (CV): the monetary transfer necessary to keep an individual at the original welfare level, following a change such as environmental degradation or improvement. Alternatively, it can be expressed as equivalent variation (EV): the monetary transfer which equals the actual welfare change due to e.g. environmental degradation/improvement. Both are valid measures, but take different perspectives on the change: before and after respectively. Under certain conditions, and for goods and services bought on markets, they can be approximated with the consumer surplus (CS) as revealed by an ordinary demand curve.[2] This is shown in the figures below: The price paid is p and the quantity exchanged on the market is q. Given the demand curve, the consumers are left with a surplus (CS) which is the excess of willingness to pay over actual payment.

Figure 5.1.1 Consumer Surplus

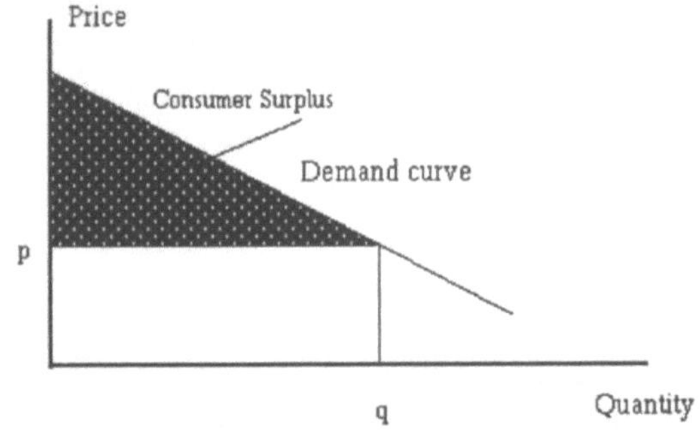

CBA is a normative exercise aimed at providing policy relevant conclusions, aiding, but not dictating, environmental decision-making. CBA ultimately rests on ethical values. The idea that results emanating from CBA are somehow "objective" is not advocated here.[3]

2. See Freeman (1979) or Hufschmidt et al (1983).
3. The theoretical foundation of CBA is discussed in Mäler (1974, 1985). A less technical discussion is contained in Cooper (1981) and Smith (1986).

The emphasis on market-orientation versus planning orientation may vary in CBA for reasons of principle and practice.[4] The view taken here is one of CBA as a tool for design, implementation and evaluation of development projects from the point of view of governments and donor agencies.

The CBA often entails a financial analysis (using market prices) from a household, company or government perspective as well, which should have a direct interest for the concerned parties. The major difference is that externalities are not taken into account in the financial perspective. The contrast between the financial and the economic perspectives provides guidance for public action.

Without losing touch with consumer preferences, there is a need for government to define crucial national parameters to ensure consistency across analyses. This concerns the valuation of future vs present costs and benefits, the pricing of unskilled labour and foreign exchange, and the weight given to impacts on various income groups.

Closely related to CBA is cost-effectiveness analysis (CEA). This is used when the benefits cannot be properly quantified, or when a goal has been laid down on political grounds. CEA aims at finding the least cost means of achieving that goal.

There are several possible perspectives for a CBA of a project. The general cases could be classified in three groups:

(1) looking at a planned project in advance (ex-ante appraisal);
(2) looking at an operational but not completed project (on-going evaluation);
(3) looking at a completed project (ex-post evaluation).

Given this initial perspective, most CBAs contain a sequence of analytical steps such as the following;

1. *The choice of evaluation criteria.* The gathering of data should be done in the context of what one needs to know in order to make good decisions. This is simplified if we can bring together the streams of future costs and benefits to one point in time, and expressed in a common unit, as far as possible. The basic concept here is the Net Present Value (NPV). Evaluation criteria are discussed further in section 5.1.1.

Assessing distributional consequences is a part - implicitly or explicitly - in the use of economic evaluation criteria such as the NPV as it contains a sum of individual costs and benefits, based on willingness to pay. Obviously, the willingness to pay

4. The planning perspective is the dominant one in the literature, with Dasgupta et al (1972) and Little & Mirrlees (1974) as prime examples. The more traditional market-oriented approach is found in Mishan (1982). The latter wants to minimize the role of national parameters determined politically.

will reflect the ability to pay. This appears particularly relevant in a developing country context and will be discussed in section 5.1.2.

2. *Identification of costs and benefits*. A common mistake in the appraisal situation is to limit unnecessarily the number of alternatives considered. Often, only one single project idea is presented. A thorough CBA critically looks at the available alternatives and may therefore result in a much more interesting conclusion than simply "accept" or "reject".

In all cases, it is important to consider the delineation of the geographically and economically relevant area. The *with-and-without* (project) approach should be used. This means including in the analysis only the factors that change because of the project. Irrelevant variables, such as investments already undertaken for other reasons ("sunk costs") should be eliminated.

3. *Quantification of costs and benefits*. This usually presents problems since our knowledge of the underlying natural scientific relationships is quite incomplete. For example, we know little about the effect of land degradation on crop and grass yield and little about the health consequences of many chemical substances polluting the air and our waters. However, decisions still have to be made, and CBA can be a useful aid in organizing available information. By use of sensitivity analysis (discussed in section 5.1.4) one can also test to what extent uncertainties matter for decision-making purposes.

4. *Valuation of costs and benefits.* This entails applying "social price tags" on the effects that have been quantified. Whereas financial prices are the market prices that affect individuals, the economic prices should reflect willingness to pay. When the supply of a commodity, say US dollars, is highly regulated, the financial and economic prices may differ substantially. Black markets are common expressions of this divergence between consumers' preferences and politically determined financial prices.

The extent to which one can actually capture environmental effects in monetary terms will differ depending on their nature and their relationship with existing markets. In some cases, one has to look for indirect market relationships between environmental values and ordinary markets. Recreational values are one important group here, since recreation often entails expenditure on ordinary goods as well. In the complete absence of a direct or indirect market one has to construct artificial markets to reveal people's valuation of environmental consequences. These methods will be presented in section 5.2.

5. *Discounting* using a real social rate of discount. This is a controversial subject and will be dealt with in detail in section 5.1.3 below.

6. Setting an appropriate *time horizon*. In principle, an infinite length of time should be considered. In practice, CBAs often limit the horizon to 20, 30 or 50 years, because effects of a project tend to decline after some time. The choice of time horizon is also related to the choice of discount rate. The higher the discount rate, the lower the weight attached to long-term effects.

7. Considering *uncertainties and risks*. This point is problematic for all environmental evaluation, economic and non-economic, CBA or non-CBA. There are numerous suggestions about how to deal with this and we shall present some in section 5.1.4.

8. *Policy conclusions* should be drawn in terms of the criteria set up, and considering the set of planning goals that the decision-maker (national government, aid agency, village council, peasant household etc.) may have defined. Commonly, a list of unquantified or unvalued impacts - intangibles - are presented along with the main economic result. The sign and approximate magnitude of these intangibles have to be assessed. Value judgments will always be involved in the execution and interpretation of CBA. Efficiency considerations have to be weighed against other social values. This does not diminish the value of having certain part of the "option map" quantified. Gains in relation to other goals can then be explicitly traded off against losses of net present value.

Some of these steps are more difficult than others in general. We will therefore devote special sections to (a) planning perspectives and evaluation criteria, (b) income distribution, (c) discounting and (d) risk and uncertainty.

5.1.1 Planning Perspectives and Evaluation Criteria

Most likely, a national government or an aid agency will want to consider a number of objectives apart from environmental ambitions. These could be growth in consumption, improved income distribution, full employment, regional balance, national self-reliance and so forth. Confining our discussion to economic criteria may appear more limiting than it actually is; these objectives can be built into the CBA. If there are still other concerns that a decision-maker may want to address, this does not render the exercise useless. On the contrary, it is particularly when facing such a multitude of goals that CBA is helpful in reducing the number of variables to consider.

The role of CBA will differ according to the institutional environment in each country. The USA is the prime example of a nation where CBA has come to occupy a central role in resource allocation in the federal budget.[5] In general, it is unlikely to determine allocations between "socio-political" sectors (such as health, education, defence) on the one hand and "productive" sectors such as agriculture, industry and infrastructure on the other. These choices are politically determined. However, when it comes to the setting of priorities for development among - and particularly within - the "productive" sectors, CBA has a role to play. One may want to consider alternative options for a project regarding:

- location;
- size;
- specific target groups;
- timing;
- choice of technique(s).

Testing alternative designs against each other, one has to know what to look for. On what basis can one determine a project to be "better" than another? This entails choosing evaluation criteria. Although these criteria do not end the discussion, they neatly summarize a substantial amount of information in a compact format.

The fundamental cost-benefit criterion is the Net Present Value (NPV): The value today of all benefits minus the value today of all costs. If this is positive, the project makes a social surplus. There are also derived criteria, as presented below.

The *present* commonly signifies a point in time immediately preceding the initiation of a project (Gittinger, 1982), but nothing prevents the analyst from choosing another point in time. The point chosen will not affect the ranking of projects, only the size of the NPV (Layard & Walters, 1976).

The Internal Rate of Return (IRR) is the maximum interest that a project can pay for the resources used in the project and still recover its investment and operating expenses (the IRR makes the NPV = 0). This can be compared with a national norm (if there is one) that projects are expected to reach; a "cut-off rate".

The Benefit-Cost Ratio (BCR) is the present value of all benefits divided by the value today of all costs. If this is more than one, the project has a social surplus.

The choice of appropriate criteria will depend on whether there is a funding constraint, and whether the projects being compared are independent or mutually exclusive. However, the NPV is safe to use. We will not go into the details of when each of these

5. An Executive Order requires that cost-benefit analysis be conducted for regulations having an annual impact of USD100 million or more on the economy (Smith, 1986).

criteria are useful and what their limitations are.[6]

It should be noted that using IRR to rank projects (independent or exclusive) may give the wrong result. This is because the IRR only measures the rate of net benefits generated by the project, but not their size. Thus, a small but high-yielding project could take precedence over a competitor yielding greater net benefits but at a lower rate. There are also cases where a unique IRR cannot be determined. Using the BCR to compare projects of different sizes may also give an incorrect signal to policy makers. However, it is useful when comparing alternative uses of a given budget which is exhausted in all alternatives.

These evaluation criteria all involve comparing flows of costs and benefits over time. This implies using a social discount rate. Many critics of CBA have argued that discounting is a cause of much environmental damage, and that the rate should be manipulated (raised or lowered) or abandoned completely. We will return to this discussion in section 5.1.3.

5.1.2 Income Distribution

A fundamental basis for CBA is the assumption that people themselves are generally the best judges of their own welfare. Their preferences are reflected in their willingness to pay (WTP) for improvements or willingness to accept compensation (WTAC) for deteriorations. This immediately raises the concern that these measures reflect the prevailing distribution of income. If this is seen as unsound - and most people would argue that it is in developing countries - there seems to be a case for introducing a corrective device. We will refer to this device as *distributional weights*.

The treatment of income distribution has received extensive discussion among economists. Three approaches can be distinguished:

(a) To ignore the issue without further comment. This approach is rarely defended, but often practiced;[7]

(b) To explicitly confine the economic analysis to one of efficiency rather than equity. Possibly present the distribution of significant costs and benefits among income groups (households or regions) but to refrain from introducing explicit

---

6. Gittinger (1982, pp. 299-361) gives an easy introduction, Helmers (1979, pp. 91-111) goes a bit further.

7. A survey of twenty CBA studies of soil and water conservation projects showed that only four had any discussion whatsoever of income distribution issues. None of them proceeded to weigh these groups against each other (Bojö, 1989).

distributional weights;[8]

(c) To introduce distributional weights explicitly to illustrate switching values. Switching values are values on the income distribution weights that make the decision switch from "accept" to "reject" according to some evaluation criteria, e.g. that NPV should be positive. The weights are to be derived by repeatedly facing decision-makers with the necessity to weigh efficiency and equity together.

The majority view among academic economists is one centered around alternative (c). The most influential works on applied CBA - Dasgupta et al (1972) and Little & Mirrlees (1974) - have similar ideas in this respect.[9]

Whereas position (a) above could hardly be defended, several arguments have been raised in favour of (b) rather than (c). Firstly, it has been argued that distributional objectives are better met by general fiscal policy (taxes, subsidies, etc.) than by project selection and design. If income distribution is optimal, there is, of course, no need for weighting. However, this is a doubtful argument given the administrative realities of Third World countries. Tax collection is often inefficient and there are political constraints to what can be achieved that way.

Secondly, it has been argued that there exists no "objective" way of weighting one group against another. Thus, the exercise becomes arbitrary and may bring CBA into disrepute. However, the traditional mode of weighing together WTP implicitly weighs all individuals "equally", given the prevailing income distribution, so there is no escape from value judgments. It is then better to present such judgments openly and see what difference they make.

Thirdly, the distribution of costs and benefits among various groups is very difficult to detect. This is indeed a problem, and may be the major reason why so many empirical analyses simply disregard the issue. But this is not a valid excuse for not trying and at least to acknowledge the problem.

Fourthly, it may be considered naive to assume that decision-makers would explicitly pronounce weights to be given to various income groups or regions, and to be used consistently for making project decisions. This is a valid point. We are not aware of any instances where a government has adopted systematic social weights in practice. However, this should not prevent the analyst from illustrating the use of such weights.

Finally, it has been argued, also by proponents of social weights, that their naive use can

---

8. See Harberger (1971), Gittinger (1982) and Mishan (1982) for a defence of this position.

9. See also Cooper (1980), Helmers (1979), Irvin (1978), Pearce & Nash (1981), Squire & van der Tak (1975) and Weisbrod (1968) among others. The theoretical roots can be traced back to de V. Graaff (1957) and Samuelson (1950).

make inefficient projects pass on distributive criteria. Helmers (1979) has suggested that only projects showing an acceptable economic rate of return before social weighing should be subject to income distribution analysis. However, this assumes that a clear distinction can be made between efficiency and equity. As we have argued above, this is not the case.[10]

In summary, good arguments have been raised for the inclusion of income distribution as a concern in CBA. There is almost unanimous agreement among economists in this respect. Still, the issue is often dodged in empirical studies.

In practical terms, it is usually very difficult to identify the differential impact other than in very broad terms. Two or three groups may still be much better than one. There are also good theoretical reasons to regard a spectrum of income differences to be acceptable according to society's standards of remuneration for education, skill and effort. This greatly simplifies the task, since a unit weight can then be assigned to a large portion of the population. In summary, we would suggest that:

(1) The search for any significant distributive effects should be mandatory in CBAs;

(2) That any significant effects should be presented to the decision-makers:

(3) That such effects should not be weighed implicitly but that switching values could be illustrated. For a project with an NPV below zero, this is done by calculating the weight(s) that would make it turn positive, given the social discount rate. This could entail setting the distributional weight to zero for some groups. This is in fact often done with people outside national boundaries, but could also apply to particularly rich persons.[11]

5.1.3 Discounting

Discussions about discounting are sometimes confused by a lack of understanding of the difference between *nominal* and *real* values. Nominal values are expressed in current prices, e.g. the cost of a litre of milk today, say USD 1. Real values are constant prices, i.e. they remain fixed to a particular point in time. Assume that the nominal price of milk was USD 0.5 ten years ago. If inflation has been 100% in ten years, the real price has been constant, while the nominal has doubled.

---

10. See Mäler (1985) for a formal discussion of the impossibility of separating allocative and distributional issues.

11. Empirical illustrations of the incorporation of equity considerations are given in Helmers (1979, ch 10), Little & Mirrlees (1974, pp. 238-242) and Squire & van der Tak (1975, pp. 63-67).

This section concerns the comparison of values in real prices over time. Inflation is a separate issue and need not concern standard CBA, since a general, uniform rise in the value of all costs and benefits will not affect the result in terms of our evaluation criteria: the NPV will not change its sign although the absolute magnitude will differ depending on what year's prices are used. This does not mean that changes in *relative* prices are excluded; if the cost of e.g. firewood is expected to rise 10% more than inflation per year, this increase in real price should be reflected in our accounts.

Few issues in environmental economics have stirred so much heated debate as the discounting of future costs and benefits to present values;

> "Devotion to economic discounting is suicidal. How soon is it so? 'In the long run,' an economist would say, since disaster is more than five years off." (Hardin, 1977, p. 113).

Economists did not - contrary to widespread opinion - invent short-sightedness and greed, but they have studied the weighing of future values as revealed by people's actual behaviour. Many economists have in fact looked upon discounting as (at least partially) an expression of human irrationality. Already Pigou noted that many socially worthwhile projects were:

> "... handicapped by the slackness of desire towards distant satisfactions. The same slackness is responsible for that over-hasty exploitation of stored gifts of nature, which must make it harder for future generations to obtain supplies of important commodities." (Pigou, 1920, pp. 27-28).

However, Pigou did not advocate a zero discount rate.

One reason why the debate about the social discount rate is so complex, is that it is cluttered with issues that should properly be dealt with under a different heading. We shall try to sort these out and return to them in other sections. The remaining issues will be difficult enough.

Approaches to Discounting

Most people find it natural to regard the value of a dollar today as greater than the value of a dollar in ten years. This goes even if the future dollar can be received with absolute certainty and with compensation for inflation. As mentioned already in section 2.2, several reasons could be thought of for this position:

> (1) A dollar could be invested now and could therefore be worth more in real terms in ten years (there is an opportunity cost in terms of return on capital foregone);
>
> (2) If I am richer in ten years than now, an extra dollar will mean less to me then

(the marginal utility of income will diminish);

(3) I am impatient to use the dollar now rather than later (the pure rate of time preference).

These perceptions have been formalized by economists and led to three major, but not distinctly separate, approaches in the determination of actual rates:

(1) The social opportunity cost of capital (SOC) approach which looks for empirical evidence of (before tax) profits on alternative investments opportunities.[12] The main argument is that public investments displaces other investment with this return.

(2) The consumption rate of interest (CRI) approach which is based on market data revealing consumer preferences for consumption today versus tomorrow. Empirically, this entails looking at returns (after tax) to the investor on risk-free bonds, etc.[13]

(3) the social time preference rate (STPR) approach. This takes the rate to be mainly a political parameter set on the basis of (a) the per capita income growth perspective, (b) the rate at which utility of increases in marginal income diminishes and, sometimes (c) an assumption of the pure rate of time preference among consumers.[14]

From the perspective of sustainable development, as discussed in section 2.2, the "impatience" of the current generation is not a desirable guide for investment behaviour.

The reader may be impatient to know what this means in practice - what rates are actually arrived at? Many authors appear hesitant to offer any numerical advice. Helmers (1979, p. 179) arrives at a figure of 7-8%, assuming a consumption growth rate of 2-3%. Little & Mirrlees (1974, p. 297) suggest a low of 4-5% (or the return on the international money market) and a high of 10-15% for the more advanced LDCs. A survey of 20 empirical studies of conservation projects (Bojö, 1989) found that most authors used a rate of 10-15%, usually with unclear rationale.

It is sometimes suggested that *different* rates should be applied to different projects, depending on the nature of the costs and benefits of the project (Price, 1973). However,

---

12. See Gittinger (1982) and Helmers (1979) for a defense.
13. See e.g. Lind (1982). Lind combines this approach with a shadow price on capital to reflect the displacement effect. There are also examples of combinations of approaches (1) and (2). In Mäler et al (1980) an unweighted average of SOC and CRI is used to derive the social discount rate.
14. Little & Mirrlees (1974) and Squire & van der Tak (1975) represent this approach. Dasgupta et al (1972) have a similar perspective but reject the pure rate of time preference revealed through markets as a guide for social decisions.

this would encourage arbitrary choices of rates, perhaps in order to manipulate the result. To make CBAs comparable, they need to apply certain national standards, one of them being a consistent social rate of discount. Furthermore, differential rates would create inefficiencies, as they would encourage overinvestment in sectors with low rates.

Usually, the same rate of discount is used throughout the period of analysis in applied CBA studies. This is mostly a matter of convenience, since the information about future changes in SOC, CRI or STPR is lacking. This does not detract from the validity of discounting in principle, but makes it even more interesting to test for different rates.

Having looked at the rationale for discounting and some approaches to finding an actual rate, we proceed to some suggestions for special considerations in the case of environmental projects.

A Special "Environmental" Rate?

It is sometimes claimed that environmental effects are particularly prone to underestimation. Therefore, these should be discounted at a particularly low rate (Cooper, 1981). A related argument is that the discount rate should be adjusted downwards to reflect environmental risks (Brown, 1983). Environmental concerns have also led to suggestions for a high rate to reflect the risk of environmental damage. Discounting the costs of projects with a particularly low rate is consistent with discounting the benefits with a particularly high rate (Prince, 1985). Are there good reasons to adjust the discount rate to reflect environmental concerns?

First, it is true that our knowledge of environmental processes is rather limited, especially regarding long-run effects. But is this a concern for the choice of the social discount rate? It appears more reasonable that this is a concern at the stages when costs and benefits are quantified and valued, and when uncertainty and risk is considered. It is not a particular concern as to how one weighs the future against the present. If there is reason to believe that environmental damage may have been underestimated, one should adjust the base case assumptions, or test other estimates and see how this effects the net benefit. This is a more explicit way of adjustment than to manipulate the discount rate.

Second, there is something odd about trying to separate *environmental* effects from other effects on human welfare. Even if that could be done in practice - which would be difficult - it would entail valuing the same losses in income differently. Consider e.g. a loss of USD 100 in income due to losses in crop yield as a result of erosion and the same loss due to the crop rotting because of lack of appropriate storage and transport to the market. Why discount the one loss differently from the other?

Third, the effect of lowering the discount rate because of environmental concerns may have the ironic effect of producing a result opposite to what was intended. A lower rate will make more projects produce a positive net present value. This may cause an increase in pollution and natural resource degradation because of increased investment activity.

Finally, the suggestion of applying a particularly high discount rate to account for environmental concerns runs into problems. It implies that risk grows progressively over time. This may not be an appropriate assumption.[15] In summary, the arguments for manipulating the discount rate because of environmental concerns have been rejected.[16]

5.1.4 Risk and Uncertainty

Formally, a distinction could be made between risk and uncertainty; risk being "quantifiable uncertainty" in the sense that a probability distribution for the outcomes can be estimated. In practice, we tend to have a spectrum of more or less uncertain variables such as the effect on fish of water pollutants and the price of firewood over the years to come etc. Pure uncertainty (no possibility of assigning probabilities to various outcomes at all) is a very unusual situation. Thus, we will treat the subjects of risk and uncertainty as one in this context.

Risk implies that the NPV of a project is not a single number, but rather a set of values with an associated probability distribution. The theoretically correct approach is to calculate the expected value of the distribution of ***utilities*** of various outcomes. This is done by multiplying the utilities of various outcomes with their probabilities and summarizing them and choosing the project with the greatest expected utility.

The nature of the utilities that are associated with the various outcomes reflects the preferences of the individual and correspond to the attitude toward risk. Consider the game of betting US $50 for the chance of gaining US $100 with a 50% chance and getting US $0 with a 50% chance. The expected value of the game is 0.5 x 100 + 0.5 x 0 = 50. Thus, the expected gain is equal to the price for participating in the game and the net expected gain is zero. If the individual is willing to accept this project he is said to be risk-neutral, while if he declines the offer he is said to be risk-averse. It seems that most people are risk-averse. Another question is, however, whether society should actually apply the same perspective. The answer depends on the nature of the project.

Consider the lottery above and assume that the individual would be interested in participating if the price falls to US$ 40. Then the cost of bearing the risk of participating in the game is US$ 50 - 40 = US$ 10. If the individual is risk-neutral, then

15. The risk factor increases as an exponential function over time. The addition of a 5% risk premium to a 5% "base rate" adds approx. 5% ((1 + 0.1)/(1 + 0.05)) to the discount factor the first year, but approximately 10% ($(1 + 0.1)^2/(1 + 0.05)^2$) the second year and so on.)

16. Several points made here largely coincide with arguments raised in Markandya & Pearce (1988).

the cost of riskbearing is zero, while if he is risk-averse, the cost is positive.

In general, the cost of riskbearing is defined as follows. The *certainty equivalent* is defined as the amount that received with absolute certainty is considered equivalent to an alternative probability distribution of outcomes. The cost of risk is the difference between the expected value of the probability distribution and the certainty equivalent.[17]

Assume that the real net present value of the project is not correlated with the general state of the economy. This means that there is no systematic covariation between the outcomes of the project and the national income. Then it can be shown that sufficient risk spreading, e.g. if the project is borne by many individuals through general taxation, would reduce the cost of riskbearing and if there are enough individuals, society should be risk neutral (Arrow & Lind, 1970).

However, there is an important qualification to be made in the case of environmental effects. The costs of adverse effects may in practice be borne not by the general tax payer but by individuals directly exposed to e.g. pesticides, poisonous water or air pollutants from factories. Effects on health or income may be quite drastic. Environmental costs often take the form of "public bads". This is the mirror image of public goods - as discussed in chapter 3. The salient feature is that one person's risk due to e.g. health hazards of bilharzia due to a dam project, is not diluted by more people sharing this risk. This characteristic of environmental effects invalidates the position of risk neutrality also from society's point of view.[18]

There are cases when environmental projects may act as an "insurance": if an industrial depression forces people to turn back to the land for subsistence agriculture, the value of a soil conservation project will appear in a different light. In such a case the cost of riskbearing is in fact negative and could be captured by using an "insurance premium".

Usually, individuals are confronted with "risky" situations in many different circumstances. If their behaviour is consistent, their attitude toward risk should be the same in all these circumstances. Therefore, it should be possible to estimate the cost of risk in one situation from observations on individual behaviour in other situations. This is the approach taken in many studies of the value of health risks. For example, Thaler and Rosen (1976), estimated the attitude to risk from analysing wage differentials in the Chicago building industry. These estimates were later used for the calculation of the value of risk to health from air pollution. Another way of getting information on risk attitudes is through contingent valuation. This technique is discussed in section 5.2.3

Currently, the usual technique for dealing with uncertainty is sensitivity testing. This

---

17. This concept of the cost of risk bearing is much used in the analysis of financial markets, see e.g. Brealey & Myers (1984).
18. This was first analyzed by Fisher (1973). For further elaboration, see Mäler (1985).

means varying the assumption on a particular point to see how sensitive the resulting value is to this change. Of particular interest are the switching values, i.e. the assumptions that will make the NPV change sign or the IRR to change position visavi the established reference rate (the "cut-off rate").

If a variable has been estimated through a sampling procedure, the values tested ought to bear some relation to the dispersion of the variable, e.g. testing +/- one standard deviation. In other cases, reasonable fractions of the most probable assumptions should be tested. There may be cases where one is faced with a bimodal uncertainty, e.g. flooding of a valley or no flooding in the absence of a dam construction in the upper watershed. This type of situation is best handled by tabulating the possible outcomes and their assigned probabilities.[19]

In summary, CBA can not "solve" the eternal problem of uncertainty, but it has practical ways of demonstrating what various assumptions, based on the best available information, imply in terms of an activity's net worth.

5.2 Valuation Approaches

The valuation we are concerned with here is one from the perspective of society: the economic perspective. This does not make the private or financial perspective uninteresting. On the contrary, a discussion about social intervention should be based on a comparison of these perspectives.

Having discussed the steps involved in CBA, we are ready to look at some applied techniques. These are grouped in three sections; valuation using:

(1) conventional markets;
(2) implicit markets;
(3) artificial markets

Each of these has several sub-categories.[20]

5.2.1 Valuation Using Conventional Markets

Four types of analysis will be exemplified under this heading:

---

19. See Dorfman (1962), Mishan (1982) or Raiffa (1968) for decision strategies under uncertainty.
20. The presentation here has been inspired by Hufschmidt et al (1983), Dixon et al (1986) and Dixon & Bojö (1988). See also Freeman (1979).

(1) changes in production;
(2) replacement cost;
(3) preventive expenditure;
(4) the human capital approach.

The fact that conventional markets are used does not necessarily mean that market prices are adopted without alterations. When significant distortions are present, appropriate shadow prices will have to be estimated.

Common examples from developing countries include the use of a lower shadow wage than the financial wage for unskilled labour. This reflects the fact that the opportunity cost in terms of production lost elsewhere in the economy is often low. Another example is the use of a lower value for domestic currency vs. foreign currency than the official one.

Transfer payments may also have to be adjusted for, in order to sort out differences between financial and economic costs. A subsidy to fertilizer or pesticides will hide the full cost to the user, but must be added back to account for the economic cost. On the other hand, a tax on an input which is not based on efficiency considerations should be eliminated. The provision is that the cost exclusive of the tax is the best measure of opportunity cost.

Consider e.g. the purchase of tree seedlings for an afforestation project. If our project displaces the consumption of seedlings somewhere else in the economy, the opportunity cost is the value of these to the alternative buyer. This may well be the market cost including tax. However, if our project simply results in more seedlings being produced, the opportunity cost is the supplier cost, exclusive of tax.

5.2.1.1 Valuation of Changes in Production

Many environmental impacts have a direct bearing on production values. Pollution may directly damage the production of fish, potable water or irrigation water, soil erosion diminishes the value of crops grown in an area etc. Most of the case studies in chapter 7 provide details of how such changes can be valued in practice. The examples concern soil conservation of crop land, range management, agroforestry, forestry and water quality management. A rich source for additional cases is Hoekstra & van Gelder (1985).

This approach represents a straightforward extension of conventional CBA. The difficulties lie not so much in the economics, but rather in supplying these calculations with meaningful data on underlying ecological relationships through e.g. Environmental Impact Analysis. This points to the need for interdisciplinary communication.

Central to the identification of costs and benefits is the with/without project perspective. This means that only such things that actually change with the project should be considered. Conceptually this is clear, but empirically, the analysis is often confronted with projects that have gone ahead without collecting base-line data. Thus, there is no clear point of reference for assessing the project's impact.

The analyst will then have to identify a suitable control area instead. It is extremely difficult to find one that is different only in the aspect that is subject to analysis, or where other factors can be controlled statistically. However, this uncertainty should not be overdramatized to mean that such comparisons are useless. Even crude indications are preferable to complete ignorance.

5.2.1.2 Replacement Cost Technique

What is the value of nutrients lost from agricultural land in Zimbabwe? That is the question dealt with by Stocking (1986) in an FAO study. Since it is extremely difficult to calculate the value in terms of lost production, he chose another route. The recent discovery in Zimbabwe of a unique set of extensive data on soil losses, and their correlation with losses of nitrogen, phosphate and organic carbon, made it possible to estimate the annual nutrient losses for various soils and farming systems. The national figures of nutrient losses were aggregated on the basis of area estimates of the respective management systems. Subsequently, the cost of replacing them by commercial fertilizers could be calculated.

A similar approach is used by Kim & Dixon (1986) in a study from Korea, which appears in section 7.1.2 below. The costs of replacing soil and nutrients lost are taken, by Kim & Dixon, as a "minimum" value of the benefits of preventing these losses. Another example is the case of replacing material corroded by acid downfall. A study on this is presented in section 7.5.3. Finally, the cost of replacing structures damaged by flooding appears as a benefit item in a case from the Philippines (7.3).

It should be pointed out that this approach rests on the assumption that replacement is worth doing. If individuals, in fact, undertake replacement, they have revealed a WTP for environmental improvement that is at least as high as the replacement cost. They may be willing to pay more to mitigate remaining environmental damage, but this is not always possible. For example, inorganic fertilizer cannot completely substitute eroded soil.

However, if individuals do not undertake replacement activities, this shows that their WTP is below this cost. This is of course based on the assumption that individuals have correct information about environmental damage, a condition not always fulfilled.

It is important to remember that the replacement cost method is a proxy method in the absence of a more direct measure of the welfare loss incurred.

5.2.1.3 Preventive Expenditure Technique

Sometimes a value of the benefit of environmental improvements can be approximated by studying the expenditures that people are willing to incur to prevent environmental hazards.

This method has mostly been used in industrialized countries - e.g. to see what expenditures on insulation and extra glass windows that people where willing to take to decrease noise levels, or expenditure on improved ventilation to decrease the exposure to radon in houses.

Examples from developing countries are that many people are willing to pay a substantial part of their income to buy bottled water, filtration devices, and install private wells to avoid health hazards by utilizing river water. Another example is the expenses that farmers incur when installing protection structures against siltation from upstream erosion (Dixon et al, 1988).

However, there may also be secondary benefits and costs from preventive expenditures that will make the estimates only a starting point; better ventilation decreases radon hazards, but also increases the costs for heating the house, while the risk for molding may go down. As this example shows, each case entails an assessment of both direct and indirect impacts of the measure to prevent environmental damage. Preventive expenditure is also discussed in section 7.1.2.

5.2.1.4 Valuation of Human Capital

Poor environmental quality can have a significant impact on health. The damage function relating a certain pollutant to individual health is often obscure, but this is not our concern here.

An explicit discussion on health and longevity valuation often cause resentment: the value of human life and health is "infinite" some say with indignation. However, there is no way denying that decisions are made every day in our society that implicitly place a price tag on morbidity and "statistical lives" lost. In other words, a particular individual's life is not priced, but reducing the probabilities of death and sickness certainly has a finite price in practice.[21]

The traditional approach in this field is the human capital approach. The basic idea is to calculate tangible results of impaired health by summing the net present value of losses of earnings for the individual (ideally reflecting the loss of production value to society) and medical costs for treatment.

The ethical problems of this approach are obvious, since it implies that you are basically worth what you earn, plus what it costs to treat you. However, one could argue (Hufschmidt et al. 1983) that the human capital approach could be used to demonstrate lower bound values of environmental improvements, explicitly stating the ethic on which such estimates rest.

The monetary value to society differs depending on the time perspective. While the person is alive the gross value of earnings represent a loss to society. After the person's death, the net of the production minus consumption is a measure of society's loss, in this limited perspective. This value could of course be negative.

The greatest cost of all in relation to poor health and premature death - the psychological cost - will not be captured. However, even knowing something which is far off the mark may be helpful, as long as the direction of the bias is known.

An alternative to the human capital approach which is more satisfactory from a theoretical point of view, is to capture willingness to pay for health benefits by implicit or artificial markets. These techniques are discussed from a theoretical perspective in sections 5.2.2 and 5.2.3. An empirical example is found in section 7.6.2, where direct interviews and market data on expenditure on housing and medical care is used to derive environmental values. Because of the difficulties involved in valuing the benefit of health, such projects are more likely to be evaluated using a cost-effectiveness approach (see section 5.3).

5.2.2 Valuation Using Implicit Markets

The basic idea behind this set of techniques is that there are links between the consumption of ordinary goods sold on markets and the consumption of non-marketed goods, including environmental values. Thus, changes in environmental quality will also be reflected in prices of ordinary goods, such as land and houses.

---

21. Such values are e.g. used by the State Road Agency in Sweden and several other countries as a guide for road planning (Mattsson, 1984). See Mäler & Wyzga (1976), Freeman (1979), OECD (1981), Mishan (1982) and Hufschmidt et al (1983) for a more elaborate discussion and empirical studies.

In principle, the same applies to the wages demanded by labour. This has inspired a considerable number of studies regarding health hazards and wage differences in the USA (Åkerman, 1987). However, the informational requirements are very strong - labour must be well informed of the impact of health hazards and other factors influencing wage levels must be controlled for. In practice, the usefulness of this method becomes very limited.

The techniques presented under this heading are in general rather data demanding. They are also based on relatively well functioning markets with substantial flows of information and flexibility. Since such conditions are rarely encountered in developing countries, our presentation is brief. However, more market oriented economic policies will gradually provide a better and better foundation for the use of these methods also in developing countries.

5.2.2.1 The Travel-Cost Approach

This method has been used extensively in the USA and to some extent in Europe to value recreational assets. The pioneering work is Clawson Knetsch (1966). Examples from developing countries are so far rare, but one case from Thailand is given in Dixon & Hufschmidt (1986).

To the extent that development projects concern the preservation or exploitation of wilderness areas, this method may be of interest. It does require the collection of substantial data on e.g. number of visitors, their origin, travel costs etc. This must be gathered in the actual area affected. This type of data may be available partially from existing visitors' books, but usually one must contact visitors for more thorough interviews.

Developing country governments may be interested in capturing the revealed consumer surpluses[22] by appropriate pricing policy and development of facilities.

An illustration of using the travel-cost method, to compare preservation versus forest harvesting of a wilderness area, can be found in section 7.4. While that particular case study concerns one single recreation area, it is quite possible to build models covering a multitude of recreational options. It is also possible to calculate the value of marginal changes in environmental quality rather than the complete destruction of an entire facility. This has already been done in Stevens (1966) and shown theoretically in Mäler (1971).

22. The consumer surplus is the difference between the consumer's maximum WTP and the actual price.

5.2.2.2 Land and Property Value Approach

The basic idea behind this approach is that prices of land and property illustrate- among other things - the valuation of environmental quality. A major difficulty in applying this technique to developing countries is the relative scarcity of monetary land and property transactions in many cultures. To the extent that they occur, they may not be recorded in a fashion required for economic analysis.

The property value method has attracted considerable attention, particularly in the USA since the early 1970s. It has been used to assess the valuation of air pollution and marginal willingness to pay for pollution abatement. Sometimes this technique is called the "hedonic price" technique. Hedonic prices are implicit prices of the characteristics of a property or piece of land, e.g size, location and environmental quality. However, to utilize this method a well-functioning market should ideally be available with among other things:[23]

(a) well-informed agents who perceive environmental differences;

(b) a significant number of transactions per unit of time in relation to the size of the market;

(c) good data availability concerning all relevant variables that influence property price.

This is rarely the case in developing countries. However, this does not mean that the approach is useless. One may still be able to assess orders of magnitude of people's valuation by comparing the price of similar houses or pieces of land in polluted versus non-polluted neighbourhoods.

An empirical example is given in an air pollution study in section 7.5.1. The range management study (7.1.3) makes reference to property valuation, but it is less clear how that was done.

5.2.3 Valuation Using Artificial Markets

In search for consumers' WTP it is not always possible to make inferences from actual behaviour as in the approaches presented above. Instead, one may have to measure consumer preferences in hypothetical situations or by creating artificial markets. This

23. Mäler (1977) gives a more comprehensive list of demands on this method.

approach is often called the Contingent Valuation Method (CVM), and has inspired a rapidly growing number of empirical studies, mostly in the USA. A comprehensive review is contained in Mitchell & Carson (1989).

The strength of these methods is that they can be applied to a variety of situations where no other data is available, or is difficult to get. To the extent that other methods are viable, interesting comparisons can be made between the results from different methods (see e.g. the case studies in section 7.4, 7.5.1, and 7.5.2)

People do not only derive direct values from the use of an environmental asset. They may also attach an option value[24] to the potential use of a particular environmental service. In addition, they may attach an existence value (Krutilla, 1967) to an environmental service, unrelated to their own actual or even potential use. As there are commonly no markets for option and existence values, the only way we can explore their significance is through CVM.

Artificial markets have been used to test individual valuation regarding water and air quality, aesthetic beauty, recreational values, preservation of open farmland, existence values of natural environments, disposal of hazardous waste, risk in relation to air travel, car travel, cigarette smoking and nuclear energy.

The techniques described below may at first appear "artificial" or "strange". However, one should not compare the situation with one where an ordinary market is operating, but rather consider the fact that one is trying to simulate a market where there is none, but where vital values are hidden. Before one discards such methods as "unrealistic", one should carefully consider what the alternative is: How else can these values be captured?

Bidding games entail direct questioning of individuals concerning their WTP (or willingness to accept compensation for an environmental deterioration: WTAC). Typically, the process involves the following steps:

(1) The interviewee is presented with a set of information about the situation and available choices (e.g. the village communal grazing land and the choice of continued free access and ensuing deterioration vs. controlled grazing managed by a village association);

(2) A starting bid is offered by the interviewer (e.g. "would you be willing to pay USD 1 as a membership fee to a grazing association in your village, with the purpose of achieving grass land rehabilitation in accordance with the programme described?");

24. The term is due to Weisbrod (1964). A good review of the ensuing debate is given in Reiling & Anderson (1980).

(3) Depending on the initial reaction, the bid could be lowered or raised in predetermined ways to capture the final bid;

(4) An average bid is calculated on the basis of the sample and extrapolated to the relevant population;

(5) Attempts are often made to analyse determining factors behind bids through multivariate regression on variables like sex, age, income, education, etc.

Empirical studies making use of bidding games for recreational and air pollution valuation can be found in sections 7.4, 7.5.1 and 7.5.2.

Costless choice is a variety on the theme of artificial markets. An example presented in Hufschmidt et al (1983) concerns the choice between the clearing up of a city dump (spreading rats, flies etc.) and a cash offer. The cash offer was given in 5 intervals to 1/5 of the group each. A group of 50 persons were interviewed in a poor squatter area. None out of 10 accepted a USD 5 offer, but all out of 10 accepted a USD 25 offer. These limits were then used as minimum and maximum values of the individuals' valuation (WTAC) of the cleaning up of the city dump.

A common criticism levelled at direct questioning methods is that individual respondents may lack the necessary information. Proponents of this view may favour the Delphi Technique using a pool of experts. These are asked independently to place a value on, say, the cleaning of a factory's wastewater.

The first round of expert estimates is fed back to the group. Each member then independently revises his own estimate, without knowing who has said what. Successive rounds may make the estimates converge around a mean. This method was developed by the Rand Corporation in the USA and has been applied primarily for forecasting.This approach has its own problems. Following Cooper (1981), we would like to point to the limited value of technical expertise in making social judgments. The experts have an advantage in better information about e.g. biological damage of certain emissions. But this does not make them experts at rating the value of this damage to individuals affected.

Biases in Artificial Markets Approaches

The usefulness of the techniques described will always have to be assessed given a specific problem. However, some brief general remarks will be made here. There are a number of "biases" involved in direct questioning of WTP or WTAC. These biases may distort the result and make it less useful for decision-making. Such biases include:[25]

---

25. See e.g. Brookshire et al (1979) and Desvousges et al (1983).

(1) Hypothetical bias: Respondents are placed in an "unusual" situation. The ability and interest to fully emerge oneself into the specific situation will differ.This puts high demands on a serious presentation of the environmental options.

(2) Strategic bias: The respondent may perceive that he has an interest in misrepresenting his true preferences. For example if I don't have to pay myself I may overstate my WTP for something I desire (the "free-rider" problem). Theoretically, this effect could be troublesome, but empirical tests have reinforced a more optimistic thinking on this.

(3) Information bias: The selected set of data presented to the respondent may of course influence his choice and therefore the expressed WTP. One way of dealing with this is to let the parties in a conflict study the information presented and comment on it. This will ensure balance and impartiality.

A specific consideration is that many people in developing countries live in an economy that is only partially monetized. The subsistence farmer asked about his WTP will weigh this sacrifice not against his total income, but against the monetary and perhaps almost non-existent part of his total income. A suggestion to overcome this is to ask for "willingness to donate labour" rather than WTP (Cooper, 1981), or why not "willingness to donate maize"? This type of question may also make more sense to persons unfamiliar with monetization of most goods.

In summary, there are many difficulties pertaining to the use of artificial markets. However, these can to some extent be statistically controlled and to some extent minimized through careful survey design. The appropriateness of these techniques will vary, depending on the purpose of the study. They should at least be considered and carefully assessed in cases where individuals' willingness to pay cannot be read off an existing market. Artificial market methods can also serve as a complement to other methods when these are applicable.

5.3 Complementary and Other Methods

The appropriateness of a particular method of economic evaluation depends, of course, on the task at hand. The framework presented above is very flexible and can easily accommodate methods that are sometimes presented as "alternatives".

An *environmental impact assessment* (EIA)[26] can be seen as a complement, even as a necessary foundation for a proper CBA. The EIA specifies the impacts for the CBA to evaluate. One difficulty with this method is that an ambitious analysis produces a mass

26. See e.g. Clark et al (1978), FAO (1982) and DSE, 1985).

of multi-dimensional information which is difficult to interpret for anyone else then the specialist. In response, ranking procedures have been developed where different effects in different dimensions have been given "scores", that are supposedly commensurable. This takes the exercise into a route directly leading to CBA.

Cost-effectiveness analysis has already been mentioned as a useful approach when benefit estimation is found to be impossible or simply not demanded. Certain goals may be given by the decision-makers without any explicit benefit estimation. This may, for example concern certain environmental standards such as emission of a pollutant. The role of the economist is then to find the least cost solution to the problem. An empirical example of a cost-effectiveness approach is given in section 7.1.2 (soil conservation).

The *opportunity-cost approach* measures what has to be given up in order to preserve an unpriced asset. Consider, for example, a beautiful wilderness area that could be exploited to generate hydropower. However, the dam and the installations for electric distribution, roads, buildings etc. would substantially damage the area. Once the dam is built, the change would be irreversible in economic terms.

The benefit of preservation is very difficult to estimate. A cheap and quick way of producing relevant information is to calculate the opportunity cost of preservation. In other words, the cost of supplying the electricity (or its services) to the people through some other means, e.g. through a coal-fired plant or by planting trees for firewood.

Let us assume that the coal-fired alternative (all environmental effects properly valued) would incur an additional cost of USD 10 million expressed as a present value. The decision-makers will than be faced with the question: "Is it worth more or less than USD 10 million to preserve the wilderness area?" This may be a significantly easier question than the question: "How much is preservation worth?"

Other cases when this approach may be useful is when different locations for a road, an industry, a port or an urban are discussed. By comparing the costs of development at different sites, a trade-off could be made with anticipated environmental effects.

Goal achievement (or objective contribution) matrices have been suggested as alternative planning tools (Akroyd, 1985; Birgegård, 1975). But the contribution to other goals than economic growth such as income distribution, employment creation, regional balance etc. can also easily be added onto the CBA framework as weights or restrictions as in section 5.1.

Planning balance sheets (Lichfield et al, 1975) is a method based on the CBA framework, but with the ambition to explicitly show how various parties are affected: how costs and benefits balance for them. PBS also shows considerable attention to non-quantified impacts and their integrated presentation to decision-makers.

Rather than entering into a detailed separation of CBA versus other approaches we think that the critics should test available alternatives according to a number of criteria for a "good" method. It is suggested that such criteria could include:

(1) Analytical cost - should not be greater than the value of the information produced;

(2) Comprehensiveness - the degree to which the approach takes relevant impacts into account;

(3) Comprehensibility - the degree to which the method and its results could be usefully interpreted by the users of the information;

(4) Democratic basis - the degree to which individuals' own preferences are reflected;

(5) Relevance for decision-making - the degree to which the information makes a difference to policy makers.

Finally, multi-dimensional problems will often require a multi-dimensional method. The costs and benefits of sulphur oxide control, for example, have been investigated by OECD (1981), using a combination of methods described above to capture effects on materials, crops, health and aquatic systems. A common theoretical framework is needed to ensure consistency, but the data available will often determine what method can be used for empirical estimates.

5.4 Criticism against CBA

Although the critics of CBA constitute a very heterogeneous group, they will be grouped here in two categories;

(1) Those who reject the foundations of CBA;
(2) Those who are critical to its practical usefulness in dealing with environmental matters.[27]

Some people object to CBA on moral or philosophical grounds:

"... to undertake to measure the immeasurable is absurd and constitutes but an

---

27. The first group is exemplified by Elzinga (1981), Schumacher (1973), Söderbaum (1986) and Swaney (1987). The second group by Coddington et al (1972), Goodland & Ledec (1987), Hudson (1981), Pearce (1976) and Weiss (1978). More examples are discussed in Pearce & Nash (1981).

> elaborate method of moving from preconceived notions to foregone conclusions ... The logical absurdity, however, is not the greatest fault of the undertaking: what is worse, and destructive of civilization, is the pretense that everything has a price or, in other words, that money is the highest of all values." (Schumacher, 1973, pp. 37-38).

This statement confuses several issues;

> (1) Whether we like it or not, decisions are continuously made that entail "pricing the priceless". We may not be able to stick a precise tag on each item, but somehow comparisons have to be made. CBA is a useful tool in sorting out these comparisons, albeit only partially;

> (2) The choice of money as a yardstick is based on practical considerations. Money is widely used by people to compare values. It does not imply that money is more important than anything else.

Other critics have pointed to the substantial data requirements entailed in carrying out CBAs. This is true, but it is difficult to see this as a particular problem for CBA. What other method could handle this problem better? CBA is a method of quantifying values to the extent possible. It does not imply that this is always possible. The fact that one must often in practice settle for a cost-effectiveness analysis has already been mentioned.

Another critical point concerns the "narrowness" of the traditional CBA perspective. We believe that a book such as this is part of the answer: CBA does not need to be "narrow". Widening the scope is not so much a matter of conceptual problems, although we have pointed to some above. But the major problems often rest with the supply of meaningful environmental data as well as the use of CBA results. Even so, we think CBA can be a useful way of organizing information.

In summary, there is reason to quote with sympathy from Williams (1973) who concludes a lengthy discussion on the critique against CBA with the following passage:

> "In contemplating CBA, I prefer the philosophy embodied in the answer that Maurice Chevalier is alleged to have given to an interviewer who asked him how he viewed old age; "Well there is quite a lot wrong with it, but it isn't so bad when you consider the alternative."
> (Ibid., p. 58).

6. Management of Environmental Resources and Environmental Policy

6.1 Introduction

We have in previous chapters argued that the basic problem in managing environmental resources is the problem of incentives. Environmental resources are often such that it is not in the best of interest of the individual to act in a way that is best for the society at large. The basic objective of environmental policy is therefore to create an economic environment in which the *incentives are correct,* that is, to create a system in which the best interest of individuals, households, companies, local communities, organizations, state agencies, etc. coincides with the collective or public interest. Obviously, the design of mechanisms to improve the incentive structure will depend not only on the characteristics of the resource, but also on the general economic and legal background. In western industrialized countries, for example, taxes will often work in different ways as compared to the situation in a typical developing country. However, we believe that it is possible to give some general guide-lines for the design of incentives improving policies, which would apply to most resources and most countries. Before that we will, however, return to the discussion in chapter 3 concerning common property resources.

6.2 Common Property Resources

Common property resources are such resources that are owned and managed collectively by a group of individuals, organizations or even countries. Usually, each individual is assumed to have the freedom to use the resource according to his own plans. Furthermore, some of these resources are resources with free access, i.e. any individual or organization has the right to exploit the resource. Examples of such resources range from the local village pond to local grazing ranges, to urban airsheds, to oceanic fisheries and to the global climate. Thus, common property resources is a concept that covers a very wide variety of resources. However, the established wisdom analyzes the management of all these resources using one and the same model - the tragedy of the commons (or the prisoner's dilemma game). In order to gain a proper understanding of the policy analysis, it is essential also to understand this conventional wisdom and also its limitations.

The story of the tragedy of the commons (Hardin 1968) goes roughly as follows. Consider a grazing range that is used by members of a village. Each member will, naturally, look only after himself and plan to herd as many animals as would maximize his own net benefits. However, in doing that he will contribute to overgrazing of the range and thereby inflicting harm to the other members of the village. Each individual will therefore, unintentionally, harm the rest of the village and the result will be a deterioration of the grazing range. Another way of looking at the same phenomenon is given by the simple game of prisoner's dilemma. Consider for simplicity the case when there are two herdsmen sharing a common grazing range. Assume that each of them must decide to have a big or a small herd. If both choose to have a small herd, the range will be sufficient to feed the two herds without any danger of overgrazing and both will make positive gains, say $100 each. However, if one of them chooses a big herd, he will increase his payoff substantially but at the cost of overgrazing which will hurt the other herdsman. Assume that the gains will be $200 to the herdsman with the big herd and that the other will loose $10 as a consequence. Finally, assume that if both decides to carry big herds, the payoffs will be zero for both. We can summarize this in the following matrix:

Table 6.2.1 Payoff matrix: Size of Herds

	Small	Big
Small	(100, 100)	(-10, 200)
Big	(200, -10)	(0, 0)

Here the two rows, small and big represent the size of the herd of the first herdsman and the two columns small and big represent the sizes of the herd of the second herdsman. The numbers represent the payoffs to the two herdsmen, with the payoff to the first herdsman as given by the first number.

It is clear that if the second herdsman selects small, it would be profitable for the first herdsman to select big as he then would increase his profit from 100 to 200. If the second herdsman selects big, it is also to the advantage to the first herdsman to select a big herd, as 0 is bigger than -10. Thus, irrespective of what the second herdsman selects, it is in the advantage of the first herdsman to choose a big herd. As the situation is completely symmetric, it is also to the advantage of the second herdsman to choose a big herd, irrespective of what the first does. The outcome, or equilibrium, will be that both herdsmen choose big herds with the consequence that the range will be overgrazed and both will experience substantial losses in payoffs. Obviously, it would have been better for both herdsmen to choose a small herd. This is therefore an example of a situation where individual rationality contradicts collective rationality.

It is quite clear that this model fits many real situations, for example the use of an urban airshed for disposing flue gases, oceanic fisheries, highway congestion, global climate changes. On the other hand there is growing evidence that it does not explain the way many *local commons* is managed (Feeny et al, 1990). Thus there is a need for a better understanding when the simple model of the tragedy of the commons is appropriate and when it is not. Without such a better understanding, policies designed to improve the allocation of resources may be counter productive.

The growing number of cases describing efficient management of local common property resources indicate that institutional and cultural factors may be such that they support efficient management of resources, even in cases where the payoff structure is as described above. However, these institutional and cultural factors need to be explained in order for us to have a *real* understanding of the phenomenon. Why is it that cultural norms and associated institutions will develop in such a way to support efficient management of resources? Obviously, there are in general many reasons for such development, but a quite obvious one, and which is overlooked in the simple formulation of the tragedy of commons concerns the time element. Since a discussion of the time element will give insights into policy issues, we will offer a brief discussion here.

The model of a common grazing range above was based on the implicit assumption that the two herdsmen will use the range only once. In reality, they will be sharing the resource for quite many years to come and they know that the quality of the range in the future will depend on their success today in reaching an implicit agreement in preserving it. Assume that the two herdsmen has initially chosen small herds. Assume further that one of the herdsmen in some time-period is tempted to increase his herd to a big herd. He knows, however, that if he does so, the other will, one time-period later, do the same with the result that the range will be overgrazed forever. In making the decision to increase the herd, the cattle owner must compare the present gain from a larger herd ($200 - $100) with the future annual losses ($100 - $0). If the herdsman does not discount the future too much, he will find it profitable not to increase the size of the herd.

Thus, if we take into account the fact that the herdsmen will meet each other repeatedly[1] collective rationality may not be inconsistent with individual rationality. This follows from the fact that one herdsman can "punish" another herdsman by reverting to a non-cooperating behaviour if the other herdsman breaks the implicit agreement. Furthermore

1. Rigourously, they have to expect to meet each other either an infinite number of times or an indefinite number of times, not knowing which time will be the final. This is essentially the Folk Theorem in the theory of repeated games (Fudenberg and Maskin, 1986).

the threat of punishment is credible, as it can be shown to be profitable for the punisher to carry out the threat.[2]

It is now easy to understand that this mechanism can be regarded as a social norm. Members of a community have over a number of years developed strategies that support collective rational management of the resource, strategies that ultimately will be regarded as social norms - *you should choose a small herd.* On the basis of such social norms, communities will develop institutions that will monitor the use of the resource and punish those who misuse the resource.

Thus it seems that common property resources will be managed rational. However, that misses the point. Only if the individuals have met repeatedly for a long period of time and expect to meet each other repeatedly in the future in a stable environment, will these social norms and cultural institutions be sustainable and efficient management the result.

Assume that a community has developed the necessary cultural institutions and the appropriate social norms for managing a common property resource efficiently. The ensuing cooperation is, however, extremely unstable in the sense that changes in the external environment - central government interventions, changes in world market prices, technological breakthroughs etc - or endogenous changes such as population growth, may easily destroy the basis for the social norms. When the gains for the members of the community change substantially because of changes in the external environment, they may be interpreted by the members as a general break down in social norms, and therefore induce such a break down. Furthermore, the external changes will induce a new "status quo",[3] which will be the base for new social norms. Thus, common property regimes that are easily disturbed by external factors or which are so "young" that social norms have not developed, should be expected to manage resources inefficiently. On the other hand, self-sustained common property regimes should be expected to be much more efficient.

There is another distinction that is needed in order to understand some common property resources. The common grazing range has the characteristic that all community members have the parallel interests in the sense that an improvement in the grazing conditions is beneficial to all members. However, quite often, there are multiple uses of a resource and these uses are not only competitive but also demanded by different sets of individuals. An airshed, for example, is used both for disposing wastes (air pollution) and for providing life supporting services (air for breathing). The airshed is a common property

2. In technical terms, it can be shown that the strategies are in "sub-game perfect equilibrium."

3. In our simple example, each member of the community had only two strategies to choose between. In a more realistic situation, each member has many strategies and there may be many equilibria that would be candidates for being elevated to a social norm. An external disturbance will in general call for a switch from one equilibrium to another, and the transition time may be quite long.

resource in the sense that all polluters can use it freely for disposing wastes and also in the sense that each individual can use the air freely for breathing. Obviously, the atmospheric emissions will damage the individuals breathing the air but not vice versa. Therefore, the argument presented above on the development of implicit social norms cannot be applied.

If there is only one individual breathing the air and only one polluter and if the transaction costs are small, we could, following Coase (1960), expect an agreement between the polluter and the pollutee. Such an agreement would include payments from the pollutee to the polluter. However, if there are many victims to the air pollution, the situation is different. Now, each individual would hope to be a free rider (which is another but equivalent way of describing the tragedy of the commons), and therefore try to reduce the own payment at the expense of the others. The result would obviously be that the pollutees would be asking for too small reduction in the pollution. If the initial rights is with the pollutees, the polluters would try to bribe them in order to be allowed to pollute the atmosphere. However, each pollutee would in this case be in a position to veto any agreement, and the result would probably be too little pollution. In both cases, it is the same mechanism working as in the simple case of the tragedy of commons. We could try to resolve the problem by once more pointing to the need to take time into account. If the pollutees expect to be in the same situation indefinitely in the future, we could expect that an equilibrium would emerge that would entail an efficient amount of pollution. However, this is more unlikely now, partly because of the time it would require to reach a social code in this way (we can not look back to a history of cooperation on air pollution problems among pollutees) and partly because of substantial transaction costs. Therefore, some government intervention seems necessary to improve the management of this kind of common property resources where there are multiple conflicting uses.

In designing policies for improving the management of environmental and natural resources, it is therefore vitally important to find out whether the resource is a common property resource and whether the resource is currently managed by a functioning set of social norms. If that is the case, any policy intervention may be counter productive and result in deterioration of the resource. On the other hand, if there are no social codes regulating the resource use, there is a prima facie argument for intervention. Furthermore, this argument is strengthened if the resource has multiple conflicting uses. We will in the sequel limit ourselves to such resources.

One common property resource is the airshed. In the next section air and water pollution problems, and possible policies for these in the context of industrialized countries are discussed. However, most of our arguments carry over directly to the context of the developing world. Furthermore, some of the conclusions can be directly applied to other environmental resources such as fisheries, surface water, etc.

6.3 Air and Water Pollution

6.3.1 Introduction

Air and water pollution problems arise mainly because the atmosphere and water courses are not and cannot be privately owned. This means that each individual or organization has no incentive to take into consideration the effects of his use of the medium on other individuals or organizations. Take the example of a negative externality. The social cost, which is equal to the sum of the costs to all individuals, is greater than the private cost to the individual using the air or water for waste disposal. The implication of this is that decision-makers will not take into account the societal cost but only the lower private cost when making decisions on how much to dump in the environment.[4] The main problem facing society is then to change the incentives in such a way that the individual polluters have to take the full social cost of pollution into account.

In order to accomplish this change in incentives, societies have developed a range of approaches, which roughly can be classified into two groups:

- negative incentives or command and control

- positive incentives or economic instruments.

An approach built on negative incentives refer to a system by which the polluter is required to reduce pollution and is punished if not doing so. An approach built on positive incentives refer to a system by which the polluter is rewarded if he reduces pollution. The two systems thus correspond to, in the first case, the stick and, in the second case, the carrot. Under certain conditions, the two approaches are equivalent, but most often they will differ and sometimes differ substantially with respect to their environmental and economic consequences. These differences will now be discussed.

A possible way of changing the incentive structure is often referred to as an environmental policy instrument, or for short an instrument. An instrument can be an emission standard i.e. a maximum limit of the amount of a particular pollutant a plant is allowed to emit, accompanied by a punishment scheme when the standard is violated. Another

---

4. We will always dump something into the environment. This follows from the principle of mass balances. Everything material that goes into economic activities - consumption, capital accumulation, etc. - must eventually come out in the form of residuals or waste. This means that the larger the size of the economic activities, the larger must be the amount of wastes. However, the damage to the environment need not be directly related to the amount of wastes, as the wastes may be transformed into less harmful substances. For an analysis of the materials balance principle and its consequences for economic theory, see d´Arge, Ayres and Kneese (1972) and Mäler (1974).

example of an instrument is a system of licences for operating certain production processes. It may also be an emission fee, i.e. a charge the polluter has to pay based on his emissions. Subsidies for adopting a cleaner technology or deposit and refund systems are further examples of policy instruments. The emission standard and the system with licenses are examples of control and command instruments, while the others are examples of economic instruments.

In the discussion to follow the marginal abatement cost and the marginal damage cost will be used repeatedly. We have in previous chapters discussed various ways by which the cost of environmental damage can be estimated. The marginal damage cost is simply defined as the extra cost incurred to society if pollution increases with one unit. It should be clear from the discussion in previous chapters that we cannot, in general, expect to be able to estimate the marginal damage cost function. However, we will use it as an analytical tool and thereby gain insights which do not necessarily depend on our ability to estimate the environmental damage function.

Abatement cost is the opportunity cost that society experience when pollution is reduced. However, pollution or the discharge of residuals or wastes can be reduced by a great number of techniques. We can differentiate between the following approaches:

1) End of the pipe abatement

2) Changes in the production process

3) Change of raw material

4) Change in energy commodities

5) Reduction in consumption and production

When one talks about pollution abatement, it is usually the end of the pipe abatement one thinks of. Municipal sewage treatment plants is one example of end of the pipe treatment, as are scrubbers to remove sulphuroxides from the stack gases and the catalytic devices on cars. Such measures were the first to be applied when it was discovered that pollution was a major social problem. Most estimates of cost of abatement are simply estimates of the cost of using end of the pipe treatment. However, such estimates can be quite misleading and in particular, such estimates may be too high. The reason is that, at least in a well functioning market economy, costs will be dispersed through a large number of adjustments and the result of these adjustments will be to lower the social cost of abatement.

Take the example of sulphur emissions. Most (but not all) emissions of sulphur oxides is a by-product of energy transformations - production of electricity from burning fossil fuels. Then consider a coal fired power plant which is required to reduce its sulphur emissions. What may be done?

First, the various end of the pipe devices may be installen in the plant, e.g. scrubbers that will catch the sulphur in the stack gases and transform it into liquid or semi solid substances. Given information on the efficiency of the scrubbers and their investment and operating costs, the cost of reducing the sulphur emissions per ton sulphur reduced may be calculated.

Beside this end of the pipe treatment, the plant can also change the combustion technology. An increase in combustion efficiency will reduce the demand for fuels and thereby reduce the emissions. Furthermore, a change to a different combustion technology, e.g. fluidized combustion, may further reduce the emissions. Still a possibility is to consider a change in the quality of the energy commodity, e.g. to change to more expensive coal with less sulphur content.

All these measures will increase the cost of power production in the studied plant. If only this plant is required to reduce its emissions, then it will probably reduce its production, which will further reduce the emissions. If this fall in production is compensated for by production increases in other plants, the net effect on the overall emissions depends on the nature of the expanding plants. If these are nuclear, hydropower or if they are burning natural gas, then there will be no increase in sulphur emissions (but increases in other environmental problems). The corresponding cost component consists of the cost of increasing the production in the other plants (including the environmental costs) less the cost of producing it in the plant we are studying. Thus, in order to estimate the cost of reducing the sulphur emissions in one power plant we need to include the environmental costs. Thus, there is no sharp division between cost of abatement and cost of environmental damage.

If all power-plants in a region are required to reduce the emissions, then the price of electricity is likely to rise, which will reduce the demand for power. This will carry a cost - the cost of reductions in consumers′ surplus for energy. This cost represent the cost of reducing indoor temperature, the increased cost of producing commodities that use electricity as input, etc.

Apparently, the cost of abatement is a rather complicated concept. It includes a variety of different adjustments in the economy to the requirement that the emissions must be reduced. If the emission reductions are relatively small and limited to a small part of the economy, then the cost of "end of the pipe" technology may be appropriate, but if the requirements are far reaching and the environmental policies cover broad segments of the society, this is not enough. A systematic modelling of the affected sectors of the economy is required, and quite often, a general equilibrium approach may be necessary.[5]

6.3.2 Criteria for the Choice of Policy Instruments

The following five criteria are of importance in choosing between different approaches for changing incentive structures:

- *Static efficiency.* This criterion concerns the cost of achieving a desired environmental improvement by applying a certain instrument. The lower the cost, the more attractive is the instrument.

- *Dynamic efficiency.* This criterion concerns the ability of the instrument to cope with (unanticipated) changes and with the incentives to develop new and better technical solutions to environmental problems.

- *Information requirements.* In order to exploit different environmental policy instruments, the policy maker needs in general different information to implement them. The more available the information is, the more attractive is the instrument.

- *Measurement and monitoring costs.* Different instruments require different monitoring and since monitoring is costly, and sometimes impossible, this is an important aspect in choosing between different instruments.

- *Political and ethical feasibility.* For example, different instruments can have (but will in general not have) different impacts on income distribution.

6.3.3 An Evaluation of Policy Instruments

In general it is possible to achieve a desired environmental improvement by using many different instruments. We have already classified these instruments into either being of the command and control type or being an economic instrument. This distinction is not always possible to maintain in all situations. However, it is quite often a very useful classification and it has become a standard in the international literature.

In order to illustrate the role of the criteria given above, let us consider two instruments, one of the command and control type and one being an economic instrument. Let us take

---

5. See Carlsson (1988) for a system analysis approach to estimating the cost of reducing sulphur and nitrogene emissions in Sweden, and Bergman (1990) for the use of a computable general equilbrium model for estimating the cost of reducing the carbondioxide emissions in Sweden.

an emission standard as one example and an emission fee as the other. The first instrument requires that the polluters do not exceed certain emission standards, and if they do, they will expect some kind of punishment. Let us assume that the punishment is sufficiently high and that the monitoring is sufficiently good to make it unprofitable for plants to violate the standards. The second instrument require that the polluter has to pay a certain amount per ton of the pollutant emitted. Once again, let us assume that monitoring is sufficiently good so that the polluter has no way of escaping the fee.

Let us temporarily assume that policy makers, government agencies, companies and other relevant parties have all necessary information on the cost of abating emissions in all plants (present and future) and on the social costs of the emissions. We further assume that there is no uncertainty about these costs. Under these assumptions, there is no substantial difference between the two instruments as far as static efficiency is concerned. Both instruments can be designed so as to achieve the same reduction in pollution and to the same cost. The reason is of course that the government agencies have sufficient information to select the emission standards and the emission fees in such a way that the same environmental improvement is achieved to the same cost.

Let us now drop the extreme assumptions on the information the government agencies have. Then a discussion on the choice between the two instruments become both relevant and interesting. In fact, it can be shown that if the agency has information on abatement costs and damage costs but if this information is uncertain, then it is impossible in general to recommend on the basis of cost efficiency one instrument before the other.

6.3.4 Cost Efficiency

Let us assume that there are two plants, A and B, emitting the same pollutant and that the environmental damage is due to the total annual emissions. What matters from the environmental point of view is obviously not how much one of the plants emits. The only relevant number is the total emission of the pollutant. How should the total emissions be divided between the two plants?

If it is only the total emissions that are of interest from the environmental point of view, should not the society be indifferent to which source, A or B, that abate the emissions? It does matter, however, since the society has other objectives as well, apart from reducing emissions. It also wants to provide the members of the society as much of other desired goods - material consumption. This is obviously of special importance in developing countries. That is equivalent to trying to achieve the desired emission reductions to as low cost as possible. It therefore matters how the emission reductions are allocated between the sources.

In diagram 6.3.4.1 below, the costs of abating emissions in the two plants are illustrated by the marginal cost curves. The emissions in the two sources are measured along the horizontal axes. The marginal cost curves give the cost of reducing the emissions with one unit. The curves are downsloping indicating that large abatements increase the cost of abating a further ton of the pollutant.

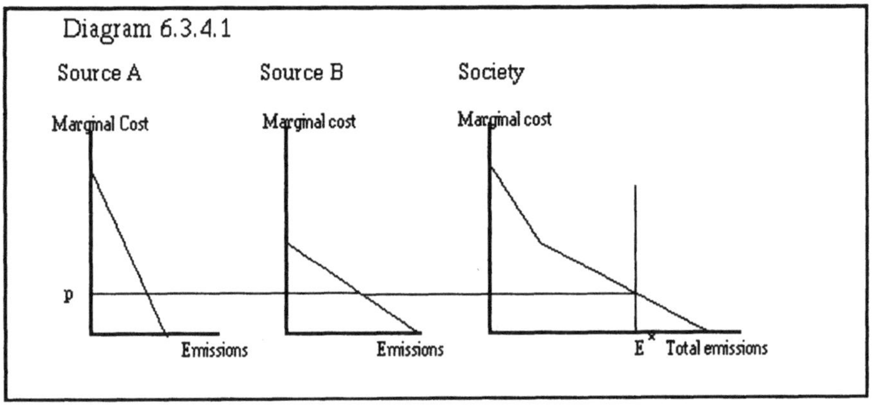

In the initial situation there are no restrictions on the emissions and both sources would increase their emissions until *their* costs are minimized. That will occur when the marginal cost of abatement is zero. The emissions will therefore be of the sizes indicated by the intersections between the marginal cost curves and the horizontal axes (in the two left most panels). Assume now that we want to reduce the total emissions to E* (in the right most panel). It does matter how this reduction is allocated between the two sources. If the whole reduction is to be undertaken by abatement in source A only, the cost in source B will be zero (as the marginal cost). But the cost in A will be quite high. By reducing the abatement in A somewhat, there will be substantial savings because the marginal cost is high. If abatement is increased in B, the cost increase will be small because the marginal cost is small. In fact, *as long as the marginal costs differ between the sources it is possible to reduce the total cost by reallocating abatement between the sources.* This is the basic conclusion - for minimum total cost or *cost efficiency*, marginal cost must be the same in all sources.

The curve in the right most panel in the diagram corresponds to the marginal cost when abatement is allocated in the cheapest way possible between the two sources, i.e. when the marginal cost is the same in the two sources. In fact the curve in this panel is obtained as the "horizontal" addition of the curves in the other two panels. We can use this curve to estimate the marginal cost corresponding to different amounts of permitted emissions. If the total emissions must be limited to E*, the marginal cost should be equal to p in both sources.

Assume then that we know this curve i.e. the aggregate marginal cost curve. Then, if we want to limit the total emissions to E* we know that the marginal cost should equal p at both sources for cost minimization. How can this be accomplished?

If the social planner knows the individual marginal cost curves, then he can obviously demand that the individual sources reduce their pollution to the levels compatible with efficiency. However, this approach has two serious problems - the planner does not really know the individual marginal cost curves and, furthermore, these cost curves will change whenever prices, technology, and other factors change. Therefore, other approaches for implementing cost efficiency must be looked for.

One such approach would be to tax the emissions at the rate $p per ton pollutant. Each source would then find it in its own interest to reduce the emissions until the marginal cost equals the tax. If the marginal cost is smaller than the tax, it would pay for the company to reduce the emissions in order to save on the tax payment, while if the marginal cost is greater than the tax, it would pay to increase the emissions in order to save on the abatement cost. Thus, the result would be a cost efficient outcome. Note that it is not required that the planner has detailed information on the individual marginal abatement costs and that even if external factors such as technology changes, the result will be cost efficient. However, what is required is that the planner knows the aggregate marginal abatement cost curve and by how much the emissions should be reduced.

Another approach would be for the planner to decide on the total amount of pollution allowed and then issue transferable pollution permits to the two sources. Then, it is possible for the two polluters to start to trade permits with each other. If the initial distribution of the permits is such that the marginal abatement cost (at full utilization of the permits) is higher at one source relative to the marginal abatement cost at the other source, a mutual profitable trade is possible. The source with the higher marginal abatement cost could gain by buying permits from the source with the lower costs. Since the buyer is willing to pay more than the marginal cost in the other source, the trade is beneficial also to the seller. In equilibrium, the two sources will have exploited all gains from trade which means that both have reduced their pollution to a level at which their marginal abatement cost is equal to p.

Using the system of transferable permits, one would expect that the target emission reduction will be achieved and in a cost efficient way. Furthermore, one would expect that if the market works well, the equilibrium price on the permit would correspond to p*, the optimal emission tax. If the price would exceed p*, then at least some sources would experience that their marginal cost is lower than the price and would be tempted to sell permits which would reduce the market price. If the ruling market price is lower than p*, then it would be cheaper for at least one company to buy more permits and thereby increase the demand and the price. In equilibrium, therefore, the price will be p*.

This presupposes that the market will be perfect. However, in general, only a few agents will operate on the market and they will not have complete information on the marginal costs of each other. Therefore, one should not expect that the market will generate a uniform price. But an experiment,[6] carried out on the emissions of volatile organic compounds in Gothenburg indicated that even in such a case, the trade in emission permits will result in efficient outcomes, although there is no unique market price. In fact, every transaction on the market will reduce the overall cost and therefore increase efficiency.

What is then the difference between a system based on tradeable permits and a system with an emission tax? There are several important differences and we will discuss a few of them. Let us start with the very important fact that the planner or policy maker never has complete information on neither the abatement costs nor the damage costs. This lack of information has a very profound influence on the rational choice between an emission tax and a system with tradeable emission permits. We can illustrate this in the diagram below.

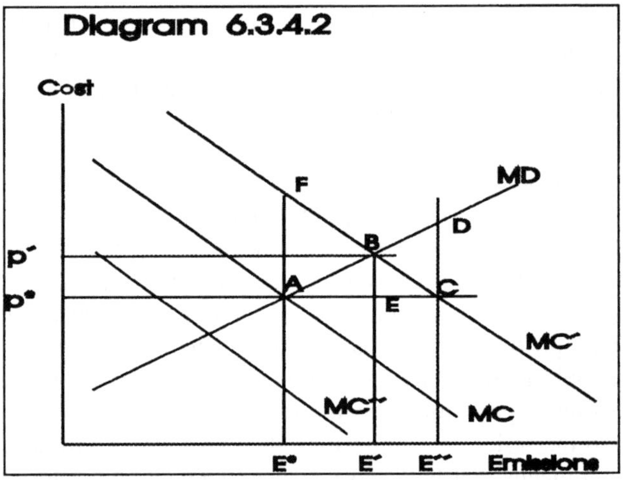

Here we have assumed that there is only one source, but since both tradeable permits and an emission charge will lead to cost efficient emission reductions. The case with tradeable permits corresponds to a command and control approach, in which the planner prescribes an upper bound on the emission level. We can generalize the analysis by including many sources but that would not yield any more results.[7]

The social planner has to decide on how much emissions should be reduced and in what

6. See I. Ståhl, L. Bergman and K.-G. Mäler, 1988.

7. The following analysis is based on Weizman (1974). See also Dasgupta, Hammond and Maskin (1980) and Dasgupta (1982). The analysis is usually called p vs q because it deals with the choice between prices and quantities in controlling an economic system.

way. He has estimated a marginal cost curve - MC - for abatement but this estimate is uncertain. In fact, we assume that what is known is that the curve is either MC′ or MC′′ (we could easily have made a more realistic picture but with no change in the results). The estimated curve is simply the average of MC′ and MC′′. We assume that the social planner knows the marginal damage curve MD with no uncertainty. Based on his information the planner will find that the optimal emission level will be E*, because at that level marginal cost of abatement equals marginal damage cost. The total expected abatement and damage cost is minimized at that level.

Assume now that the planner decides to control the pollution by using an emission tax with the tax rate p*. If the true marginal cost curve would have been MC, everything would have been fine. But the true curve is either MC′ or MC′′. Assume MC′ turns out to be the true curve. Then the optimal tax rate should have been p′ and the optimal emission level E′. Because of having used the curve MC extra costs are incurred to society. Let us find these costs.

At the tax rate p*, the emissions will be E′′ instead of the optimal emission level E′. This means that the environmental damage will be greater than in optimum. More precisely, the extra damage cost is equal to the area below the marginal damage curve (remember that the area under a "marginal" curve gives the "total"), or the area E′E′′DB. On the other hand, there will be savings in abatement cost as the emissions are larger. These savings are equal to the area under the marginal abatement cost curve or E′E′′CB. The net increase in cost because the true marginal abatement cost curve is MC′ and not MC is thus

E′E′′DB - E′E′′CB = BCD.

Thus the triangle BCD measures the extra cost when using an emission tax when the true marginal cost is higher than the expected. A similar expression can easily be found in the case the true marginal cost curve is MC′.

Note that the triangle BCD will be greater the flatter the MC′ curve is and the steeper the MD curve is. The intuition behind this is simple. If the marginal abatement cost curve is flat, the emissions are very sensitive to the tax rate and a small mistake in setting the tax will mean a big difference for the emissions. If the marginal damage cost curve is very steep, then the environmental cost will be very large because of the difference in emissions. The loss will thus be proportional to the elasticity of the marginal cost curve and inversely proportional to the elasticity of the marginal damage curve. In fact, this is true in a much more general setting than the one we have used here. Let us now look at the case when we use a tradeable permit system. Then the planner prescribes the maximum pollution. Given his information on the marginal cost curve MC and on the marginal damage curve MD, he will find the optimal emission level E*. He will then require that the emissions never exceed this level.

Assume then that MC′ is the true marginal cost curve. The true optimal emission level is as before E′. By limiting the emissions to E* society is experiencing higher abatement costs than would have been optimal. The extra abatement cost is, once again, equal to the area under the marginal cost curve or E*E′BF. On the other hand, the environmental damage cost will be smaller. The reduction in the damage is equal to E*E′BA. The difference

$$E^*E'BF - E^*E'BA = ABF$$

is a measure of the extra cost from using a command and control approach when the marginal cost curve turns out to be MC′ instead of the estimated MC.

The area ABF is larger the steeper the marginal cost curve is and the flatter the marginal damage cost curve is. The general result is that the expected loss from using a command and control approach is proportional to the variance in the marginal cost and to the elasticity of the marginal cost curve and inversely proportional to the elasticity of the marginal damage cost curve.

Which approach should be used? Should we use a command and control approach and prescribe an upper bound on emissions and then let the market through a system of tradeable permits allocate the emissions efficiently among the sources? Or should we impose an uniform emission tax?

According to the analysis above, the answer depends on the elasticities of the marginal abatement cost function and the marginal damage cost function. If there are reasons to believe that the marginal damage cost curve is very steep while the marginal cost curve is not, one should choose the command and control approach. This may be the case when there are thresholds in the environment so that a small increase in the emissions will cause strong harmful effects on the environment. On the other hand, if the environmental damage is not that sensitive to the annual emissions, a tax may be preferable. This is the case when the environmental harm is caused by the accumulated emissions. The precise control of the annual emissions is in that case not needed, but it is the emissions in the long run that are important.

All of this rather lengthy discussion of environmental policy instruments and cost efficiency is based on the assumption that only the total emissions matter from an environmental point of view, i.e. that the environmental damage is a function only of the total emissions and not their spatial distribution. However, quite many pollution problems are such that the spatial distribution matters.

Take for example, the effluent from a sewage treatment plant. This effluent, when discharged into a river will, through microorganisms in the water, decompose. This process will, however, consume free dissolved oxygen in the river and thereby damage the reproduction of some fish species, reduce the clarity of the water and in general reduce its quality for recreation or for drinking. On the other hand, the flowing water will be reaerated and will therefore sufficiently far downstream recover its level of dissolved oxygen.

The damage from the discharge of effluent will obviously depend on the location of the sewage treatment plant. If the plant is located close to the mouth of the river, the damage will be rather limited as the oxygen level in the receiving sea will compensate the lack of oxygen in the river. On the other hand, a treatment plant far from the mouth will potentially create oxygen deficiency in a very long stretch of the river. Thus, it does matter where the discharge of the effluent take place.

From a cost efficiency point of view, this situation would require that the sources of the organic wastes - the effluent - reduce their discharges in relation to the damage from the individual discharges. The plant close to the mouth should be required to reduce its discharges relatively little compared to the plant upstream the river.[8]

In this case, a policy using emission tax should be designed in such a way that upstream plants have to pay taxes for its discharges at a higher rate than plants closer to the mouth. In principle, each should be charged with its marginal damage cost. We could also think of tradeable discharge permits, designed in a way such that the discharge of one ton of organic wastes from the upstream plant can be freely exchanged to the discharge of x tons in the downstream plant, where x represent the relation between the marginal damage from discharges in the downstream plant to the upstream plant.

It is obvious that both these systems - the system with individually tailored tax rates and the system with fixed exchange rates between individual permits - will require more monitoring and more administration than a system with an uniform tax rate or a system where permits can be exchanged one to one. However, even a flat tax rate will be superior to a system with uniform discharge reductions.[9] We will see an example of this in the section on international environmental problems.

Air pollution from traffic offers another example when it matters where the emissions take place. Different areas of a city may have different sensitivity to the concentration of air pollution and the concentrations will differ between different monitoring stations because of winds. Thus, it matters where traffic is reduced in order to improve the environment. One could still think of a system with differentiated tax rates (which will be cost efficient) and one could also think of a system with tradeable permits but which will not be exchanged one to one. For a discussion of such systems, see Tietenberg

8. For an illuminating discussion of the cost efficiency aspects of discharges of organic wastes in a river, see Kneese and Bower (1968) and in particular their discussion of the Delaware study.
9. See Kneese and Bower (1968).

(1985) and the references given in there.

The discussion above was based on the assumption that there existed well defined abatement cost functions, i.e. functions relating cost of abatement to amount of abatement (although we have assumed that these functions are not necessarily known with certainty). However, in many realistic cases, emissions are due to random events within a production process. A valve may break which will give rise to an increase in pollution or a plant may start to burn and thereby releasing toxic substances. In both these cases, the events were not planned or foreseen. The only thing that may have been known was the probability of the events. Now as long as it is only the average or expected emissions that matters, this is of no concern. Normally, this is not the case. We are much more concerned than proportional with the peak load of pollutants in the ambient environment because the marginal damage cost function has a very steep slope. It is quite possible to discuss cost efficiency in this situation and compare different policy instruments essentially in the same way as we did above. However, the analysis becomes more complicated so we will only summarize some important conclusions (see Mäler 1974 for an analysis of emission taxes).

- Emission taxes have a substantial advantage as compared to command and control instruments.

- A simple tradeable permit system will not work.

- A more complicated permit system with many different permits, each for a period of definite length, may work.

Before leaving the discussion of static efficiency, two further concepts should be mentioned: Polluters Pay Principle (PPP) and Victims Pay Principle (VPP). These are principles that define two different cost sharing mechanisms. With PPP, the polluter is assumed to pay all abatement costs, while with the VPP cost of abatement is paid by the victims of pollution. Sometimes, however, the principles are defined differently. PPP, is e.g. defined to cover the case when the polluter not only pays the abatement but also compensate the victim for his damage cost. The first interpretation is the most common one and we will use it in the sequel.

OECD adopted in the beginning of the 1970's the Polluters Pay Principle as a basis for environmental policy. There were three reasons behind this decision. First, there was the ethical view that the polluter should bear the cost (and usually the cost would include the damage cost). Second, it was thought that a violation of PPP, by subsidizing abatement, might be a form of non-tariff barrier to international trade. Finally, it was also argued that PPP would be necessary for static efficiency. However, the last argument is wrong. It is possible to design a system (although a quite complicated system) involving VPP, which would produce a cost efficient outcome (Kneese and Mäler, 1973). However, when we turn to dynamic efficiency there will be a difference between PPP and VPP.

We have here discussed command and control approaches versus taxes from the point of view of static efficiency. This is perhaps the most discussed and best known aspect of the design of environmental policies. However, there are other, perhaps even more important aspects. We now turn to some of these.

6.3.5 Dynamic Efficiency

In the long run, the most important aspects of the choice of policy instruments are the incentives to develop new and better technology and the influence on economic development. Both these aspects have only been rudimentary studied by environmental economists, in spite of the fact they may have substantial influence on the future well-being of man. We will, therefore, only offer a couple of remarks on these aspects.

Consider a plant that is emitting a pollutant in the air. Its marginal abatement cost curve is given by MC in diagram 6.3.5.1. Assume that the environmental policy is based around a command and control approach, i.e. that the plant is restricted to emit E tons of the pollutant each year. The total abatement cost, due to this requirement, is then equal to the area under the MC curve, or EBC.

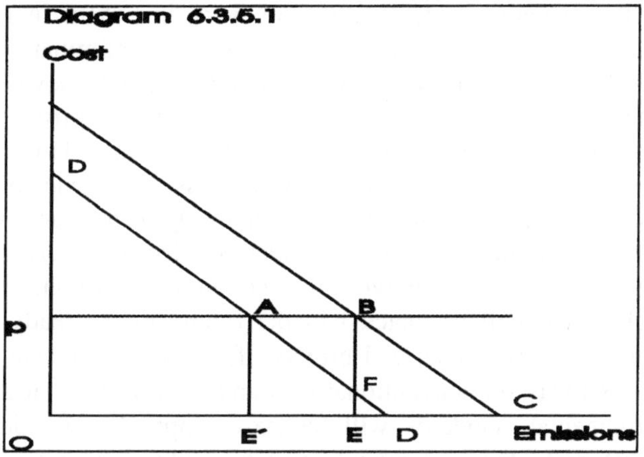

Assume now that it is possible for the plant to develop a new technology that would reduce the abatement costs and that the new marginal abatement cost curve is MC′. If this new technology has been introduced, the abatement cost would be equal to the triangle EDF. The savings from the new technology is then equal to the area DCBE. It is strictly equal to the reduction in abatement costs.

The situation is different when we have an emission tax. Assume the tax is p. Then the total cost to the plant with the old technology is ECB (abatement cost) plus OEBp (tax payment). With the new technology, the cost is E′DA (abatement cost) plus OE′Ap (tax payment). The cost saving from the new technology is then DCBA. This is strictly greater than the cost saving with command and control, because the plant will not be able to reduce its abatement cost by using the new technology, it will also be able to reduce its tax payment by reducing the emissions. Thus it seems that an emission tax gives stronger incentives to develop and apply new, cleaner technologies than a command and control approach.

What about a tradeable permit scheme? Will it give the same result as an emission tax or a command and control approach? It depends. If the permits are given once and for all to the sources, but after that they are bought and sold on a market, the result will be similar to the result with an emission tax. The permits will now have an economic value and by adopting a new and cleaner technology, the plant can sell some of its permits and earn money. If the price of the permits does not change because of the new technology, the result will be exactly as in the case with an emission tax. However, if several companies adopt new technologies, the total demand for permits will fall and so will their price. Thus, the return from adopting new cleaner technologies will drop and so will the incentives to develop better methods of production. Thus, in general tradeable permits will give smaller incentives for technical development than a tax but larger than in a pure command and control system.

These aspects on technical development are very important in relation to long term environmental goals. Assume that a country want to eliminate the conventional car engine and replace it with a more environmentally friendly device at some date in the future. The parliament may make a law saying that ten years from now, no sales of cars with the conventional engine will be allowed. Is such a law credible? Assume no technical development takes place and ten years pass. If the sales of new cars were to be banned, the consequences would be drastic, not only to the car manufacturing industry but to the whole economic system. A democratic elected government would obviously try to change the law in order to avoid the economic catastrophe. Therefore, in order to be useful, a law that will be enacted in the future must already now be regarded as credible in order to have beneficial effects. If, on the other hand, the parliament had introduced a tax today on conventional cars and with a rule that any car that will pass stricter environmental standards will be tax-exempt, the situation would have been completely different. The car manufacturers would then have strong incentives to develop as fast as possible cars that would pass the new standards in order to avoid the tax burden. And, the policy is credible because it is in operation at the moment (or rather soon thereafter) it has been decided.

It is also clear that any environmental regulation will reduce the return on the capital investment in a plant which in the long run may reduce the capital formation and thereby the economic growth. Studies of the American environmental legislation with the help of a dynamic computable general equilibrium model (Kopp and Hazilla, 1989) indicate that this effect can be substantial. It is quite obvious that an emission tax will reduce the return more than a pure command and control system, including a system with tradeable permits. Therefore, one would à priori expect an emission tax to reduce the growth of the economy still further. However, emission taxes should be looked upon as part of the much wider portfolio of different taxes on labour, capital, value added etc. Obviously, it is possible to design the total tax system in such a way that the negative effects on capital investments from an emission tax is offset by changes in taxes on profits. In fact, Sweden introduced in 1990 a system of taxes on sulphur and nitrogen emissions which is a part of a much bigger tax package, including reduction in capital taxes, reduction in labour taxes and increases in value added taxes. In economic jargon, the package takes away the "income effect" of the emission taxes but keeps the "substitution effect". By this is meant the following. An emission tax has two effects on a company emitting a taxed pollutant. First, its overall profitability decreases because the cost increases. This decrease in profits may have as an effect a reduction in output and therefore also in emission. This is the income effect. However, even if there is no income effect, there is the much more important substitution effect. It is cheaper to use environmentally cleaner technologies, including increased abatement, increased use of cleaner inputs. Thus one could design a tax package including emission taxes that would have no income effect but still give rise to substantial substitution effects. By that, one could increase the chances of sustained growth.

It is not as clear that a system with tradeable emission permits will have similar negative effects on the rate of return on capital investments as will an isolated emission tax. That depends on the way the initial permits are distributed among the companies concerned. If the distribution is determined by an auction each year, then the system with tradeable permits will have exactly the same effects as a system with emission taxes. If the permits are auctioned out only initially, then in later periods, the holding of permits will be part of the assets of the firm, and an increased holding of such assets will not necessarily lead to a deterioration of the profitability of the company. Finally, if the initial distribution is determined by "grandfathering", i.e. if each source is given a number of permits proportional to their actual emissions, then some companies will be able to increase their wealth through the system, and there is no reason to believe that tradeable permits will reduce profits more than a simple command and control policy. Furthermore, a system based on tradeable permits or based on command and control can be coupled with reforms of taxes in general in order to negate the income effect, and thereby not put any breaks on the growth potential of the economy.

One could restate some of the conclusions above in terms of Polluters Pay Principle and Victims Pay Principle. With Polluters Pay Principle, the polluters will be the ones who make the direct gains from technical progress, while with the Victims Pay Principle it is the victims who would gain. However, it is the polluters who make the decisions on technology and it is therefore clear that with PPP, the polluters have greater incentives to find new technical solutions to environmental problems than with VPP. Thus, in a dynamic context, one could make a strong argument for using PPP instead of VPP, in order to reduce the cost of preserving the environment.

6.3.6 Monitoring and Other Practical Aspects

The discussion in the previous section was based on the implicit assumption that emissions can be monitored continuously. In many cases, this is far from being a realistic assumption. Trivial examples are given by littering, and garbage disposal. Obviously, it will not be possible to monitor each individual 24 hours a day, which means that he can throw away a beer can without being observed. A less trivial example is the release of volatile organic substances from a refinery. Most often, these substances are emitted through faulty valves, bad ceilings in oil tanks etc. The emissions of these substances is an example of diffuse emissions. It is not possible to define one point at which the emissions are released, and so it is impossible to monitor the emissions with any precision. Another example is given by non-point sources. The emissions from a car driving through a city cannot be monitored directly and neither can the runoff of fertilizers in agriculture to a lake. Perhaps still more common is that even if monitoring is possible, such monitoring may turn out to be extremely expensive. Monitoring the sulphur emissions from the oil-burners in family houses is technically feasible but unthinkable from an economic point of view.

However, even if direct monitoring of emissions is not feasible, most of the analysis in the previous sections is applicable, because usually we do not need direct monitoring of the emissions. Take for example the emission tax. If we cannot monitor the emissions directly, we can always find a system of taxes on inputs and outputs combined with a system of subsidies that will have exactly the same incentive effect as the emission tax (this theorem was proved in Mäler, 1974). This theorem implies that we can always find a combination of taxes and deposit-refund systems that will make it profitable for the company to reduce its emission as much as it would with an emission tax.

The case of a sulphur tax may be illuminating. We have concluded above that we cannot monitor all sulphur emissions directly. What is the alternative? First, tax the sulphur content of the imported and domestically produced fossil fuels. The sulphur content of the fuels can be measured with adequate precision. Next, give a rebate to those who can prove that they have reduced the sulphur-emissions by some technical device, scrubbing the stack gases, changing the combustion process etc. Such reductions can also be easily monitored. The system is in principle a deposit-refund system. You pay for the sulphur you buy (embodied in the fuel) and get a refund when you show that you have taken care of the sulphur.

Mercury or cadmium in batteries are a source of serious environmental problems. Here, a deposit-refund system may do the work. We cannot tax the actual disposal of batteries in the environment but we can use a deposit-refund system that will have exactly the same effect as if we were taxing the disposal of the batteries. By taxing the sales of the batteries and refunding the tax (less a charge for administration cost and cost for ultimate disposal), we are indeed taxing the disposal of the batteries. Furthermore, since there is a difference between the tax and the refund, corresponding to the cost of ultimate disposal, producers of batteries will have incentives to develop new types of batteries that are less harmful to the environment and therefore not taxed or taxed at a lower rate. For a general discussion of deposit-refund schemes, see Bohm (1980).

Another example is given by automobile exhausts. We have already concluded that we cannot monitor these exhausts. Can we define a tax base so that the exhausts are taxed indirectly? In Sweden, the parliament introduced in 1987 the following system in order to promote cars with catalytic converters. Cars with such converters require lead free gas. The standard leaded gas would soon destroy the converter. This means that one could try to use two instruments - taxes on gasoline and taxes on cars - in order to achieve an indirect taxation of automobile exhausts. This was done in the following way. First, a tax differential was introduced between lead free gas and leaded gas. Second, a discount in the sales tax was introduced for cars with a catalytic converter. The tax differential on gas and the discount in the sales tax were calculated in such a way that one would approximately be taxing the exhausts from cars not equipped with catalytic converters at a rate that would make it profitable for consumers to buy cars with catalytic converters. The result was that during the first year, more than two thirds of all sales of new cars were sales of cars with catalytic converters.

These examples (and the theorem in Mäler, 1974) show that it is possible to transform an emission tax to an equivalent system of taxes and tax discounts. However, this is not necessarily true for a system with tradeable permits. Take the last example. A tradeable permit system would include permits, either to drive or to buy gasoline. In both cases, the transaction costs would be extremely high, and make the system unworkable. On the other hand, a system with tradeable permits for sulphur emissions may work. Here the permits would be permits for buying sulphur embodied in fuels. In the case sulphur has been removed from the stack gases by some device, the plant would be entitled to a corresponding number of extra permits, which then can be sold. Here there is an obvious parallel to a system with an emission tax.

Even with random emissions of pollutants e.g. accidental spills of chemicals, one can think of systems that would work similarly to emission taxes. For example, compulsory insurance systems may work or a system with insurance bonds (Perrings, 1989).

Thus, it seems that economic instruments may have an important role in the design of environmental policies even in cases where emissions cannot be monitored directly.

What the environmental economist must do is to try to understand as well as possible the effects of a first best (but perhaps practically impossible) design of the policy and then find combinations of practically possible instruments that can achieve the same result.

There are a few other practical differences between different instruments which deserve being mentioned. The first concerns inflation. If an emission tax is fixed in nominal term, i.e. in $ per ton emitted, and there is a rapid inflation going on, then the emission tax will soon be eroded since the real value of the tax rate will fall as the inflation continues. Thus, it is necessary to fix the tax rate in real terms. This has hardly ever been done and the result is that some workable and desirable systems are no longer working. In Sweden, a deposit refund system was introduced for cars a decade ago. A special tax was levied on the sales of the new car, but a part of that tax was refunded when the old and worn out car was returned to an official handler of old cars for proper disposal. The idea was to give people incentives to see to it that old cars were not left in the nature. However, the tax and the refund were fixed in nominal terms, and the inflation very soon reduced the corresponding real values to almost nothing.

With a tradeable permit system, inflation does not create any direct problems (in addition to the general mess in various markets rapid inflation usually achieves). Here the market prices of the permits will follow the inflation automatically, and the system will not be eroded over time.

Another practical aspect concerns changing environmental objectives. One would expect that the demand for ambient environmental quality will rise with income (i.e. the damage cost will increase) and the policy should therefore be made flexible so that it easily can accommodate a desire to reduce pollution further. Both a system with emission taxes and a system with tradeable permits are flexible enough to accomplish that. With emission taxes, the parliament has to raise the real rate of the tax and with tradeable permits, the state can simply buy permits on the market. In the latter case, the permit price will increase and the overall effect will be a reduction in pollution. Of course, it would also be possible to achieve the same result through a "devaluation" of the permits. A permit to emit 1 ton of sulphur may be transformed into a permit to emit only 0.7 ton, and thereby reducing the overall pollution with 30%. However, this last approach may have some severe drawbacks if companies anticipate such devaluations. Furthermore, the first approach has the major advantage that the government has to make an explicit comparison of the cost of buying permits with the benefits from reducing the pollution.

6.4 International Economic Problems

6.4.1 Introduction

In 6.3 we studied a common property resource - an airshed, a watershed, that could not be expected to be managed efficiently without government interventions. In this section we will continue this study, but focus on such resources that are internationally shared. For such resources, there are no government that can intervene in order to improve on the allocation of resources. Everything that can be achieved must be achieved through voluntary cooperation. The purpose of this section is to analyse conditions for such cooperation.[10]

It may be useful for this analysis to classify resources according to the economic incentives for cooperation that they give rise to. We will therefore separate between

- upstream - downstream resources

- regional reciprocal resources

- global resources

By upstream-downstream resources we mean a resource that one or more countries can use (i.e. pollute) without damage to themselves, but with damage to other countries. The Rhine river is one such example. When Switzerland pollutes Rhine, downstream countries will be damaged. But also airsheds with persistent winds belong to this category. Countries upwind will then create harmful effects in countries downwind. In order to be complete, we should look at various cases of upstream-downstream resources. One such case is when there is one upstream country and one downstream country, another when there are many upstream countries and one more case when there are many downstream countries. The reason why it is important to separate these different cases from each other is that they give rise to different economic problems. The second case differ from the first in that we now have to look at the cost efficient allocation of emission reductions among the upstream countries. The third differ from the first in that we now have free rider problems among the downstream countries. However, we will not analyse these cases separately because we will gain insights from studying regional reciprocal resources. Instead we will focus only on the case with one upstream and one downstream country.

By regional reciprocal resources we mean resources that are shared by many countries

---

10. For a more complete discussion, see Mäler, 1990

and such that the resource in one country will affect all other countries. This is the generalization of prisoner´s dilemma game to the case with many actors.

Finally, global resources refer to resources that are shared by all men - climate, the ozone layer, the deep oceans etc. Most of the conclusions we will reach on regional reciprocal resources can be generalized to the case of global resources, and we will therefore not study them in detail.

6.4.2 Upstream-Downstream Resources

Let us look at a very simple case, the case when one upstream country is polluting a river flowing into a downstream country. The upstream country can abate the pollution and the marginal abatement cost curve is the curve MC in diagram 6.4.2.1. The pollution causes damage in the downstream country and the marginal damage cost curve is the curve MD. Assume now that transfers can freely be made between the two countries. This implies that from an efficiency point of view, the countries should strive for a reduction in pollution which will minimize the sum of abatement cost and damage cost. By using international transfers, one could then distribute the gains between the two countries in any way that is desirable. By using transfers, we can *separate* the allocation issue (i.e. the size of the abatement in the upstream country) from the distribution issue (who will get what benefits). Without transfers, such separation is not possible and it may no longer be desirable to minimize the total cost.

Cost minimization implies that the marginal abatement cost should be equal to marginal damage cost, i.e. emissions should be reduced to the level E* in the diagram.

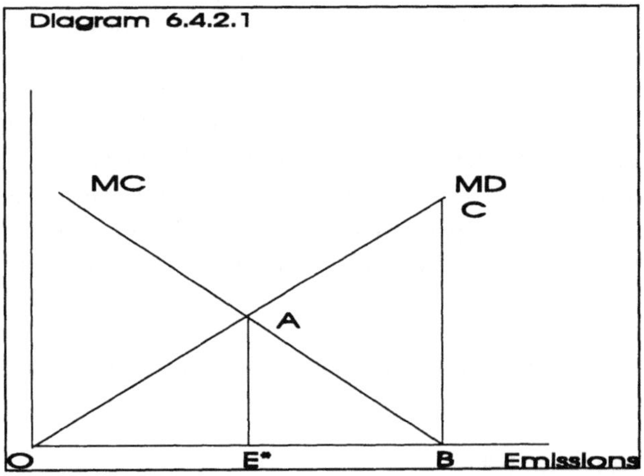

Initially, the upstream country is emitting as much as it can, i.e. up to the level OB. If the countries agree to minimize the total cost, the upstream country should abate the amount E*B, which will cost the upstream country E*AB, i.e. the area under the marginal cost curve. The downstream country will gain since its environmental damage will be reduced. The gain corresponds to the area E*ACB, i.e. the area under the marginal damage cost curve. Thus, the downstream country will gain and the upstream country will loose. Obviously, the upstream country will not accept such an outcome but ask for compensation. Only if an agreement is beneficial to both countries will it be accepted. Note the difference from the situation of a national pollution problem. In such a case, the state could dictate that the upstream polluter should abate pollution. As regards international pollution problems, there is no supranational authority that can dictate the upstream country to abate. An agreement must be based on voluntary cooperation, and such cooperation requires that all parties expect to gain from it.

In the case illustrated in the diagram, both countries can gain from a reduction in emissions. If the downstream country compensates the upstream country, it will still gain from the agreement since the reduction in the damage cost is greater than the abatement cost. Thus, it seems that in international pollution problems, we cannot rely on the polluters pay principle but instead on the victims pay principle (VPP). The victim country has to "bribe" the polluting country to abate pollution. However, note that this does not necessarily imply that VPP must be adopted in domestic environmental policy. In fact, the adoption of VPP for solving international problems simply means that the downstream country should compensate the upstream country, but not the polluting firms in the upstream country. The design of the environmental policy within the upstream country is up to that country.

This result is the standard result in the discussion of transboundary pollution problems. It is simply the Coase theorem (Coase, 1960) applied to one particular class of problems. However, the Coase theorem was based on the assumption that there where property rights that were well-defined and could be transferred by law. In transboundary pollution there does not exist a supranational agency with the right to enforce property rights. In the analysis above, it was tacitly assumed that the upstream country has the right to pollute the downstream country and that the downstream country must compensate the upstream country for any abatement. I do not know of any actual transboundary pollution cases where this has not been the case. On the other hand, there seem to be very few empirical studies looking at international environmental problems from the point of view of the distribution of property rights.

6.4.3 International Commons

Assume that the two countries share a common resource - for example a common airshed. Country i emits z_i to the airshed and the total emission is $z = z_1 + z_2$. The damage in each country is now a function of the total emissions z, that is

$$D_1 = D_1(z_1 + z_2)$$

$$D_2 = D_2(z_1 + z_2).$$

Let the emission in country i be z_{i0} before any cooperation has been agreed upon, and assume that country i has to reduce its emission to z_i because of cooperation. The cost of the abatement is given by

$$C_i = C_i(z_{i0}-z_i), \quad i = 1, 2.$$

In this case, cooperation could reduce the total cost to the two countries. In fact, the countries could agree to reduce the emissions in such a way as to minimize the total cost, i.e. to agree to reduce the emissions to the point where

$$C_1 + D_1 + C_2 + D_2$$

is minimized. If the situation is symmetric, i.e. if the cost of abatement functions and the damage cost functions are the same in the two countries, both countries would gain the same amount. However, if the abatement functions or the cost functions differ between the countries, then one country may gain more than the other. In fact, we could think of cases (and we will shortly study one real case - the case of acid rains in Europe) where one country would be a net looser while the other a net winner. Obviously, no country would voluntary enter an agreement which is expected to bring about a net loss for the country. The only feasible outcome is therefore that the winning countries compensate the loosing countries by some kind of transfers (exactly as in the case with an upstream - downstream pollution), so that all countries are net winners.

This is however not enough. Both countries would still have incentives to deviate from the agreement, by being a free rider. In that sense, this resembles the prisoner´s dilemma game or the tragedy of the commons discussed in the introduction to this chapter. In the case of the upstream - downstream pollution problem, no country could gain by being a free rider. With an international common, on the other hand, free riding behaviour may in the short run be beneficial. However, in the long run it is still true that cooperation will be desirable. If the countries can monitor each other perfectly, a deviation could be met by deviations from other countries. The result will be that both countries will expect future losses. If they don´t discount these losses too much, they will find it profitable not to defect from a cooperative agreement. This is a simple application of the Folk theorem on repeated games, see e.g. Kreps (1990). Thus, with perfect monitoring of emissions we would expect a stable efficient outcome (assuming, of course, that countries that are net losers because of the agreement are compensated). Moreover, if the situation is not completely symmetric, one country may loose unless there is a side payment made from the other country. Thus, even in the case of shared common resources there may be a need for international transfers.

6.4.4 The Acid Rain Game

In order to illustrate the arguments above, we will study two existing international agreements over transboundary problems - the first being the protocol under the Geneva convention on sulphur reductions and the second the Montreal protocol on reductions of use of chlorofluorocarbons (CFC´s). We will use the simulations in Mäler (1989b) for a study of the sulphur protocol.

It is well known since at least twenty years that sulphur oxide emissions will contribute to acid rains with detrimental consequential effects on forest growth and ground as well as surface water. However, it is also well-known that not only sulphur but also nitrogen oxides contribute to acid rains. We will, for simplicity exclude nitrogen from the discussion.

Although, it may appear as though the European problems of acid rains are rather specific, the constructs and analysis that will be presented in this section have a much wider application. The problems of global warming and the emissions of greenhouse gases have essentially the same economic nature and the discussion on sulphur emissions will throw light on this larger issue.

Sulphur oxides are emitted when fossil fuels are burnt and in some industrial processes. In the atmosphere, the oxides are oxidized into sulphates, which can be transported by winds for very long distances. Ultimately, they are removed from the atmosphere by rain - wet deposition, and by contact with plants, surface water etc. - dry deposition. In either case, the deposition of the sulphates will increase the acidity of the surface water, the top soil etc. and will have detrimental environmental effects.

As the winds will blow in various directions, this is a case of a reciprocal externality, although because some winds are more prevailing than others, the situation is not completely symmetric. Some countries are more upwind than others and some are more downwind. The extent to which a country is a net receiver of sulphates is given by a transport model. In the case of sulphur, the annual transport between countries can be described in terms of a matrix A with coefficients $a_{i,j}$ indicating the amount of sulphur deposited in country j from the emission of one ton of sulphur in country i. Since most of the sulphur emitted in a country will be deposited in the same country, the diagonal elements of the transport matrix (i.e. the elements that give the proportion of the emissions that will be deposited in the country of origin) will in general be large compared to the non-diagonal elements. We will now use this transport model to construct a simulation model for the economics of acid rains in Europe. The discussion will necessarily be more technical than the previous discussion. Readers with no interest in technical details may want to skip the next few paragraphs and turn to the results in the end of this section.

Let E_i be the emission of sulphur in country i and let E be the corresponding vector $[E_1, E_2, ..., E_n]^T$ (T denotes the transpose) of sulphur emissions. Let the deposition of sulphur in country j be Q_j and the corresponding vector $Q = [Q_1, ..., Q_n]$. Then we have

$$Q = A^*E \text{ or}$$

$$Q_i = \Sigma_j a_{i,j}E_j, i = 1, ..., n$$

Let the cost of reducing sulphur emissions in country i be

$$C_i = C_i(E_i).$$

and the monetary damage from the deposition Q_j be

$$D_j = D_j(Q_j).$$

If the initial deposition is Q_{oj}, then the benefit to country j from having the deposition reduced to Q_j is

$$D_j(Q_{oj})\text{-}D_j(Q_j).$$

A Nash non-cooperative equilibrium is defined as an emission vector E' such that E_i' maximizes

$$NB_i = D_i(Q_i) - D_i(Q_i) - C_i(E_i)$$

subject to

$$Q_i = \Sigma_j a_{i,j} E_j$$

for each i. Thus, in the Nash equilibrium, each country is maximizing its own benefit without regard to the consequences in other countries. This can be interpreted as a rationality requirement on the countries. The countries will do as best as they can for themselves, given what the other countries do. A necessary condition for a maximum is that

$$C_i' = - a_{i,i} D_i',$$

(where ′ denotes the derivative) for all i. That is the marginal abatement cost equals the marginal damage cost times the proportion of the own emissions that is deposited in the own country.

We now have a complete game theoretic model for the European emissions of sulphur. In order to use it for illustrative purposes, the unknown cost functions and damage functions must be numerically specified and a relevant transport model need to be found. Within the European Monitoring and Evaluation Programme - EMEP - a transport model has been estimated and used for producing "sulphur budgets" for Europe. The matrix A above has been estimated on the basis of the sulphur budgets for 1980 - 85.

Cost of abatement functions have been estimated by IIASA (the International Institute for Systems Analysis in Laxenburg, Austria). Although these estimated abatement functions have some serious drawbacks, we will use them for this application. However, there are no consistent estimates of damage functions from acid rains available. In order to overcome this problem, we will follow a simple calibration procedure.

Let us assume that 1984 was a year which can be characterized as a Nash equilibrium, i.e. there was no cooperation between the European countries to reduce the emissions of sulphur dioxides. Then it follows from above that the marginal damage cost in each country would be equal to the marginal abatement cost divided by the appropriate diagonal element in the transport matrix. Since we know the marginal abatement cost from the IIASA cost functions, and since we know the elements of the transport model from the EMEP sulphur budgets, it is possible to calculate the marginal damage cost for each country in 1984. If we then further assume that the marginal damage cost is constant and independent of the amount of deposition, we also know the slope of the damage cost curve for each country. We have then a completely specified game model for the sulphur emissions in Europe, the resulting depositions of sulphates and the economic consequences of sulphur abatement, as well as of sulphate depositions. By using this simulation model, several important insights may be derived.

First, let us consider the case when the sum of the net benefits over all European countries is maximized. This will be called the full cooperative solution. The consequences for some countries of this solution is summarized in table 6.4.4.1.

Table 6.4.4.1. Net benefits from the full cooperative solution

Country	Emission reduction	Net benefit Mill. D-Mark[11]
Czechoslovakia	75	152
Finland	14	-2
GDR	80	11
FRG	86	328
Poland	27	599
Sweden	4	606
Soviet Union	2	1 505
United Kingdom	81	-336
Europe	39	6 290

Although one should not take these numbers too seriously, some insights may be gained from the table on the nature of international environmental spillovers. One can first note that substantial gains can be made from cooperation. Moreover, in view of the calibration procedure, it is quite certain that the gains are understated in table 6.4.4.1. The full cooperative solution would require an average reduction of the sulphur emissions in Europe with almost 40%. This is more than what corresponds to the sulphur protocol of the convention on long range pollutants on sulphur emission reductions, the so called 30-club with 30% reductions. More interesting is probably that the net benefits from cooperation are very unevenly distributed among the countries. Some countries will even experience negative gains, that is, losses from cooperation. This is mainly due to the geographic location of these countries; some are more upwind than others so that they will not have as big net benefits as those countries that are more downwind. An extreme case is provided by United Kingdom, which is very much upwind, and therefore would have to abate their emissions substantially, while not benefiting from the abatement in other countries. Sweden is an example of a downwind country, only having to reduce her emissions with 4%, and making substantial net benefits. The USSR is a special case because it is large and very little of its substantial emissions will blow to the

11. The reason we are measuring the net benefits in German Marks is that the IIASA cost functions were estimated in that denomination.

other European countries.

Why should United Kingdom be willing to sign an agreement by which it would loose more than 300 million D-Mark? We are obviously back to the earlier issue of polluter pays principle versus victim pays principle. The only reason UK would be willing to accept this burden is that she would expect to gain something in some other area. Let us stick to the assumption that it is possible to measure this other gain in D-Mark, that is, assume that the transferable utility can be measured in this currency. Then UK needs a gain worth more than 300 million D-Mark in order to sign the full cooperative agreement. In fact, in the full solution, four countries (Finland, Italy, Spain and the UK) would experience losses that must be compensated in order to induce these countries to sign the agreement. However, the net benefits in the rest of Europe would be more than sufficient to cover their losses. The situation is however more complicated, because if United Kingdom does not sign the agreement, while the other countries do, UK will benefit from the reduction of emissions in the rest of Europe, while she does not have to bear any burden. It may pay UK to become a free rider. Assume that all the four countries that would experience losses decide not to sign an agreement but that the rest of Europe decides to go ahead and maximize their total net benefit. The result is shown in table 6.4.4.2.

Table 6.4.4.2 Net benefit from coalition formation

Country	Emission reduction %	NetBenefit Mill. D-Mark
Cooperating countries		
Czechoslovakia	75	125
GDR	80	- 47
FRG	86	78
Poland	27	544
Sweden	3	478
Soviet Union		1 377
Total for cooperating Europe	37	4 933
Defecting countries		
Finland		5
Italy		150
Spain		5
United Kingdom		87
Total		247
Total for Europe	28	5 180

Not only have the losses for the four countries disappeared but they have even turned into substantial gains. These are the gains from being a free rider to enjoy the benefits from the cooperation among other countries without having to make any sacrifices. However, these free rider gains can be achieved by all countries. Sweden could, by defecting, achieve a gain (although very small) since Sweden does not have to abate much of her emissions in the full cooperative solution. Similarly for every other country - they all stand to gain by not signing the agreement hoping that the rest of Europe will cooperate. The outcome will obviously be no agreement that includes all of European countries. The free rider incentives in this model are so pervasive, that we should not expect a full cooperative solution to emerge.

Note that exactly the same mechanism will be working in the case of unidirectional externalities when there are more than one country receiving pollution from other countries and the downwind countries have to compensate the upwind countries.

6.4.5 A Long Run Model

Before continuing, it is of interest to note the rather simplifying assumptions that have implicitly been made on the acidification processes in discussing the repeated game. We have assumed that it is the annual deposition of sulphur that matters and that each year starts afresh. In reality, there is an accumulation of sulphur in surface waters, groundwater and soil, which only slowly will disappear because of wash out or because of the buffering capacity of the environment. Thus, current deposition will have detrimental environmental effects not only now but also far in the future. The speed at which sulphur is removed from the environment depends of course on the media. A stream with low pH[12] may recover quite fast because of the replenishment of the water. For a lake it may take much longer time and still more for ground water and the soil. In order to simplify, let us assume that there is a fixed amount per ha of sulphur that the environment can assimilate. This amount is known as the "critical load", and is defined as "a quantitative estimate of the exposure to one or more pollutants below which significant harmful effects on specified sensitive elements of the environment do not occur according to present knowledge" (Nilsson 1986)).

In order to take that into account, one can construct a model that makes the annual change in the accumulated sulphur in the environment equal to the annual deposition less the assimilating capacity of the environment. In view of the definition of critical loads, it seems possible to interpret this assimilating capacity as the critical load. Thus, the stock of sulphur will change over time reflecting both the deposition of sulphur and the removal of sulphur. It is then natural to assume that the annual damage from sulphur is a function of the stock of sulphur and not the annual deposition. In this way, the situation can be modelled as a dynamic game, in which each country tries to minimize its present value of future abatement costs and damage costs.

In dynamic games of this type, it is important to separate between different kinds of strategies, depending on the information structure. If no country is expecting new information on what the other countries are doing in order to abate their emissions or on the deposition in its own country, then each country will formulate an abatement policy that it has no reason to abandon in the future, i.e. it will be followed for ever. In this case we have "open-loop" strategies. If each country expects to be able, at each moment of time, to get correct information on the deposition in the own country or changes in

12. The acidity of water is measured in pH. Water that is neutral, i.e. neither acid nor alcalic has pH equal to 7. The more acid the water is, the lower is the pH.

emissions in other countries, then the country can formulate its policy strategy in such a way that the actual emission abatement at any point of time depends on this information. In this case we have a closed loop or feed back strategy.

One can show that if one restrict the strategies to open-loop strategies, there exists a unique Nash non-cooperative equilibrium, i.e. a plan for the whole future for each country that is "best" for the country, given that the other countries are following their equilibrium strategies. Moreover, the equilibrium strategies are such that the emissions will in the long run approach the levels that are compatible with the critical loads. Thus, if countries are not receiving more information than what they have now, we should expect a long run equilibrium such that the stock of sulphur in the environment will not grow further.

However, it is a rather strong assumption that countries will not receive any new information on emissions and depositions. Therefore, a more realistic equilibrium should take as its base the use of closed loop strategies. Thus countries would adjust their emissions according to the information available on the stock of sulphur in the environment. What kind of adjustments of the emissions would constitute an equilibrium in closed loop strategies? There exist an infinite number of different equilibria in closed loop strategies. However, one can show that there exists at least one equilibrium that would correspond to countries choosing cooperating strategies if side-payments are allowed to compensate the countries that would loose from using such strategies. In principle, these equilibrium closed loop strategies supporting cooperation are very close to the trigger strategies discussed in the theory of repeated games. If a country discovers that the stock of sulphur increases more than would correspond to cooperation, the country would break the cooperation with the result that all countries would be punished, including the defecting country. It can be shown that this threat is sufficient to make it unprofitable to break cooperation (this is once more a conclusion of the Folk theorem mentioned above).

Moreover, it can also be shown that these cooperative strategies also in the long run implies emissions that would be compatible with the critical loads. Thus in the long run, the emissions in a cooperative equilibrium and in an open-loop non-cooperative equilibrium will be the same. However, the convergence toward the critical loads emissions are faster with the cooperative strategies and the resulting stock of sulphur will be smaller.

Thus, analyzing the incentives from a dynamic point of view seems to change the conclusions reached earlier. However, the conclusion that there is a need for international transfers remains. Unless countries that are loosing from cooperation are compensated, no cooperation with them will be established. But given these compensations, there are in the long run incentives for the countries to cooperate. Even if there are incentives to be a free rider, these incentives will gradually diminish when the horizon goes to infinity. Furthermore, in the long run, emissions will be adjusted in such a way as to become compatible with the critical loads (this is, however, only true for the "acid rain game" and not necessarily true for global warming or the depletion of the ozone layer).

One should add that the analysis above has been built on the implicit assumptions that transboundary spillovers can be monitored. This is, however, not that simple. For the transboundary transport of sulphur, the present state of art of monitoring requires monitoring the emissions and then using a transport model to find out the average transportation of sulphur from one country to another country. For other kinds of transboundary problems, monitoring of emissions alone may be sufficient. For example, if we consider the global warming problem, it is the emissions that are important, because emissions of greenhouse gases will have the same effect on the global climate irrespective of where they take place.

6.4.6 The Design of Agreements

We have so far only analyzed the incentives to cooperate and found that in the short run countries have incentives to free ride, but that in the long run, they will if the appropriate transfers are made, find it profitable to cooperate. It remains to discuss how the cooperative agreements should be designed.

First of all, such agreements should be made as flexible as possible in order to make it possible for countries to adapt to changes in external conditions. The protocol on 30 percent reduction of sulphur emissions from their 1980 levels is an example of an agreement that does not meet the flexibility requirement. If international relative prices change drastically, some countries would find enormous potential gains from expanding activities emitting much sulphur. However, according to the agreement they will be prohibited from doing that. Their incentives to break the agreement would therefore be quite high. Furthermore, the cost of achieving the reduction in depositions is unnecessary high. It has been estimated that the same reduction in depositions could have been achieved at half the cost if the agreement would have been cost effective (see Mäler and Olsson 1990). If, instead, the agreement had been based on the much more natural ecological point of view of reducing the total deposition of sulphur in Europe the cost of the agreement would have looked quite different. It could have involved a European "bubble", that would put a limit on the total transboundary flux of sulphur, but with emissions rights transferable among European countries. Mäler (1989) analyzed such a mechanism and found that it would support an almost efficient allocation of sulphur emissions. Moreover, such a mechanism would be flexible in the sense that each country would have much more flexibility in adjusting to changes in economic conditions.

6.4.7. The Montreal Protocol[13]

The Montreal Protocol on Substances that Deplete the Ozone Layer (1987) was the first international agreement on truly global environmental problems. Let us study this protocol from the point of view of the theoretical discussions in previous sections. The objective of the protocol is to reduce the releases of chlorofluorocarbons (CFC's) and halons into the atmosphere as these substances destroy the ozone layer in the stratosphere and thereby increasing the ultra violet radiation reaching the ground. The protocol includes

i) upper bounds of CFC consumption (at specific dates) for a signatory,

ii) upper bounds of CFC production (at specific dates) for a signatory,

iii) possibilities of transferring production reduction requirements among signatories,

iv) ban of imports of CFC's from non-signatories,

v) ban of exports of CFC's from a developing country at a specific date.

At least three questions pertaining to efficiency aspects can be raised in connection with this protocol. The first concerns the number of signatories. The second question is closely related and has to do with non-compliance. The third question finally asks whether the resulting reduction in CFC use and production will be cost effective or not.

We have seen earlier that for a global common like the ozone layer, there is in general strong incentives for a party to become a free rider by either not signing the treaty or by trying to cheat on the treaty it has signed. However, it can also be shown that not all countries would be free riders. In the symmetric case (i.e. in the case when all countries have the same cost of abatement functions and damage cost functions) we can understand this by the following argument. Assume that all countries initially are cooperating. Then one country would discover that it would benefit from being a free rider and leave the cooperation. Then one more would leave cooperation and so on. However, the gains from becoming a free rider decreases with the number of free riders, and the benefits from cooperation will increase as the number of cooperating nations goes down. Thus we should expect that there will be a cut off number at which no further country would benefit from being a free rider while no free rider would benefit from starting

13. The discussion in this section is to some extent based on P. Bohm, 1990, and S. Barrett, 1989.

cooperation. This implies that we might get incomplete cooperation, i.e. a subset of countries cooperating, while others are staying out of cooperation.[14] Thus we should expect incomplete cooperation to occur frequently when countries try to solve regional or global environmental problems. This theoretical prediction is also confirmed by the observations we can make of existing treaties and agreements. The Montreal Protocol, for example, has not been signed by all countries, and not even by all countries that are really concerned by the growth of the holes in the ozone layer. However, in general countries are not identical with respect to the payoff from cooperation and this is obviously true for the case covered by the Montreal Protocol. The holes in the ozone layers tend to be above the two poles and the consequent increase in radiation will therefore affect people living far north or far south more than those living further away from the poles. We saw when discussing acid rains that in general there will be a need for transfer payments in order to induce cooperation. Thus, we should predict that northern countries (i.e. Europe and North America) and southern countries (New Zealand and Australia) would be willing to pay other countries to reduce their use of CFC´s. These predictions are also confirmed by the developments of the Montreal Protocol, in which funds for technological transfers have been set up in order to compensate developing countries for not using CFC´s.

Let us now briefly review some other economic problems in connection to the Montreal Protocol. The most important requirement on a signatory of the treaty is that the consumption and production of CFC´s (the difference between consumption and production is foreign trade) of that signatory must not exceed certain levels after certain dates. The signatories may, however, transfer CFC production requirements among them.

The first thing to note is that requirements to reduce the production of CFC´s can be transferred between countries *but not requirements to reduce consumption.* Even if all countries would have signed the protocol, we would not have reached a global efficient reduction of CFC consumption since these reductions cannot be freely transferred among countries in order to equalize marginal costs.

Perhaps more important is the fact that countries cannot offset an increased use or production of CFC against a destruction of old CFC in for example refrigerators or freezers. The incentives to rational manage such old commodities in order to limit the release of CFC´s into the atmosphere are therefore unnecessarily low. The incentives to

14. This possibility of incomplete cooperation was first pointed out by d´Aspremont in the context of cartels among oligopolists. Barrett adopted the idea and applied the idea to an analysis of the Montreal Protocol (Barrett 1989). Carraro and Siniscalco (1991) did an extensive theoretical analysis on these issues, and in particular noted that it might be beneficial for non-cooperating countries to subsidize cooperation among the countries already cooperating and that it also might be beneficial for cooperating countries to bribe other countries to reduce their emissions.

construct new products so that the CFC´s embodied in these products can easily be recovered or destroyed are also too small because of this.

Finally, we should add that these criticisms against the Montreal Protocol on balance may not be too strong in view of the rather low costs of reducing the use of CFC´s. When we now turn to a discussion of the emissions of greenhouse gases and possible effects on the climate, inefficiencies will be of much greater importance.

6.4.8 Climate Change and Limiting the Emissions of Carbondioxide

It has been known for almost one hundred years that emissions of carbondioxide and the resulting increased concentrations of the gas in the atmosphere will trap heat that otherwise would have been radiated away from the earth. This trapping will eventually raise the average temperature of the earth. Thus the increase in the concentration of carbondioxide in the atmosphere will work like a greenhouse. It is now known that other gases in addition to carbondioxide, such as methane, CFC´s and dinitrousoxides, also will act as greenhouse gases. The climatologists are all agreeing that the greenhouse effect is real and that increased emissions of the greenhouse gases will eventually bring about a change in the climate of our earth. The main uncertainties today are how fast the atmospheric concentrations of the greenhouse gases will increase as a result of the emissions (mainly because the exchange of carbondioxide between the oceans and the atmosphere is not perfectly known) and the possible effects from increased cloud covers. However, taking these uncertainties into account, the climatologists predicts that under the assumption of "business as usual", the average rate of increase of global mean temperature during the next century will be 0.3° C per decade (with an uncertainty range of 0.2° - 0.5° C per decade). This increase is a more rapid increase than has been seen during the past 10,000 years. The regional impacts are very badly known. However, there are great risks that local weather patterns may change dramatically and for example reduce the precipitation in the Sahel Region. Furthermore, as the ocean water warms up, it will expand and this will give rise to an estimated rise of the sea level, perhaps with 30 - 50 cm by year 2050. This will obviously create large damage to countries with low coastal zones.

In order to avoid such a change in the climate of the earth, the emissions of greenhouse gases must be stabilized at a much lower level than today. Even if other "technical fixes" such as fertilizing oceans in order to increase their carbon uptake or artificially increase the cloud cover by using various chemicals have been proposed, the only reasonable way out seems to be reductions in emissions. However, as we have seen in relation to the acid rains in Europe and the use of CFC´s and the threats to the ozone layer, it will be difficult to achieve complete cooperation among all countries in order to achieve an efficient global climate strategy. In fact, the efficient global management of the climate is much more difficult than to achieve efficient management of regional acid rains or efficient management of the ozone layer because of two factors. First, the emissions of carbondioxide are mainly due to the combustion of fossil fuels and any reduction in these emissions must be the result in a reduction of our use of fossil fuels. This is in general, however, much more costly than to reduce sulphur emissions or to reduce the use of CFC´s. To a large extent, the industrialized world is built around the use of fossil fuels, and reduce the use of fossil fuels may need substantial changes in this part of the world. Second, countries are much more dissimilar when we look at the global scale than was the case when we looked at the regional problems of acid rains. The difference in the use of fossil fuels per capita between for example the US and India are tremendous. If India would be able to consume the same amount of oil and coal per capita as the consumption in the US, we would indeed expect a much more rapid heating of the atmosphere and much more serious consequences.

Applying the arguments presented in connection with the discussion of acid rains to the problem of climate change, we could, however, try to analyze the following possible strategy. Assume that a minimal set of countries agree to cooperate and that they agree among themselves to reduce the emissions of carbondioxide (and of course the other greenhouse gases) so that their total emissions do not exceed a load that would not jeopardize the climate further. Assume further that they decide to make their emission reductions transferable. Countries can then buy rights to emit greenhouse gases from each other. Such transactions would not change the total emissions from the group of cooperating countries, but would guarantee that the over all cost of reducing the emissions is minimized. The initial distribution of emission rights will of course be decided after negotiations, but obviously no country will agree to cooperate if they expect to be worse off from cooperation. In order to "bribe" a country to cooperate it will therefore in some cases be necessary to give that country an excess of emissions rights. Take India as an example. If India would commit itself not to increase carbondioxide emissions in the future, she would in effect abstain from future economic development. Thus, India would only join cooperation if she would obtain sufficient with emission rights so that future economic development is not curbed too seriously. Such an initial distribution of rights to India would correspond to a rather large transfer of resources from the other countries as India can sell her rights to other countries in exchange for foreign currency. A country such as the US would not have to cut down on its use of fossil fuels immediately, since it can buy up those emissions rights that India is not currently going to use. However, this transaction would raise the price of energy in the US and therefore in the long run decrease the demand for energy. On the same time, the transfers to India in the form of export revenues from selling the emission rights may give rise to economic development in India which will increase her demand for fossil fuels. There will therefore be a general rise in the price of the rights, which will further increase the pressure in the US to shift away from the use of fossil fuels and - as the demand for the rights in the US is inelastic - increase the export revenues of India. Thus the use of transferable emissions rights will enable countries to smoothly reduce the use of fossil fuels and at the same time promote economic development in those parts of the world that really needs such development. This effect of a system with transferable rights can be further strengthened if we could design the system on rights for net emissions. In such a system, a country with growing forests may offset any emissions of carbondioxide or sales of emissions permits with the carbon that goes into the growing trees. Brazil could in such a system earn extra export money from letting her forests grow.

There are obviously almost an infinite number of very difficult practical problems with the proposed system. How can one monitor the use of fossil fuels in different countries? How can the international community monitor the growth of biomass in countries claiming offsets? How should the initial rights be distributed? However, the objective with this discussion was to point out that the use of simple economics may point to solutions to problems that otherwise may have seen to be unsolvable. That is the role of economic analysis of environmental problems!

7. Case Studies

This chapter contains a survey of empirical studies, based on the different methods of analysing environmental effects outlined in chapter 5. Most of the case studies represent different kinds of projects with environmental impact, covering a range of projects like soil and water conservation, range management, agroforestry and forestry. These are presented in sections 7.1 and 7.2. One example of a multiple-objective programme is presented in section 7.3. Furthermore, a study concerning the establishment of a national reserve forest is summarized in section 7.4.

Approaches to quantify damage from air and water pollution are presented through some more briefly presented studies in sections 7.5 and 7.6. The kind of methodology applied in some of these studies might be of more limited interest for developing countries, but they are presented here as they illustrate how different consequences of pollution can be analysed.

The studies concerning the assessment of values of environmental impacts are presented in terms of the following main issues (when applicable):

- introduction to the methods used in the study
- a brief background to the project
- a description of the project
- identification and valuation of benefits
- identification and valuation of costs
- the results
- discussion of the results or conclusions

Throughout the presentation there is an emphasis on the methodology used and the data needed when carrying out the analysis. The main purpose of the presentation of the case studies is to illustrate economic analyses, but also to touch upon the uncertainties involved in handling data.

Less attention is paid to the results obtained from any specific analysis (e.g. in terms of the net present value or the internal rate of return). The reason is that the final results pertain to a specific project, while this chapter aims at providing a more general understanding of applied economic analysis.

Many development projects and environmental action plans fail, however, to have the desirable effects owing to the fact that government policies generate the wrong incentives. In contrast to the more abundant literature on the physical linkages relating to environmental degradation, relatively little attention has been given to the exploration of the kind of economic, financial, social and institutional channels through which an improper use of environmental resources might be encouraged.

In the very last years, a few case studies have appeared concerning environmental degradation from policy failures. These studies offer reviews of how the economic incentives look in some particular country or area, and a discussion about their environmental consequences. Examples of such case studies are given in section 7.7.

As regards the case studies concerning valuation aspects, the type of project or the issues of study and the applied valuation techniques are summarized in table 7.1:

Table 7.1

Section	Project Type/Issue of Study	Valuation Approach
7.1.1	Soil and water conservation in Lesotho	Changes in production
7.1.2	Soil and water conservation in Korea	Cost-effectiveness (replacement cost vs. preventive expenditures)
7.1.3	Range management in Australia	Changes in production and property value approach
7.1.4	Agroforestry in Nigeria	Changes in production
7.2	Forestry in Nepal	Changes in production
7.3	Integrated environmental project in the Philippines	Changes in production
7.4	Establishment of a national reserve in Sweden	Travel-cost and bidding game

Table 7.1 (contin.)		
Section	Project Type/Issue of Study	Valuation Approach
7.5.1	Air pollution experiment in U.S.A.	Property value Bidding game
7.5.2	Valuation of morbidity reduction due to pollution abatement in Israel	Using implicit and artificial markets
7.5.3	Corrosion damage due to air pollution in Europe	Replacement cost
7.6	Water pollution in Thailand	Changes in production

Two of the studies concerning policy failures presented in this chapter have been carried out in Brazil, one in Ecuador, and one is studying a part of Indonesia. We are well aware that there are strong reasons to believe that policy failures play a significant role for the environmental degradation in many developing, as well as developed, countries. As already mentioned, there are, however, as yet only a few studies focusing on this issue, which limited our possibilities to choose studies from other countries than those selected.

The studies focusing on policy failures are found in the following sections:

Table 7.2	
Section	Issue of Study
7.7.1	Deforestation in Brazil (study carried out by Mahar, D.)
7.7.2	Deforestation in Brazil (study carried out by Binswanger, H.P.)
7.7.3	Upper watershed degradation in Java
7.7.4	Tropical deforestation in Eastern Ecuador

7.1 Agricultural Projects

7.1.1 Soil and Water Conservation - Farm Improvement and Soil Conservation in Lesotho.

Source: Bojö, J., 1990: *Economic Analysis of Agricultural Development Projects. A Case Study from Lesotho.* EFI Research Report. Stockholm School of Economics.

Background

Environmental degradation in Lesotho - especially soil erosion - has been a serious concern for decades. There is a long, and largely unsuccessful, history of attempts to stop this process.

One result of this common concern is a soil conservation programme launched in 1985 in cooperation between the Government of Lesotho (GoL) and the Swedish International Development Authority (SIDA). This programme has had a modest beginning in the Mohale's Hoek District in southern Lesotho, but considerable expansion is planned. Current plans extend to mid-1992.

A sequence of cost-benefit studies of the project has been undertaken since 1987. The methodology and findings of the 1990 version are briefly sketched here.[1]

The FISC Project

A key feature of the project is that conservation should not be seen in isolation as something good per se but rather as a direct means of promoting higher agricultural production. Hence, the project has been styled as a "farm improvement and soil conservation project" (FISC). It uses low cost technology and is based on the concept of "people's participation".

The project encourages the use of inorganic fertilizer and hybrid seed varieties as well as the rehabilitation and construction of terraces, waterways and drainage systems. Controlled grazing, fodder cultivation, afforestation, spring development, communal vegetable gardens and fruit trees are also promoted.

The project provides training for "lead farmers" and extension and conservation agents. It has hired a number of junior professionals as "conservation organizers" and aims at leaving behind an institutional village structure capable of maintaining project advances.

---

1. A final report, which also places the project in a macroeconomic context, is contained in Bojö (1991).

Analytical Steps

The sequence followed in the study can be summarized in the following points:

- determination of evaluation criteria
- cost and benefit identification
- quantification of costs and benefits
- valuation including shadow pricing
- discounting to present value
- determination of an appropriate time horizon
- discussion of distributional aspects
- sensitivity analysis
- policy implications

The *evaluation criteria* used are net present value (NPV) and internal rate of return (IRR) (see section 5.1.1.1 for a discussion of these concepts).

The costs are initially identified as all financial costs (including overhead) pertaining to the project, incurred in Lesotho or elsewhere.

Increased production of fruits, maize, sorghum, fodder grass and firewood were identified and quantified as the main outputs. A considerable item is also the salvage value of buildings constructed. The benefits from vegetable production, etc. were considered as minor at present.

A number of so called intangibles were identified; increased crop residues suitable for animal feed, conservation benefit from up-slope tree planting, spill-over effects from training into other areas, multiplier effects from increased consumption, but also secondary costs due to increased purchases from the Republic of South Africa. These unquantified variables are not to be taken as unquantifiable. This may or may not be the case given available analytical resources and the value of quantification.

For example, the value of improved crop residue production can in principle be assessed by comparative sampling of control plots and project plots. If the crop residue are not marketed as fodder, its content can be calculated in terms of standard units comparable with marketed substitutes. If such substitutes do not exist, the value can be assessed in terms of increased production of milk, meat, etc.

The value of up-land conservation of soil due to afforestation can also, in principle, be assessed by measuring sediment and nutrient transportation to assess off-site effects on the lower cropland (positive and negative).

Quantification of crop benefits was primarily done through random sampling of farmers participating vs. non-participants. Sampling has been carried out for four years.

The *valuation* can be divided into several components.

No adjustment was made with regard to foreign exchange, as the Loti is freely traded on a par with the convertible South African Rand.

Labour was split into unskilled vs. semi-skilled and skilled. The latter two were priced with the financial wage rates given existing competitive markets. The former category was shadow priced at about 60% of the project stipulated financial wage given information about the local, informal wage level.

Material inputs are sold (net of taxes to the project) on reasonably competitive terms. The one exception is fertilizer, where the 30% subsidy was added to arrive at the economic price.

Project outputs were valued using the opportunity cost principle, i.e. the farm gate price of imported grain. It should be noted that the conventional assumption of constant real prices was not used here. Instead, available time series of nominal prices for white maize (the preferred type) and sorghum were converted to constant (1989) prices. A simple regression was made to uncover the trend. This trend was assumed to continue for the remainder of the period analyzed.

An additional adjustment was made on imported items to allow for the fact that Lesotho receives compensation for the price raising effect of the Southern African Customs Union tariffs (about 20%). Thus, imported items were multiplied with a factor of 0.8.

Discounting had to be done in the absence of any national or donor supplied parameter. The internationally quite common real social discount rate of 10% was used in the base case, subject to sensitivity testing with 1% and 19% as lower and upper bounds.

The *time horizon* for the project depends critically on the degree of maintenance of structures and improved crop management after the project's active involvement has ceased. The past record from conservation projects is dismal in this respect, but FISC's emphasis on popular participation, labour intensive and simple constructions and use of farm inputs yielding short term benefits, provide some basis for optimism. The base case considers a 50 year period. However, the level of impact varies for the different benefit items.

Distributional concerns have been clearly expressed as a motive for SIDA involvement in this particular area. The district turns out to rank as no. 6 out of 10 districts in the country, with an average rural (cash + in kind) income of 65% of Lesotho's average. Thus, the distributional concern could be more adequately addressed by expansion into even poorer areas.

On a household level, the distributional effects are mixed. Obviously, land improvements will primarily benefit villagers who actually own land (approximately 50% of villagers). Grazing improvement will also primarily benefit the half owning cattle. However, the rest of the population can participate in communal work and profit from cash wages. It was concluded that women had monopolized the work opportunities to a large extent. Severely disadvantaged groups such as the aged or handicapped remain outside the group of direct employment beneficiaries. A separate study concluded that there was no significant difference in stated income between participants and non-participants.

The sensitivity analysis concerned several key parameters: fruit tree production, crop yield decline due to erosion assumed in the "without" project scenario, net project impact on use of improved inputs, social discount rate and distributional weights.

The Results

The numerical results of the base case were a NPV of minus Maloti 3.6 million (about USD 1.7 million) and an IRR slightly less than zero. The sensitivity testing showed that rather implausible assumptions had to be made concerning fruit production, erosion-yield impact and project impact on input use to considerably improve this performance. However, the result is clearly affected by the choice of discount rate and income distribution weights.

In contrast, the financial analysis showed a very high private return on investment in fertilizer and improved seed. However, risk-aversion may be a considerable obstacle in maintaining a high level of agricultural input use, as yields vary considerably between years due primarily to rainfall.

Conclusions

A financially successful input package coupled with an economically doubtful project suggests that we have a case of oversubsidization of the farmers. Attention to credit/insurance schemes may be a low-cost alternative. The qualified and expensive expatriate staff must also be matched with more local staff to expand project impact over a greater area.

7.1.2 Soil and Water Conservation - Upland Agricultural Project in Korea.

Source: Kim, S-H. and Dixon, J.A., 1986: "Economic Valuation of Environmental Quality Aspects of Upland Agricultural Projects in Korea." In: Dixon, J.A. and Hufschmidt, M.M. (eds.), *Economic Valuation Techniques for the Environment - A Case Study Workbook.* Johns Hopkins, Baltimore.

Introduction

This study is an example of the *cost-effectiveness approach* (see section 5.3), i.e. we are looking for the least-cost method to achieve a determined objective. In this case the objective is to avoid soil and nutrient losses.

The study does not estimate the benefits from conserving soil and its nutrients. These are assumed to be greater than the costs as is the convention when carrying out a cost-effectiveness analysis. Nor is there any attempt to incorporate the intangible effects which might accrue from the project.

On the other hand, the study emphasizes the importance of considering the downstream effects of soil erosion, i.e. to include the *off-site effects*. Furthermore, one may note that the project's purpose being to maintain the soil and its nutrients in the area, this might in the long-run be regarded as a way to assure *local sustainability*.

Background

In order to meet the rapidly increasing demand for food the Korean Government implemented a programme for upland development. The expansion of agricultural production into the hilly uplands had caused damage in the environment due to the inadequate soil management technique used. Two broad categories of environmental losses were identified:

(1) the loss in productivity of the uplands,

(2) the siltation of the paddy fields in the lowlands.

The Study

The study was aimed at finding the least-cost method of avoiding soil erosion and soil-nutrient losses in the area. The prevailing method of avoiding the damage caused by cultivation was to replace the soil and its nutrients in the uplands and clear the silted paddy fields in the downlands.

The alternative method considered in this study consisted of the use of a new soil treatment. This particular method was chosen because it gave the best result in controlling soil erosion, when compared with different soil treatments (nine different types of soil treatment were investigated i.e. the results from various forms of trenching, chiselling, mulching, and vertical mulching were compared with a control plot). The method chosen, mulching, reduced the annual soil loss by up to 90 per cent.

The Economic Analysis

In the past, conventional cost-benefit analysis had been used in the area to assess the agricultural programme, but only the positive effects of increased productivity had been included. The off-site effects, or the externalities, due to the project had not been considered (see section 3.2.1 for a discussion about externalities). Hence, a comprehensive evaluation of the effects of the project was needed, in which environmental factors such as soil erosion, water run off and siltation effects on downhill streams, rivers and paddy fields were included.

In order to evaluate the two different methods, the present value of the costs associated with these were calculated and compared. Henceforth, the two methods will be referred to as *the replacement alternative* (meaning the prevailing method) and *the preventive alternative* (i.e. the new soil treatment which helps prevent the heavy soil erosion).

The study does not estimate the benefits of these two alternatives. Hence, it can only offer the prescription that if the present value of social benefits exceeds the costs associated with the least-cost alternative, the method should in fact be adopted.

Identification and Valuation of Costs

The basic data needed for the analysis were the extent of water run off, soil loss and nutrient loss that would prevail under each alternative. It should be emphasized that these factors are affected by the type of crop grown (in this case soybean or barley), as well as rainfall quantity and timing.

The costs associated with *the replacement alternative*, i.e. how much it costs each year to replace lost soil and nutrients and maintain a given level of production, were composed of the following main components:

- labour costs for spreading nutrients (including truck rental and other materials)
- cost of nutrients (measured in market prices)

- soil cost
- compensation payment from the upland to the lowland farmers to cover the decrease in productivity due to siltation (which was assumed to reflect the true cost of lost yield)
- field maintenance and repair
- supplemental irrigation costs

Soil and nutrient replacement needed to be done each year.

The costs of *the preventive alternative* were similar for some items to those associated with the replacement alternative but the amounts involved were much smaller, because of the marked decline in soil erosion under the preventive alternative. There were no irrigation, field maintenance or repair costs, but there were substantial land preparation and mulching costs.

The costs associated with implementing the preventive alternative, mulching, required that appropriate measures were taken every four years. In the first year the cost of mulching was estimated to be high, in succeeding periods, the projected cost was reduced since less labour and materials were required. In addition there was a yearly expense for mulch.

The Results

Calculation of the present values of the costs for the two alternatives was carried out, covering 15 years and using a 10 per cent discount rate (in the sensitivity analysis other discount rates were used).

When comparing the two alternatives, the present value of the costs associated with the preventive alternative turned out to be slightly more than half of the replacement costs.

Data covering crop yields for the different soil treatments implied that yields might even increase with the preventive alternative.

Discussion of the Results

Although it appears as if the preventive alternative would be attractive even if yields were the same under both approaches, there might be some reasons why all farmers had not adopted the new technique. Possible reasons are listed here (Ahmad, Dasgupta and Mäler, 1984):

- Farmers may adopt a higher discount rate which would lower the net present value.

- The costs charged to the conventional system were perhaps not cash costs that were actually paid by the farmers.

- The new technique might require large cash expenditures for mulch and credit may be a constraint.

- Perhaps yields were not actually to increase in the individual farmers' fields as indicated by the comparison with the control plot.

Hence, the fact that the new system appears economically very attractive from the social point of view may not assure its acceptance by farmers. The farmers must see the new technique as *attractive in terms of their own perceptions of costs*. If the social and private (farmer) perspectives differ, appropriate incentives may be required to secure adoption of the new system.

It should be pointed out that this study deviates slightly from the common cost-effectiveness approach due to the fact that when choosing one among the nine different soil treatments, the choice was not based on a minimizing cost-criteria (which is more appropriate). Instead the treatment yielding the lowest soil loss in kg/ha was chosen, irrespective of the costs.

7.1.3 Range Management - The Eppalock Catchment in Australia.

Source: Abelson, P., 1979: *Cost Benefit Analysis and Environmental Problems.* Saxon House, Teakfield Ltd., Westmead, England.

Introduction

This study assesses the major costs and benefits of a large conservation (range management) project. It considers the project as a means to *achieve multiple objectives*, such as improved agricultural productivity, more attractive landscapes and increased water storage.

The study includes the use of *the valuation of changes in production approach* and *the property value approach* (see sections 5.2.1.1 and 5.2.2.2, respectively). Although the study was carried out in a developed country, Australia, most of the reasoning in the study is applicable in a developing country as well. One exception is the use of the property value technique, which probably would not be feasible in many developing countries.

Background

In 1959, the Victorian Soil Conservation Authority reported that "the land in the northern part of the Eppalock catchment presented an example of extensive land destruction rarely paralleled in other parts of the State." The intensive land use which the area had been subject to over the last hundred years, had caused erosion resulting in numerous gullies, stony base surfaces on steep slopes and some dryland salting. Silt loads and irregularities of the flows of the Campaspe river had also increased.

The Project

The agriculture in the Eppalock catchment area is almost entirely sheep grazing, but some cattle grazing and cropping also take place.

The soil conservation project ran from 1960 to 1975, and involved the planning and development of the catchment, which also had indirect effects on surrounding holdings outside the catchment. Some of the capital works were designed mainly to protect the water storage capacity and water quality in the Eppalock reservoir. This involved gully control structures, protective fencing and erosion control earthworks. Other improvements related directly to agricultural development. Examples of these were chisel seeding, farm sub-division and improved stock water supplies. Hence, both individual and public efforts were included in the project.

The With/Without Project Perspective

The essential difference between the project case and the base case was the timing of improvements. Whereas all project improvements were completed by 1975, it was assumed that there would have been some activity of the Soil Conservation Authority in the area in the base case and that direct agricultural improvements would have been completed by 1990 and the soil erosion controls by 2005.

Identification and Valuation of Benefits

The cost-benefit analysis was made in 1975 and included both forecasted and projected benefits. Incorporated in the analysis were the benefits that would occur until 89/90 for agriculture and until 2005 for soil erosion control.

The major project benefits may be divided into the following groups:

(1) agricultural benefits due to improved pastures,(i.e.the increase in output of livestock)

(2) the benefits of extra dam capacity and of water yield

(3) amenities

(4) flood mitigation

(5) water quality

(6) benefits of local authorities

(7) knowledge

The quantification and valuation of these are discussed below.

1) Agricultural benefits due to improved pastures
Improved pastures increased the number of cattle, which resulted in increased output from the livestock. The annual agricultural benefits of improved pastures inside and outside the catchment, were estimated for each livestock category (wethers, mixed sheep flock and cattle).

The output from the animals was either wool or the animal itself, because the latter was also subject to trade, although to a smaller extent. The wool from the livestock was estimated as a product of the area carrying livestock, the livestock per hectare, and the output of wool per head. The difference between the annual output with project and the annual output in the base case were multiplied by the net benefit per unit of output. From this were subtracted the costs of acquiring stock times the difference in stock purchased in the two scenarios.

Potential stocking rates per hectare were considered to depend on soil type and rainfall conditions. Information about the stocking rates was provided by a survey among farmers, which indicated that there had been an increase due to the project. The survey also indicated large increases in stocking rates in a large area adjacent to the catchment.

The price used in the calculations was the historic price for the years 1960/1961 - 1975 and the forecasted prices 1976 - 1989/1990 of wool or of animal sales. The cost subtracted from the price will be further discussed below under the heading "Landholder expenditure on livestock".

2) The benefits of extra dam capacity

The value of extra dam capacity and water yield was based on estimates by engineers about the siltation that would occur without a soil conservation project.

It was assumed for the base case that normal pasture improvements and Soil Conservation Authority extension work would, to some extent, also reduce annual siltation.

The actual siltation occurred was based on a survey of parts of the lake some years after the project had been implemented. It was assumed that there had been a linear reduction in siltation, but that the siltation rate had been constant after 1967, when the main areas of sheet erosion had been stabilised. Siltation varies, however, with conditions of rainfall and run off, and measurement is complicated by the movement of silt within a reservoir.

The relationship between dam capacity and yield is complex because it depends upon the amount and the distribution over time of the inflow, the pattern of demand for water and the way in which the dam is operated. The study assumed that a 1 per cent decrease in capacity would lead to a 1.5 per cent decrease in yield.

Any reduction in the supply of water from the Eppalock dam would reduce the output of dairy farms, which were the marginal consumers of the water, paying the lowest price for it. Unfortunately the price paid by the dairy industry for the output of the dairy farm (the market price for butterfat), did not reflect the national benefit from the water. The reason was that all the butter was exported and, hence, yielded the revenue from the export market. The farmer, on the other hand, received the average of the domestic and the export price of butterfat regardless of where the marginal product was sold. Since the export price was half the domestic price, the farmer was willing to pay more for water than he would be if he had received, as did the nation, only the returns from the marginal product which was exported. The revenue the farmers received was mainly subsidized by other dairy farmers.

The net value of butterfat for export was therefore estimated in a given year as the product of the amount of butterfat produced per megalitre of water times *the net social value of butterfat*. The social value of butterfat depends upon the relationship between butterfat and butter (the percentage of butterfat per lb of butter), and the export price of butter.

3) Amenities
Between 1960 and 1975 land was chisel seeded, trees planted, numerous gullies grassed over or otherwise improved and dams constructed in the Eppalock catchment. The amenities of the area, like for example increased birdlife, were substantially improved.

Environmental benefits to residents were estimated by comparing the average prices of unimproved and fully improved properties in 1974/75. The residual difference in price was taken to be a measure of the additional environmental value of the improved land to landholders. Hence, *the property value technique* was applied in this respect (see section 5.2.2.2 for a discussion of the property value technique).

The difference in price was, however, attributed to both environmental improvement as well as increased carrying capacity for improved land, which had to be taken into account before using the figure as a measure of pure amenity. The valuation of the increased carrying capacity was consistent with the calculations of agricultural improvement discussed above.

Unlike agricultural benefits, environmental benefits were calculated only within the catchment because of difficulties of quantification for other areas.

4) Flood mitigation
The rate of run off in the catchment was significantly reduced by the extensive chisel seeding and gully regulation. Thus diminished, the flows and silt loads caused less damage to fences and farm roadways in the catchment. The total benefits of flood mitigation owing to the project was, in this case, assumed to be small, but positive.

5) Water quality
The dam water quality was assessed for bacteria levels, colour, turbidity, and salinity. Paucity of data made, however, the conclusions about with and without project differences conjectural, and there was no attempt done to quantify these effects. Weighing up the various influences, the report concluded that on balance the project had marginally decreased the quality of water in the reservoir.

6) Benefits of local authorities
Local authorities benefited from the project through reduced maintenance costs for roads, bridges and water supplies. The most important and the only ones quantified were the reduced road maintenance costs. These were based on estimates of the expenditures by local authorities in the with/without project case.

7) Knowledge
The report also considered that the project may have had a research and development effect improving conservation practice and increasing output beyond the project's area of direct influence.

Identification and Valuation of Costs

The costs may be divided into three categories:

(1) public costs

(2) landholder's land development costs

(3) landholder expenditure on livestock

These are presented below:

1) Public costs
- the Soil Conservation Authorities' capital expenditures between 1960 and 1975 and forecasted maintenance costs after 1975. A *shadow-price*, three-quarters of the actual wage for unskilled labour, was used to adjust for local unemployment and underemployment.

- expenditures by the Department of Agriculture (which tested the efficiency of pasture improvements)

- expenditures by local authorities (extra expenditures to conform to the SCA's recommended standards for roads, bridges, etc.)

- the government's share of the costs of additional fertilizer used by farmers, which was subsidized.

2) Landholders' land development costs
The main land development costs incurred by landholders related to clearing of stumps, subdivision fences, additional water supply dams, pasture seed and fertilizer.

For the base case it was assumed that similar farm development would be made, but at a slower rate than in the project case.

3) Landholder expenditure on livestock
These costs consisted of fodder, shearing, crutching, dip drenches, veterinary costs and sheep replacement.

The Results

The effects of the project, both inside and outside the catchment were established by comparison between the situation predicted to exist without the project (the base case) and the situation expected to exist with the project. The essential difference between the project case and the base case was, as already pointed out, *the timing of improvements*.

The net present value was estimated using an 8 per cent discount rate and a 30 year evaluation period. This yielded a high net present value, which still remained high when carrying out sensitivity tests by changing the discount rate, the time horizon and the valuation of key variables. The internal rate of return of the project was calculated to 25.4 per cent.

Discussion of the Results

To estimate the national benefits of the project, it might be necessary to allow for any downward *impact the project may have on* wool *prices*. This effect on price would create a loss in producer surplus but would, on the other hand, increase consumer surplus. A project does, however, only influence prices if the project is very large, so this effect usually does not have to be considered.

The project is partly financed by taxes. The *deadweight loss* arising from taxes, i.e. the difference between the loss the tax causes to others and the tax revenues to the government (see e.g. Friedman, 1985), should therefore be explored.

Moreover, many prices will usually change when imposing a tax or when a price of one good changes. In theory, we must be able to calculate all the equilibrium prices that will result, i.e. to analyse *the general equilibrium* (see chapter 4).

Losses occur in two other groups as well, but these losses arise both in the with and without project case. First, most of the difference between the revenue received by the farmers in the area and the social benefits of butter production were borne by other farmers. Secondly, as butter was subsidized, some of the difference was borne by the general taxpayer. These losses were not at all included in the CBA. Hence, there might be, despite the extensive analysis carried out, several more *side-effects* that should be included in the CBA.

Other Studies

Other studies focusing on range management are Thomas and Bennett, (1980), Dixon and Hufschmidt, (1986), and ODA, (1986).

7.1.4 Agroforestry - An Afforestation Programme in Nigeria.

Source: Anderson, D., 1987: *The Economics of Afforestation - A Case Study in Africa.* The John Hopkins University Press, Baltimore.

Introduction

This case study examines the benefits and costs of investment in rural afforestation in the arid zone of Nigeria. It illustrates the benefits that could be brought about by establishing shelterbelts and farm forestry, applying *the valuation of changes in production technique* (see section 5.2.1.1).

Furthermore, it explores the nature of the *risks* and *uncertainties* in farm forestry programmes, which is of great importance in this kind of analysis.

As the paucity of empirical research in the arid zone is considerable, the intention of the study was as much to define the kinds of research needed, as to estimate benefits.

Background

The destruction of trees in woodlands and on farms in Nigeria because of the demand for firewood, agricultural land, and livestock fodder have led to a progressive degradation of the environment and have made the soils more vulnerable to desiccating winds.

The consequences are mainly of four kinds:

- a marked decline in farm tree stock in the arid zone

- a threatened decline in soil fertility

- the harvesting of tree stocks without replenishment in other parts of the country for sale in the arid zone

- significant encroachment on and degradation of the forest and game reserves

The Project

In 1978 the federal government initiated the Arid Zone Afforestation Programme (AZAP), which was curtailed in 1984. The two main elements in the project was:

- a programme of *farm forestry* that included the establishment of a nursery network and a seedling distribution system, and the use of a agricultural extension service to encourage farm forestry

- a programme of *shelterbelts*

Identification and Valuation of Benefits

The benefits of the afforestation programme might be divided into the following four groups:

(1) the benefits of preventing declines in soil fertility

(2) increases in soil fertility as a result of improved moisture retention and nutrient recycling

(3) increases in the output of livestock products

(4) the value of the tree products: firewood, poles, and fruit

The following discussion under this heading concerns the data needed to measure these benefits. In particular the uncertainties in the data are explored.

a) The losses in trees
The main source of information about the losses in trees was field reports by foresters, which were rather approximate, relying on the foresters' judgment and experiences.

The decline in trees in some areas could be stemmed for a time by the transport of wood from areas where trees were abundant. This would give some respite to the firewood-deficit areas but would contribute to the spread of deforestation, with negative effects on soil erosion and fertility over larger areas.

b) The decline in soil fertility
This is a difficult component to quantify, the reason being the lack of relevant data on soil fertility and on the extent of erosion when tree stocks are being depleted. In addition, the process by which soil fertility is thought to decline is difficult to model, since it involves the formulation of environmental, demographic, and economic relations over regions and over time.

Another uncertainty arises because as firewood becomes scarce, rural families might turn increasingly to dung for fuel, and soil fertility may decline fast. In the analysis an assumption was made of a decline in soil fertility of 1 per cent, which agronomists and others knowledgeable about the region considered reasonable.

In the with-project case, the decline was gradually stopped and soil fertility improved as the afforestation programme began to take effect after about seven to ten years for shelterbelts and seven to fifteen years for farm forestry.

In the without-project calculations the decline was assumed to continue until net farm income became zero or negative, at which point the land would be taken out of production.

c) The present level and trends in farm output from cropping
To value the benefits in group 1,2 and 3, above, data about the cropping and livestock activities must be available. Since it may take seven to fifteen years for trees to have significant ecological effects, it was necessary to consider both the present level of farm output and the trends.

Considering trends, there is an uncertainty referring to future crop yields. Agronomic analyses showed that the future yield would probably increase, and, hence, farmer income, owing to new seed and increased use of fertilizer.

Even if this were not the case, future increases in farm income were to be expected, because population growth would probably make agricultural land more valuable. Given the size of Nigeria's present population and its growth, it was considered likely that the "land frontier" would be reached within twenty years. This would probably lead to one or more of the following effects:

-a rise in real land values

-a rise in yields

-a rise in food imports

Either of the first two changes would lead to an increase in the gross value of farm output in relation to costs. The third change were assumed to dampen the growth of land values, but the effects were reckoned to be limited. Any large and growing deficit in farm output in relation to the demand for food would lead to increases in food imports. This would raise the price of tradables in relation to the price of nontradables. The food crops being a tradable good, the gross and net values of farm output would raise over time. This justified making an allowance for a rise in the real value of farm output in the area that would be protected by the programme.

d) The output from cropping with the project
Field experiments show that afforestation programmes, have *positive effects* on crop yields: surface evaporation is decreased, soil moisture increased, crop damage from storms reduced, and there are generally favourable effects on the nutrient content of the

soil. The last effect is thought to be larger for farm forestry than for shelterbelts, since several species of farm trees are highly advantageous for nutrient recycling. On the other hand, shelterbelts are much more effective than farm forestry in reducing surface wind velocity.

There is also a possibility that shelterbelts may have *negative effects* on yields. Shelterbelts compete for moisture and nutrients with the crops on their boundaries and if shelterbelts are incorrectly oriented this may lead to accelerated air currents ("funnelling"). Some more complex negative effects may arise from the entrapment of higher-temperature air within the shelterbelts, but this was not considered significant in this study.

The only research studies undertaken in the arid zone were by a government forestry research unit at Kano. The results indicated positive effects on yields, ranging from 20 to over 50 per cent from the implementation of shelterbelts. These were consistent with the results in several other countries.

Furthermore, it has been reported in several studies that the effects of shelterbelts on crop yields are far greater in drought years than in wet years, because the incremental benefits of additional nutrients and soil moisture are likely to be greater under these conditions. Due to these empirical findings, the effect is expected to be substantial under arid conditions. Given the above results, a 15-25 per cent increment in crop yields was expected in shelterbelt areas as the trees approached mature heights, which was the assumption made in the analysis.

For farm forestry, it was more difficult to decide on an appropriate assumption because of scarcity of data. The quantitative effects of farm tree plantings on moisture and nutrients in the soil had not been measured in the arid zone.

The effect of plantings on surface wind velocity and soil moisture depends on farm tree densities over large areas and thus on farmer response. If only a few farmers plant trees in a denuded area, the effect may be negligible, but if a large proportion plant fifteen to twenty trees per hectare, the benefits may be significant. In the analysis a 5 to 10 per cent effect on crop output was assumed, which was considered plausible if farmers were to respond well to the programme.

e) The output from livestock without the project.
A rough estimate of the output from livestock was made by considering how many cattle might be supported by crop residues and by fodder from local shrubs and trees, assuming constant crop yield.

f) The output from livestock with the project.
Crop residues, farm trees, and shrubs provide dry-season fodder for livestock, which

rises in line with crop yields. A 20 per cent increase in yields in traditional agriculture produces approximately 350 additional kgs of fodder per ha. The planting of farm trees and shrubs were expected to raise this figure to more than 500 kgs/ha, sufficient to support over one quarter of a goat. This justified applying the crop yield increments discussed under d) when calculating the output from livestock in the with-project scenario.

g) Wood and fruit production.
Concerning wood and fruit production, an allowance was made for low survival rates of the planted farm trees. Surveys show that if the aim is to achieve twenty surviving trees per hectare, as many as a hundred seedlings per hectare may have to be distributed. The *marginal costs of supplying extra seedlings are*, however, *small*, while the fixed costs of establishing a nursery network and providing regular extension advice to a given number of farmers are large. It was concluded that twice as many seedlings from the same nursery network could be distributed to the same farmers with comparatively little effect on costs, resulting in a larger ecological effect.

The loss of fruit to animals and pests, waste, and the costs of gathering and marketing was also assumed to be considerable, resulting in a net value of only about 10 to 15 per cent of the gross values.

A remark needs to be made about the prices used when calculating the value of wood and fruit production. The prices used in the calculations of the value of firewood and poles were the market prices, which were assumed to rise appreciably as firewood became scarce. There was, however, *a limit being set by the costs of commercial cooking fuels* such as kerosene. From this were deducted the costs of cutting, hauling and chopping.

For the valuation of fruit production, market prices in the arid zone were converted into border prices by a local conversion factor. The latter was the ratio between the value of crop output in border prices and its value in financial prices.

To account for the fact that full ecological effects are not reached until the shelterbelts and farm trees are mature (i.e. some years after planting), a stepwise buildup of benefits was derived from foresters' estimates for shelterbelts and farm forestry.

Identification and Valuation of Costs

The costs associated with the shelterbelts were composed of the following components:

- land
- fencing
- posts

- operational costs (including seeds, fertilizers, and labour)

The land costs were estimated as the value of the land in the without project case that would be taken out of production when implementing the project.

An allowance had to be made for the possibility that some shelterbelts would fail because of unfavourable water tables, "pans", droughts, encroachment of cattle or the like. The success rates are normally 70-80 per cent.

The costs of farm forestry arise from:

- nurseries
- training and use of agricultural extension agents to disseminate the ideas and practices of farm forestry
- state management
- project management
- costs to farmers (measured as the local labour cost)

The Results

In the study, the shelterbelt and farm forestry programmes were analysed separately. The main difference between farm forestry and shelterbelts is that the buildup of benefits is slower and the yields effects are smaller in the farm forestry case.

The net present values were calculated using a 10 per cent discount rate and a 30 years' evaluation period. This resulted in positive net present values for both shelterbelts and farm forestry, shelterbelts yielding the highest value.

Different scenarios to account for uncertainties were postulated in the analysis of the costs and benefits. These were: low yield/high cost case, high yield case, no erosion, more rapid erosion (i.e. 2 per cent instead of 1 per cent), and soil restored to initial conditions plus yield jump. All of these scenarios resulted in positive net present values.

It was concluded that shelterbelts had prospects of more certain returns than the farm forestry programme, but had significantly higher costs. Farm forestry had prospects of significantly better returns but greater risks.

Discussion of the Results

It was pointed out in the study that there were considerable deficiencies in empirical data on soil condition. This emphasizes *the need for research* on subjects like changes in soil fertility, the responses of soils (and thus of farm output) to afforestation programmes, and the social, tenurial, and economic factors that affect the farmers' response to afforestation programmes.

One crucial assumption made in the preceding analysis was that farmers were to respond well to the farm forestry programme. As the costs from the programme were expected to exceed the benefits the first years, this implies that *incentives* to the farmers *for investment in and maintenance of land must be created.*

The comparison between the different scenarios raises another policy implication for afforestation programmes. It was shown that the benefits were lower when the rates of erosion rised from 1 to 2 per cent a year. The reason is that at higher rates of erosion, the value of enhancing the fertility of an increasingly degraded soil is much less. For example, a 20 per cent enhancement of yields when soil fertility has already been degraded by 20 per cent is much less valuable (in relation to the without-project case) than when soil fertility has been degraded by 10 per cent. This means that *it is advisable to protect the better soils before the threat of rapid degradation becomes serious.*

7.2 Forestry Project - Nepal Hill Forest Development Project.

Source: Fleming, W.M., 1983: "Phewa Tal Catchment Management Programme: Benefits and Costs of Forestry and Soil Conservation in Nepal." In: Hamilton, L.S. (ed.), *Forest and Watershed Development and Conservation in Asia and the Pacific,* Westview Press, Boulder, CO.

Introduction

This case study concerns the benefit and cost valuation of a forest development programme in Nepal. It is another example of the use of *the valuation of changes in production technique* (see section 5.2.1.1) in which actual market or shadow prices are used for placing values on the inputs and outputs due to the project. Apart from seeking to increase the productivity of the different land uses within the watershed, the project also reduces soil erosion. The latter effect was not, however, quantified and is not included in this analysis (for an assessment of these kinds of environmental effects see section 6.1.2.).

The project also aimed at providing *a sustainable flow of resources* like firewood and fodder.

Background

Due to the rural need for supplementary income and the urban deficits of fuelwood and fodder, the forests in Nepal have been overexploited. Most of the forests in the middle hills have been converted into shrubland, trees have been overcut and the forest floor overgrazed. Shrubland has been exploited for fodder to feed livestock and firewood removed. As a result, the water-retaining capacity of the vegetation in the hill forests has been reduced, and run off has increased, causing major damage downstream.

The Project

To help meet the fuelwood and fodder requirements of rural and urban communities and to reduce the negative off-site impacts, the introduction of systematic hill forest management was proposed. Among the project components were:

- shrubland and timber stand improvement, including additional fencing within the total forest area

- afforestation of grasslands within the forest area with mixed fuelwood and fodder species including fencing

- a separate agricultural programme (but no grazing, pasture, shrub or forest land would be converted into terraces, so the agricultural programme would not directly affect the extent of the hill forest).

Nearly half of the land area affected was terraced for agriculture, and about one-fourth was forest (including shrub and forest lands used for grazing and fodder). Subsistence agriculture was the main economic activity in the area. Principal crops were rice, maize, millet, wheat, potatoes and other vegetables. Buffalo and cattle were kept for fertilizer and milk production and ploughing. Feed for livestock was about 50 per cent agricultural residues and the rest came from the forests. In addition to fodder, the forests provided firewood and timber.

The With/Without Project Perspective

The cost-benefit analysis used to assess the project was based on estimates of the economic values of the products in a with- and without project context.

Projected use of land without the project:
An estimate of firewood production in the forests around Kathmandu and Pokhara compared to the amount demanded gave a large deficit in firewood. This was met by importing firewood, through illegal removal of wood from the surrounding forests and by using cattle dung as a substitute.

There was also great pressure for forests to be converted into grazing land which was needed for the increasing livestock population. Projections showed that with present use and increased demand from a growing population, the total forested areas would disappear within 15-20 years. Furthermore, without the project, the water-retaining capacity in the area would continue to decline due to removal of vegetation, with increasing run off causing further environmental problems downstream.

Projected use of land with the project:
It was assumed that the separate agricultural programme would increase productivity on cultivated agricultural lands at rates equal to the rate of population increase or more. The grazing, pasture, shrub or forest land would not be directly affected as no such area would be converted into terraces.

The forest project would also help alleviate shortages in firewood and livestock fodder in the Kathmandu and Pokhara valleys. Furthermore, it would reduce the illegal and destructive removal of forest in the surrounding area. It would also help improve overall agricultural productivity, once livestock dung (currently used as a fuel) was applied as fertilizer.

The forest project would also significantly contribute to the control of soil erosion, landslides and flash floods and would improve the water regime by establishing vegetative cover on hill slopes. These project benefits were not, however, included in the analysis.

Identification and Valuation of Benefits

The benefits of the programme were considered to equal *the economic value of the products* of the land with the project, minus the value of the products without the project. These benefits and the associated costs were then used to calculate the benefit-cost ratio.

The products of the land affected by the programme may be divided into the two main groups:

- fodder and grazing for livestock, which would increase milk and fertilizer production

- firewood

The value of land without the project.
Grazing land, pasture and shrubland were used to feed the animals, the products of which were milk and fertilizer (as dung) in this area. The carrying capacity of different land types were estimated, using data about the fodder consumption of animals. The production of animal products were expressed in kg/animal for fertilizer and liters/animal for milk.

In order to calculate the values per hectare of land, market prices were used to establish fertilizer and milk values. The market prices were, hence, assumed to reflect *marginal willingness to pay* as the prices were not in any respect government controlled.

Firewood was produced on shrubland and forest land. To estimate the firewood values, three methods were presented:

a) Opportunity cost of cash
In this case, the market price in Pokhara, the main market place, was used. There the project's production would contribute to approximately 20 per cent of the current firewood consumption. However, as the firewood markets were small and isolated, the market price was considered not to represent the value of firewood outside the market.

b) Opportunity cost of substitute
By this method the firewood was valued in terms of the value of alternative uses of its closest substitute (e.g. in terms of cattle dung that would be used as fuel when wood was

not available). The opportunity cost of using cattle dung as fuel can be estimated in terms of the agricultural production lost when it is diverted from fertilizer use to fuel.

To carry out this calculation, assumptions were made about the amount of dried cattle dung that is the energy equivalent of wood, and the expected increase in agricultural yield as a result of the use of the cattle dung as fertilizer.

c) Opportunity cost of time
The third method which was used was an opportunity-cost approach for the value of the time that families spend to carry firewood from the forest. To carry out this calculation, assumptions were made about the amount of firewood collected daily by each family, how much time each family spend collecting firewood, and the daily gathering wage (the opportunity cost of labour based on other employment).

The indirect substitute method yielded the lowest estimate which was chosen for the analysis.

The value of land with the project:
The calculations were similar to those described above, but based on data for the projected yields per hectare in the with project situation for forest and shrubland. The per hectare values of grazing and pasture lands were assumed to be the same as in the without project situation, but to some extent these land categories would be converted to forest through afforestation.

Identification and Valuation of Costs

These consisted of programme implementation, administration, personnel and training costs for the different activities realized by the project, i.e. afforestation, plantation, maintenance, forest protection, gully control, stall feeding, and training and research.

The Results

Present values were calculated for the two scenarios using a discount rate of 10 per cent and a 20 year time horizon. The net benefits of the programme were calculated as the difference between the total present value with the project minus the total present value without the project.

The benefit-cost ratio for the proposed plan was calculated to 1.7. Since this value was greater than 1, the project was found to be justified in economic terms.

Discussion of the Result

The results from *the valuation of firewood* are very surprising in the way the cost of the substitute turns out to be lower than the opportunity cost of collecting firewood. This would in fact mean that, if the calculations are correct, no one ought to gather firewood, but should instead use the substitute (i.e. cattle dung). Therefore, there is reason to be hesitant to use the substitute of dung in the calculation.

Furthermore, as the market of Pokhara is small and isolated, the relatively significant increase in firewood due to the project is likely to lead to a decrease in the local price. The *impact on the producer- and consumer surplus* should, in that case, be incorporated in the analysis.

Finally, *some side-effects* accruing from the project were not included in the analysis due to lack of data or because they were not considered significant at the time. These were:

Tourism and recreation
This was not a significant component of the country's economy at the time, but the importance of which was supposed to increase in the future. This is a reason for including the income from tourism associated with the improved environment as a benefit of the project.

Fisheries
Eutrophication and siltation led to a decline in fishery, a trend that was to be reversed by the project. Data on the fishery was not, however, available from the fishery industry, nor had there been surveys made to find out whether there actually was a declining trend. The fishery component was, therefore, not included in the analysis.

Hydroelectric Power
The project would increase the life of a hydroelectric power plant, but these benefits would accrue well past the project's planning period, and were therefore not incorporated in the analysis.

Other Studies

Other studies that are concerned with the assessing of a value of firewood are Matsaba (1985), Dixon (1986) and Newcombe (1984).

7.3 Integrated Environmental Project - Environmental Protection in the Philippines.

Source: Finney, C.E. and Western, S., 1986: An Economic Analysis of Environmental Protection and Management: An Example from the Philippines. *The Environmentalist*, Volume 6, Number 1.

Introduction

In this study, an analysis is made of the economic returns that are likely to arise from an environmental protection programme. It is an attempt to assess a multiple-objective programme, using *the valuation of changes in production technique* (see section 5.2.1.1), including objectives which are not easily quantified.

Due to the scarcity of reliable data and the difficulties in making projections of future trends with and without environmental protection, the study is rather approximate in nature. Still, it illustrates the data needed and the considerations that have to be done in this kind of analysis.

Background

The island of Palawan is located in the southwest of the Philippines archipelago. It is richly endowed with natural resources, like cultivable land, forests, marine and mineral resources. Furthermore, the island's flora and fauna are rich, including several rare species.

Palawan has been a relatively unspoilt island but the social and economic pressures on its natural resources and environment have begun to increase. For example, as a result of the destruction of forests the soil erosion and sedimentation of the rivers and the sea have increased. Moreover, most of the island's unique flora and fauna are exposed to danger as these depend directly on the forests.

In recognition of this, the Philippines government and the European Economic Community commissioned in 1983 the preparation of an integrated environmental programme for the island, the aim of which was to stimulate the island's economic development and preserve its ecological balances.

The Project

In the early planning work, a division of the island into ecological zones was carried out. The zoning was developed to help the environmental planning to bring out a correct land use for a given type of land. The three main ecological zones were: land, mangrove and inshore.

The proposed plan consisted of an integrated series of programmes and projects extrapolated over a ten-year period, the objective being to develop Palawan's natural resources, conserve the island's landscapes and wildlife and to accommodate the expected increased population in ways consistent with maintaining a stable environment.

Specific plan components were:

- measures to stabilise the environment, including protection of forest on the steeper uplands, better regulation of commercial logging, protective management of the coastal mangroves, measures to introduce stable systems of agriculture in already occupied areas and establishment of national parks and reserves, both terrestrial and marine, to protect Palawan's wildlife and to encourage tourism

- development activities aiming at attracting settlement to environmentally sound locations (i.e. developing roads and water supplies, education and health facilities).

The With/Without Project Perspective

The analysis of the economic benefits and costs of the environmental protection programme for Palawan was based on a comparison of the plan's expected results with those of the projected "present trends", which represented the "without protection" situation. The analysis was carried out in terms of the three main groups of the components proposed by the plan:

(1) land-based protection

(2) mangrove conservation

(3) inshore marine conservation

Identification and Valuation of Benefits

The benefits were projected for 24 years (i.e. until 2007), and were thereafter taken to remain constant. The time horizon used was 100 years.

1) Land-based protection benefits

These were identified as:

- agricultural benefits
- forestry production
- reduction of flood damage to infrastructure
- tourism

These are discussed below:

Agricultural benefits
The direct agricultural benefit of avoiding run off by catchment protection was the saving of crop land which otherwise would have been eroded away or buried by flood sediments. The major benefits would accrue from averting the large-scale loss of present and planned irrigated rice land.

The total value of agricultural benefits from protection consisted of two components:

a) Prevention of adverse effects on the land assumed to be irrigated even in the "without" situation. These benefits consisted of prevention of increases in irrigation maintenance costs and prevention of reduction in yields and net returns from irrigated rice.

b) Irrigation development of the additional land, due to catchment protection. In the steep lands where agriculture would be replaced, the change would, however, result in a direct loss of crop output, which also had to be included in the analysis.

Forestry production
The main forestry production was the timber output from the commercial logging concessions.

Based on the assumptions made about the production per hectare of forest and on World Bank price projections for tropical woods, and allowing for timber extraction costs, the commercial forest returns with and without the plan were estimated.

Reduction of damage to infrastructure
In the absence of environmental protection the main increase in infrastructure costs would accrue from the damage to bridges and roads caused by flash floods. Benefits, in terms of damage and repair costs avoided, were estimated. These did not, however, allow for the economic costs of the traffic disruption caused by road and bridge failures.

Tourism benefits
There was, as yet, little tourism in the area, because in comparison with other parts of the Philippines, Palawan is not particularly accessible. The island was, however, considered likely to have a potential for tourism, which would be lost without an adequate conservation policy. The tourism benefits were therefore included in the analysis.

An annual increase of 10 per cent of returns from the foreign tourist trade was assumed, but these were assumed to fall to only half that level if Palawan's environment was not protected. Furthermore, assumptions were made about the amount of money the tourists would spend on average and about their average stay.

2) Mangrove conservation benefits

Mangroves are a very valuable natural resource. They are a major "nursing" ground for and produce substantial catches of fish, crustaceans and shellfish. Furthermore they are a significant source of timber, charcoal and other forest products. Loss of the island's mangrove forests would therefore have severe consequences. Given that the prevailing trends were expected to continue, it was estimated that a large amount of mangrove forest would be destroyed. Conservation of the area would, however, result in long-term sustained production of timber, charcoal, fish, crustaceans and shellfish.

The mangrove conservation benefits were therefore calculated as the amount of fish, timber, charcoal and other forest products that would not be destroyed through the measures taken to preserve the mangroves, times their values in market prices. These estimates did not, however, take into account the mangrove's substantial value as a nursing ground for inshore marine fish.

3) Inshore marine conservation benefits:

The tangible benefits of inshore marine conservation are increased returns to fisheries.

The conservation measures from the programme would benefit fish production in the inshore marine zone through control of fishing and the protection of coral reefs.

The returns were calculated using data on the total annual catch times the average landed price of fish, accounting for fishing and related costs. It was assumed that fish resources were neither under- or overexploited at the prevailing rate. To account for the fish production in the future, the assumption made was that without any conservation activity inshore marine fish production would decline at an annual rate of about 3 per cent. Based on this assumption, the annual benefit from preventing this decline was calculated using market value of the fish catch. The causes of the decline would be a combination of inadequate control of fishing methods and the degradation of the mangrove and coral ecosystems.

Alternative approaches to estimate these benefits could have been to use the value of substitutes for fish, or the opportunity cost of catching fish.

Identification and Valuation of Costs

1) *The costs of land-based conservation* included:

- capital costs of reforestation and forest rehabilitation
- demarcation and other capital costs of forest preservation
- loss of crop production from the zone converted into forest
- administrative costs (e.g. the strengthening of the Bureau of Forest Development)

The costs assumed had to allow for the heavy maintenance expenditure required in the first one or two years to establish the trees and plants properly. Maintenance thereafter would be relatively inexpensive.

2) *The costs of mangrove conservation* were almost entirely composed of the same components as the costs associated with the land-based conservation, but with the difference that there was no loss in crop production. Instead there were the costs of foregone present income from not clearing the mangrove forests and obtaining immediate returns from mangrove (i.e. timber and charcoal).

3) *The costs of marine conservation* included:

- the establishment and operation costs of three marine parks

- administrative costs (e.g. the strengthening of the Bureau of Fisheries and Aquatic Resources)

Apart from the costs mentioned above there were costs associated with the environmental protection staff that would be needed for certain other agencies.

The Results

The present values of costs and benefits were calculated by using two discount rates: 0 and 5 per cent. Customarily, a discount rate of 10-15 per cent is used in the Philippines to assess projects, as capital is in short supply. Using this high discount rate was, however, expected to show that the most profitable policy was to extract the island's timber immediately. This conclusion arises from the fact that the project yielded an internal rate of return of 7 per cent, so that using a 10-15 per cent discount rate would result in a negative net present value. The lower discount rates were therefore adopted to emphasize the importance of future incomes from the forests.

Comparison between the land-based and mangrove conservation showed that the mangrove conservation yielded the highest return, because the costs associated with this were low and the benefits high (as the latter accrued from both the mangrove- and the inshore marine zone).

The overall analysis, including the marine conservation, also yielded a result justifying the implementation of the programme.

Discussion of the Results

According to the convention of cost-benefit analysis the actual discount rate used should be consistent with any of the approaches presented in section 5.1.3. The discount rate being a crucial factor, the results might otherwise be manipulated, reflecting only the desired outcome of the analyst. *The adoption in this study of the low discount rates is* in view of the fact that the discount rate is otherwise considered to be 10-15 per cent, *highly questionable.*

Apart from the benefits included in the analysis above, some more general ecological benefits were likely to arise from the project. The following benefits were not considered in the analysis (except to some extent reflected by the tourism benefits):

- retention of the forest ecosystems

- preservation of the mangrove ecosystem

- protection of the complex inshore element of the marine ecosystem, including the important coral reefs

- maintenance of the island's unspoilt natural beauty

- survival of many species of flora and fauna within these different ecosystems, which would otherwise disappear.

Other Studies

Concerning approaches for valuing non-marketed commodities like fauna, most of the studies carried out have been based on *bidding games* (see section 5.2.3). Bidding games for acquiring a hunting licence or encountering the animal have been constructed to arrive at a value of wildlife. These studies are of more limited interest in developing countries, but an example of this kind is Brookshire, Eubanks, and Randall (1983).

Furthermore, there is an extensive amount of literature focusing on fishery, but this deals mainly with approaches to establish the *optimal harvesting rate* and the closely related issue of regulation of the fishery industry. Examples of these are Somerton and June (1984), Hannesson (1975), Berkes (1985), and Spence (1974).

Finally, a remark about water development projects in general needs to be made. Before undertaking this kind of project, it is important to examine the presence of water-borne diseases in the proposed area. In a study by Rosenfield and Bower in 1978, *a cost-effectiveness approach* (see section 5.3) is applied to the control of schistomiasis, a water-borne disease transmitted by snails.

In their study, a model is used to predict the prevalence of the disease, based on empirical data from other areas. Alternative strategies for reducing the prevalence of the disease are analysed (i.e. reducing human-snail contact, modifying human activities and treating human population with drugs) and their costs estimated.

It was, however, concluded that it was difficult to separate one single disease in one such a multi-disease area, the different diseases leading to synergistic effects.

7.4 Recreation and Forestry - Preservation of Mountain Forests - The Vålå Valley in Sweden.

Source: Bojö, J., 1985: *Cost-Benefit Analysis of Mountain Forests. The Case of the Vålå Valley.* With contributions by Hultkrantz, L. Research Report, Stockholm School of Economics (in Swedish with an English summary). The report is also presented in a summary form in Johansson, P-O., 1987: *The Economic Theory and Measurement of Environmental Benefits.*

Introduction

This case study represents an example of how both *a travel-cost* and *a bidding game approach* (see sections 5.2.2.1 and 5.2.3, respectively) were applied to constitute a basis for decision-making on whether to preserve an area of mountain forests or not.

Background

In 1983, the County Board of Jämtland in northern Sweden suggested that a 120,000 hectare Nature Reserve, protected from forest harvesting, be created in the Vålå Valley. A conflict arose between the Swedish State Forest Service and the Forest Workers Trade Union on the one hand, and the tourism, nature conservation and reindeer husbandry interests on the other. The question was: what kind of utilization of the Vålå Valley would be the most rational from society's point of view?

The Study

A group of researchers at the Stockholm School of Economics undertook to use cost-benefit analysis to quantify the major aspects of the conflict.

First, the alternative of harvesting the forest in the area was examined. It was shown that this would result in a financial surplus for the Forest Service. However, this surplus turned negative when the substantial government subsidies were subtracted.

The subsidies aim at increasing employment in this unemployment stricken area. Therefore, shadow pricing was undertaken to allow for the low opportunity cost for forest harvesting employment. This diminished the deficit, but did not completely eradicate it. Sensitivity analysis showed that forest harvesting - before any environmental values were even considered - was unlikely to be profitable from society's point of view. This result points to a policy failure: the government was oversubsidizing the harvesting of marginal forests, with social losses as a consequence.

As this was the first study of its kind to be undertaken in Sweden, there was still a methodological interest in extending the analysis by bringing in environmental values. A survey was carried out in which 282 households visiting the Vålå Valley were interviewed. The interviewees were presented with maps and a description of the area and the two options at hand: forest harvesting or preservation. The description had been drafted in close cooperation with the main parties to the conflict.

The survey gathered two types of data: (a) *travel cost information* for the estimation of a demand curve for the Valley and (b) *willingness-to-pay bids* for the preservation.

The Travel Cost Model

First, a so-called *distance decay function* relating visitation frequency to a number of independent variables was estimated using ordinary least squares. In a second step, the aggregate consumer surplus for the untouched area was calculated. The result was an aggregate value of some USD 230,000 per year. Based on the interviews, potential changes in this surplus could be assessed to about 70% of this value. This is the magnitude of the potential annual loss in welfare to visitors.

The Bidding Game

The potential consumer surplus loss was also estimated using direct questions about willingness-to-pay a (fictitious) entrance fee to the area. The average bid was about USD 4.5 per person and day. Bids ranged from USD 0-17 in general, but three extreme bids of USD 21, 33 and 83 per person and day were also recorded. In general, the bids were quite plausible, representing a potential cost increase of 10-15 per cent of actual costs incurred.

Two different bidding patterns were tested, but no significant impact on mean bid was discovered. However, a considerable interviewer bias was uncovered through multiple regression including a dummy variable for the interviewer.

With data on the number of visits for the lodges in the area, the total willingness-to-pay per year was calculated to be about USD 170 000. This is comparable to the result of the travel cost analysis.

The study concluded that *preservation*, rather than forest harvesting, *would be most profitable to society.*

In addition, as already pointed out, the study revealed that the prevailing *public interventions* strongly *encouraged forest harvesting* in marginal forest areas. The employment subsidies made it profitable for the Swedish State Forest Service to cut down forest even in the case of a bad harvest. It was estimated that the subsidies in the area were between eight to sixteen times too high as to what was justifiable from the society's point of view. That is, the benefit from harvest pertaining to additional employment opportunities did far from create a social surplus when subtracting for government subsidies. The estimates reveal that in this area, the economic policies create incentives to engage in activities that is not profitable to society even before including environmental values. Thus, there is implications that considering environmental aspects or not, we have in this area (and also in substantial areas with similar conditions) an example of *a policy failure*.

Post Scriptum

In 1988, a Nature Reserve in the Vålå Valley was officially declared by the County Board of Jämtland.

7.5 Air Pollution

7.5.1 Air Pollution - The South Coast Air Basin Experiment in California

Source: Brookshire, D.S., d'Arge, R.C., Schultze, W.D., 1979: *Environmental Protection Agency. Methods Development for Assessing Air Pollution Control Benefits.* Volume II. Report no. EPA-600/6-79-001b. National Information Service, Springfield, Virginia.

Introduction

A problem in valuing non-market goods (here represented by "air quality") is that different approaches lack a common theoretical basis. In this study both *a property valuation* and *a bidding game approach* (see sections 5.2.2.2 and 5.2.3, respectively) were applied to determine if people would actually pay what they said they were willing to pay (i.e. if the results from the two approaches corresponded to each other).

A weakness of many studies on air quality is that they do not separate *the health* and *the aesthetic effects* of pollution. In this experiment, these components were attempted to be valued separately.

Background

In some Los Angeles neighbourhoods, deterioration in air quality has been relatively severe, as measured by concentrations of NO_x or total oxidants.

The population of the South Coast Air Basin areas had become well-informed through the years of the causes of air deterioration, the potential effects, and the scope of the problem. Thus, in valuing the air quality, the experiment was conducted with reasonably well-developed market information for individuals.

In order to insure comparability of results and aid in aggregation, six pairs of neighbourhoods were selected. The pairings were made on the basis of similarities of housing characteristics, socioeconomic factors, distance to beach and services, average temperature, and subjective indicators of the "quality" of housing. Thus, for each of the six pairs, an attempt was made to exclude effects on property values of factors other than differences in air quality.

The Bidding Game

The bidding game was conducted by randomly choosing homes within the paired areas.

The air quality levels for the paired areas were determined using monitoring station data in the South Coast Air Basin. Focusing on total oxidants, nitrogen dioxide, and total suspended particulates, maps were constructed, showing "good", "fair", and "poor" air quality regions as well as photographs where the pollution was visible.

The contingent bidding and site substitution data of the experiment were collected via a survey questionnaire, where the individuals answered questions about their willingness to pay for a reduction in air pollution. The survey yielded valuations by the individual for both aesthetic and health effects. The questionnaire was designed to test for *strategic*, *information*, and *starting-point biases*.

Two specific forms of information bias were investigated via a health pamphlet. This attempted to determine for a sub-sample of the respondents whether detailed information about health effects would affect bidding and substitution behavior. Strategic, information and instrument bias were concluded statistically not to be significant influences upon the results.

The Property Valuation

The data for the property value study, obtained from the Market Data Center, pertained to 719 homes sold in the 12 paired communities during 15 months, and contained information on most important structural and/or quality attributes. The property value analysis included three separate approaches.

- a comparison was made of average housing values in the sample paired communities: standardizing was conducted only for living space.

- a linear relationship between a home's sale price and its supply of housing and community attributes was estimated. The value of an improvement in air quality was then deduced from the resulting hedonic housing value equation.

- the willingness-to-pay equation, as a function of income and other household variables, allowing for non linearities was estimated.

The Results

The property value study gave an estimated average bid of $40.00 per month per household (1978) for a 30 per cent improvement in air quality, and the bidding results gave an average bid of slightly less than $30.00 per month.

Given various assumptions of location, income, aggregation by areas, specific housing characteristics, and knowledge on health effects of air pollution, both the bidding game and property value studies yielded estimates ranging from \$20.00 to \$150.00 per month per household for a 30 per cent reduction in air pollution.

By this it was concluded that *the air quality deterioration* in the area *has had substantial effects on housing prices* and that these negative price effects on housing were comparable in magnitude to what people say they were willing to pay for improved air quality.

7.5.2 Valuation of Morbidity Reduction due to Pollution Abatement: Direct vs. Indirect Measurement

Source: Shecter M., Golan L., and Kim M., 1987: *Valuation of Morbidity Reduction due to Pollution Abatement: Direct vs. Indirect Measurement.* Paper presented at the conference on "Environmental Policy in a Market Economy". Wagening. The Netherlands.

Introduction

In chapter 5.2.1.4, valuation of effects on human health was discussed in terms of *the human capital approach* and *the willingness to pay approach.* It was concluded that the human capital approach was not the theoretically correct measure but could provide a lower boundary for the willingness to pay for a reduction of a particular hazard to human health. The case study to be surveyed here, tries to capture an unbiased estimate of the willingness to pay for a risk reduction by using both an indirect approach and a direct approach. The indirect approach relies upon *the use of implicit markets* (markets for housing and medical care, see 5.2.2). This is, however, not a property value study, but it uses data on the demand for housing and medical care to estimate an indirect utility function from which the willingness to pay can be calculated. The direct method is an example of *using artificial markets* (see section 5.2.3).

Background

Air pollution has been associated with both health and non-health damages. Included in the health category are the incremental mortality and morbidity which may be traced back to pollutants in the air. This study deals only with the valuation of a reduction of air pollution-induced morbidity. However, the results from the contingent valuation must be given a broader interpretation. We will come back to that in the discussion of the results.

The focus of the study is a reduction of air pollution in Haifa, Israel. The data base for the study was obtained through a household survey. The study is thus based on household data in contrast to most other indirect approaches which are based on aggregate variables.

Due to the topographical layout, and the location of industry in Haifa, there is marked inter-neighbourhood variability in ambient air quality, of which there is some public awareness. There has been considerable media exposure regarding air pollution-induced diseases so it is likely that the respondents to the questions in the survey did not respond to excessively hypothetical questions.

The Indirect Utility Function

Most indirect approaches are based on the estimation of an arbitrary demand system with environmental quality as an explanatory variable. By invoking the principle of weak complementary,[2] it is then possible to calculate the appropriate welfare measure for a change in environmental quality (willingness to pay or willingness to accept). In the Haifa study, instead of starting out from an arbitrary demand system, the starting point is an arbitrary *indirect utility function*. This simply means that the researchers described the preferences of the citizens of Haifa in terms of a mathematical device known as an indirect utility function. Then by using wellknown theorems from consumption theory, it is possible to derive the demand functions for housing and medicare. By assuming that the indirect utility function can be approximated by a translog specification,[3] a specification of the demand functions is obtained.

The household survey was based on a stratified, cluster area probability sampling procedure. All heads of households in the city blocks in Haifa that were sampled were interviewed. In order to capture the seasonality effect of air pollution in Haifa, each neighbourhood was repetitively sampled over a year, May, 1986 - May 1987. Altogether, about 4,000 interviews were conducted, although only half of them were actually used in the study.

The data collected contained information on the following variables: net income per month, apartment area, visits to doctor per year, tax per year per m^2, housing expenditure per year, medical services expenditure per year, total expenditure, cigarette smoking, respiratory illness symptoms of head of household, respiratory illness symptoms of all other members of household, respiratory illness of head of household, respiratory illness of all other members of household, perceived air quality level, housing share, and medical services share.

On the basis of this information the budget share equations were estimated, which resulted in, among other results, that substitution elasticities between budget shares and air pollution levels could be calculated. The crucial assumption is now that the estimated parameters in the budget share equations can be used to identify and estimate the parameters in the indirect utility function. However, it seems that the authors have overlooked that one parameter in this function has been given the arbitrary value of one. This is an assumption similar to the assumption of weak complementarity, except that there is no intuitive explanation for the assumption. Anyhow, this assumption implies that the values on air pollution reductions estimated by this method , are to some extent

2. See Mäler 1971 and 1974 for the introduction of the concept of weak complementarity and Mäler 1985 for the introduction of weak substitutability and similar concepts.

3. A translog specification means that the logarithm of the indirect utility function is assumed to be approximated as a quadratic function in the logarithms of the variables.

arbitrary. In fact one can interpret their numerical findings as indicating that their results are biased downward.

The Direct Approach

In the survey questionnaire, individuals were asked to reveal preferences for air quality through contingent valuation questions. In one question they were asked about their willingness to pay to prevent (WTP^C) a worsening in air quality levels (a 50% increase in present pollution level) and in another question they were asked about their willingness to pay to achieve (WTP^E) a better air quality through 50% reduction of present air pollution levels. The vehicle for the willingness to pay was the municipal tax.

Results

The results of the study can conveniently be summarized in the following table, in which the two approaches are compared.

All amounts are in NIS (New Israeli Shekel).

Table 7.5.2.1	Air pollution study in Haifa	
	Indirect Approach	Direct Approach
WTP^C	13.41	32.1
WTP^B	2.1	33.4
$MWTP^C$	4.1	3.42
$MWTP^B$	6.7	3.23
Substitution elasticity:		
- housing	-0.32	
- medical care	0.065	

The willingness to pay concepts, WTP^C and WTP^E are the same as the ones defined above. The $MWTP^C$ and $MWTP^E$ are the corresponding marginal willingness to pay, i e the amount the individual would be willing to pay to prevent a "small" deterioration of the air quality and to pay to achieve a "small" improvement. It is clear from the table that estimates of WTP^C, $MWTP^C$ and $MWTP^E$ are of the same order of magnitude in the two approaches and that there is a significant difference in WTP^E. These differences between the indirect and direct approaches can perhaps be explained by the arbitrary assumption made on the indirect utility function, mentioned above.

The substitution elasticities show that an individual would be willing to substitute, in the long run, an increase of 1% air quality for:

(1) a decrease of 0.32% in the budget share allocated to housing; in other words, substituting better air quality for lower-quality housing services.

(2) an increase of 0.065% in the budget share allocated to medical care; that is, better air quality is substituted for additional medical care.

Discussion of the Results

This study is unique in at least three ways:

(1) It uses household or individual data both for a contingent valuation study (which is, of course, necessary) and for an indirect approach. The indirect approaches have usually been based on variables aggregated over many households.

(2) It applies two approaches on the same data set, which means that they can be compared.

(3) Its application of the indirect approach starts with a specification of the indirect utility function and not, as is usual, of a demand system.

The results show that the two approaches yield results which are approximately of the same order of magnitude, except for the willingness to pay for a 50% improvement of the air quality. In general, however, the direct approach gives higher estimates of the willingness to pay than the indirect approach. This can be explained by the partial nature of the indirect approach. It is based on the assumption that the effects of air pollution are only caught by the demand for housing and medical care. It is not too farfetched, however, to imagine other goods and services, the demand for which is affected by the air quality. For example, a deteriorating air quality may induce people to travel out of the Haifa region, and thus increase the demand for transportation. A deteriorating air quality may also induce households to spend more on cleaning the house or preventive measures. These effects are not directly related to health effects, but the results from the direct approach must be interpreted as the willingness to pay for air pollution changes in general, while the indirect approach only yields the willingness to pay for combating health effects. Thus the indirect approach, as it has been designed in this study, should yield substantially lower results than the direct approach. By including more and more goods and services in the indirect approach, the results from the two approaches should come closer.

In most indirect approaches, one has to make assumptions which basically mean that individuals have the same preferences. However, in this particular study, it would have been possible to avoid that assumption by including more variables characterizing the household, besides the smoking habit. For example, it would have been interesting to see the effects of profession, working habits, recreational habits etc. on the results and whether the inclusion of such characteristics would have changed the results significantly.

7.5.3 Air Pollution and Corrosion Damage.

Source: OECD, 1981: "Atmospheric Corrosion of Materials.", In: *The Costs and Benefits of Sulphur Oxide Control.* Paris.

Introduction

The study surveyed here is part of an OECD study from 1979 on corrosion due to sulphur oxide emissions in northern and western Europe. It is based on an analysis at the Swedish Corrosion Institute.

The study represents an example of *the replacement-cost technique* (see section 5.2.1.2).

Background

The rate of corrosion of materials is determined by both natural (humidity and temperature) and man-made factors. When considering corrosion of metals, the most important man-made factor is the pollutant of sulphur compounds. Considerable work has been done to establish the corrosive effects of one of these compounds in particular, i.e. sulphur dioxide (SO_2).

The Study

As the natural factors are similar in the climatic zone of Europe, where the study was carried out, any difference in the corrosion rate was assumed to be caused by man-made factors (of which air pollution is the most important).

Furthermore, only corrosion damage caused by sulphur dioxide was analysed (the reason being the importance of the effects of this compound and the availability of quantitative data).

Although several materials were intended to be included in the analysis, the number was finally limited to two. This was due to the low corrosion rate or the minor importance of the other materials. The materials included in the cost assessment were:

(1) zinc and galvanized steel

(2) paint coatings on steel and galvanized steel

The study of corrosion damage was carried out in two steps. In the first step, the damage functions were established. In the second step, the monetary value of the corrosion was assessed, and the damage functions were used here to predict the materials corroded. The corrosion was valued according to *the present material prices*.

Establishing the Damage Functions

The relationship between corrosion damage and exposure to the air pollutant was explored by regression analysis. This was established for 1) the corrosion rate of zinc/galvanized steel and the SO_2 concentration in the atmosphere 2) the length of life of paint on zinc and on steel and the SO_2 concentration in the atmosphere (based on data on time between repaintings). The findings provided *the damage functions* used in the study.

The Costs of Corrosion

The total cost of corrosion was estimated as the cost of replacing the corroded materials. The following components were needed to arrive at an estimate on a yearly basis:

1) cost estimates for surface treatment (cost of painting or galvanizing, based on OECD Annual Statistics from 1960 onwards) including the basic material cost of galvanized wire only

2) the amount of treated material (for all materials, it was assumed that they were used in proportion to the population) in the various regions

3) the length of life of painting and galvanizing (measured in years)

The costs were then calculated multiplying component 1 by component 2, dividing by component 3.

Discussion of the Results

The cost of corrosion was calculated for three SO_2 emission scenarios. The influence of SO_2 was thus obtained by comparing the incremental costs of these different scenarios (for a presentation of these, see the full study). The results from the study were comparable to results from other studies on the cost of corrosion.

The authors conclude that sources of error are the exclusion of materials older than 25 years, no consideration of withdrawal of materials from use, the exclusion of certain materials and the assumption of constant production of corroding materials between

1975 and 1985.

Another weakness of the study rises from the fact that the materials were valued in the present material prices. The appropriate approach when carrying out this kind of study would be to include the value of the use of the materials, a value that is neglected in this study.

7.6 Water Pollution - Water Quality Management in Thailand

Source: Phantumvanit, D., 1982: "A Case Study of Water Quality Management in Thailand". In: Ahmad, Y.J. (ed.), *Analysing the Options.* United Nations Environmental Programme. UNEP Studies, 5.

Introduction

In this study, the damage costs due to water pollution are compared to the abatement costs. A model is used to simulate the damage on the environment under different climatic and hydrological conditions.

The study may be regarded as representing yet another example of *the valuation of changes in production technique* (see section 5.2.1.1).

Furthermore, it aims at finding *the sustainable use* of the water as a receptor of effluents.

Background

The pollution, resulting mainly from sugar mill effluents in the Mae Klong River, north-west of Bangkok has been severe, leading to the death of fish, cockles and shrimps.

In order to alleviate the pollution of the Mae Klong, the Government has requested every sugar mill to install an individual water treatment system, consisting of aerated ponds and cooling towers, and to ban the establishment of new sugar mills.

The Study

The potential damage costs due to water pollution were investigated, in order to compare them with the abatement costs of a pollution control programme. The method relied on available scientific findings complemented by direct questioning.

Damage Costs

The damage arising from water pollution was subdivided into that affecting cockle farms, shrimp farms and agriculture.

The damage to the *cockle farms* relied on data from a field survey, reporting that the cockle loss was as high as 81 per cent in the sampling area.

Data on the production from *shrimp farms* gathered from the district official record and discussions with the leaders of the fishermen in the area, indicated the total loss to shrimp farming due to pollution.

The damage to *agriculture, effect on domestic water consumption and other areas* were more difficult to evaluate. Although studies were undertaken to investigate the damage to agriculture, it was difficult to differentiate these from long-term damage to soil quality induced by flood (the area is flooded almost every year during the rainy season).

In order to help meet the domestic water consumption, hundreds of wells were dug for ground-water supply. With regard to health, a field survey revealed that the local residents had been affected by the odour of polluted water and some had suffered from skin diseases. Based on the field survey an attempt to estimate these damage costs were made.

The abatement costs consisted of the capital investment costs and the operating costs for the required waste treatment facilities.

Water Quality Routing Model

A computer programme was adopted, simulating the biochemical oxygen concentrations and dissolved oxygen profiles using a conventional water quality equation (see e.g. Kneese and Bower, 1973). The programme was designed to cover varying climatic and hydrological conditions during a 12-month period. The model broke the river system down into elements, based on the different sub-systems of the river.

The Results

The relationship between the damage costs and the water quality was examined.

It was concluded that the treatment level had to be kept above 75 per cent, in order to maintain the river quality above 4 mg/l of dissolved oxygen, above which no damage costs were assumed.

Conclusions

The understanding of the assimilative capacity of the Mae Klong and the available water quality simulation programme helped the authorities to define regulatory limits of the water pollution. It was concluded that the present policy of limiting the expansion of sugar-milling capacity was unjustified, since the existing facilities comprised a treatment level of 96,6 per cent.

Other Studies

In Dixon and Hufschmidt (1986), another study is presented, which in more detail examines different water pollution control options. Furthermore, in Peskin and Seskin (1975), a number of water quality studies are compiled and briefly discussed. The theoretical basis is given in Feenberg and Mills (1980), and in Smith and Desvousges (1986).

Another study of the Mae Klong river concerned the consequences to a waste-producing firm, if the case was brought to court by a party claiming compensation for damage (Hufschmidt and Hyman 1982). In the study the compensation costs were compared to the costs of fighting the case (i.e. the transaction costs, including legal fees, purchase of information etc., times the probability of winning the case).

As the probability of losing the case was very high by past experience, it was concluded that the party responsible for pollution had a very strong incentive to pay the compensation.

The transaction costs for the plaintiff were also calculated. These varied depending on whether the plaintiff was a firm or a household, and, hence, the incentive for the damaged party to bring the case to court.

7.7 Environmental Degradation and Policy Failures

7.7.1 Deforestation in the Amazon - Regional Development Policies

Source: Mahar, D., 1989: *Government Policies and Deforestation in Brazil's Amazon Region*. The World Bank. Washington D.C.

Introduction

In his study, Mahar traces the evolution of *regional development policies* for Amazonia over the past 25 years. It is apparent that when designing the regional development policies in the Brazil's Amazon Region, little or no thought was given to the unique physical environment in the area. As a result, the individuals have been given the wrong incentives as regards any sustainable use of the environmental resources in the area.

Background

The most recent estimates of deforestation in the Brazil's Amazon region indicate that almost 600,000 km^2 of Amazon forest have been cleared since the mid-1970s. This is an area larger than France. About 80 per cent of the deforestation has occurred since 1980.

Mahar refers to the primary causes for the deforestation in the Amazon region as being mainly small-scale agriculture, cattle ranching, logging, road-building, hydroelectric development, mining, and urban growth. Although the relative contribution of different activities to the deforestation in the area is not known with precision, Mahar argues that the rapid expansion of the agricultural frontier, in particular the conversion of forest to pasture, has been an important cause.

Pasture is the predominant form of agricultural land use in the region, where the conversion of forest to pasture occurred at a rate of approximately 8,000 - 10,000 km^2 per year during the 1970s. Land devoted to annual cropping, the second most important form of agricultural land use, probably increased by about 2,000 km^2 per year between 1970 and 1980. Cropping is typically a small-farmer activity.

Logging has also grown rapidly in Amazonia over the past two decades. Between 1975 and 1985, regional roundwood production increased from 4.5 million m^3 per year to 19.8 million m^3.

The Regional Development Policies

In 1966 and 1967 the Government started a plan for development of the region known as "Operation Amazonia". Besides legislative acts and decrees, there was included in the plan a road-building programme aimed at linking Amazonia with the Northeast and South (the "Belem-Brasilia highway"). Official estimates suggest that the total human population of the zone increased from 100,000 in 1960 to some 2 million ten years later, and that the cattle population increased from practically nothing to 5 million during the decade.

The increase in population associated with the Belem-Brasilia highway generated demand for secondary and feeder roads, which in turn attracted more population, and so on. The most powerful tools to attract people and enterprises to the region have been through investment tax credits and subsidized credit. Moreover, the construction of the Cuiaba-Porto Velho Highway, the programme "Polonoroeste" and the establishment of growth poles in the area have further increased the migratory flow to the Amazon. These measures are discussed below.

Investment tax credits

These allowed registered Brazilian corporations to take up to a 50 per cent credit against their federal income tax liabilities if the resulting savings were invested in projects located in "Legal Amazonia" and approved by SUDAM (Superintendency for the Development of Amazonia). The tax-credit mechanism proved very attractive to investors and by late 1985 some 950 projects had been approved by SUDAM. Of this total, 631 projects were in the livestock sector. The performance of these livestock projects did, however, fall short of expectations.

Moreover, there are examples in the area of many projects being exploited solely for their fiscal benefits. In other cases, entrepreneurs intentionally delayed project implementation in order to obtain additional tax-credit funds from SUDAM through successive project "reformulations". Changes in ownership have also been very frequent, since a transfer of ownership also transfers the right to receive tax-credit funds.

Estimates suggest that the environmental damage associated with cattle ranching, may account for as much as two-thirds of total deforestation in the region. An effort to halt further deforestation was mounted in 1979 when SUDAM officially declared its intention not to approve any new livestock projects in rainforested areas. Such projects have, however, been approved in subsequent years.

Subsidized credit

Subsidized rural credit has long been used by the Brazilian government as a means of compensating agriculture for foreign exchange overvaluation and import controls. After 1974, the volume of subsidized rural credit increased dramatically, and the volume committed to Amazonia increased almost tenfold in real terms between 1974 and 1980. Although the effects of subsidized credit on the behaviour of farmers and ranchers in Amazonia are difficult to quantify, the following general conclusions may be reached:

- The availability of subsidized rural credit facilitated the acquisition and deforestation of large tracts of land in Amazonia, particularly in the latter half of the 1970's.

- The special credit lines which served to increase the unit subsidy element for undertakings in Amazonia vis-a-vis more developed regions of Brazil probably attracted some resources which would have otherwise been invested in farms and ranches located in the less fragile natural environments.

Since 1980, the volume of official rural credit has, however, been significantly reduced.

The Cuiaba-Porto Velho Highway and "Polonoroeste"

In 1968, a few years after the completion of the Belem-Brasilia highway, the construction of another penetration road in the area of Rondonia was started. This was followed by a ten-fold increase in the annual migratory flow in the 1970s. Most of the deforestation in the area of Rondonia is the result of clearing for agricultural purposes along the main highway.

Owing largely to inadequate infrastructure, technical and financial assistance, agricultural research and marketing facilities, most of the early settlers engaged in traditional, and environmentally-unsound farming practices. Moreover, by the rapid growth of Rondonia's feeder roads network and, hence, the access to remote areas, the deforestation process was greatly facilitated.

Recognition of the growing socioeconomic problems in Rondonia led to a proposal by the Government to implement a new programme, known as "Polonoroeste". The principal objective of this programme was to reduce forest clearance on land without long-term productive potential and to promote, instead, a more widespread adoption on the part of migrants of sustainable farming systems based on tree crops.

The actions carried out under "Polonoroeste" do not, however, seem to have succeeded in slowing down the deforestation, and the intended shift of farmland into tree crops did not take place.

Instead there was, and still is, an undesirably rapid conversion of forest into pasture, the reasons being:

- the federal Institute of Forestry Development (IBDF) has not been able to enforce *the "50 per cent rule"*, prohibiting landowners in Amazonia from clearing more than half of their holdings;

- *subsidized credit* that would be made available to finance purchases of modern inputs have not been made available to the extent demanded, and even when credit has been available, many farmers have been reluctant to use it because the subsidy element has not been high enough to offset the risks associated with the cultivation of tree crops;

- *certain land and tax policies* have encouraged unnecessary deforestation and inappropriate land use, one example being the rural land tax, which is reduced according to the degree of utilization of land, where the latter is measured in terms of crop yields, cattle stocking rates, etc;

- some of INCRA's (the National Institute for Colonization and Agrarian Reform) policies have encouraged inappropriate land use, one example being its policy of *accepting deforestation as evidence of land improvement*; and

- *the potential gains from speculation in land* have been very high in Rondonia because of rising real prices of land, and because of low maintenance cost the land speculators prefer to keep their land in pasture.

The "Big Projects" Era

In the mid-1970s, the Government essentially abandoned the road-building and directed settlement strategy, and instead started to emphasize the development of large-scale export-oriented projects in the livestock, forestry and mining sectors in 15 "growth poles" scattered throughout Amazonia.

The mining activities were not undertaken with regard to the natural environment, one exception being the Carajas Iron Ore Project which was developed with close attention to its possible environmental impacts. The overall impact on the Amazon rainforest of the "big project" policy seems, however, to have been negative.

Conclusion

Mahar concludes that the individuals who have settled down in the Amazon region and who have engaged in activities that increase deforestation, have merely responded to incentives created by the Government. For example, as in the case of the Rondonia region, without the resources to pay for fertilizers and other modern inputs needed for cultivating tree crops on the poorer soils, settlers often have found pasture formation the only option available.

In addition, it has been revealed that cattle ranching, apart from the negative effects it has on the rainforest, is intrinsically uneconomic under conditions generally prevailing in Amazonia. The reason for this is its high potential for degrading the soil.

It should be added that there is currently increased awareness in Brazil about the environmentally unsound policies that have been pursued in the country. There is also a need to reduce public spending in general. Measures have therefore been taken to reduce those subsidies which have clearly encouraged the improper use of environmental resources. In particular, the subsidized credit for settlement in the Amazon has been reduced, as has subsidized investment for new cattle ranches.

7.7.2 Deforestation in the Amazon - Fiscal and Legal Provisions

Binswanger, H.P., 1989. *Brazilian Policies that Encourage Deforestation in the Amazon.* Environment Department Working Paper, No. 16. Environment Department. The World Bank, Washington, D.C.

Introduction

As in the study surveyed in section 6.7.1, the present study concerns deforestation in the Amazon. Binswanger identifies in his study several fiscal and legal provisions in Brazil that encourage the Amazon's deforestation by increasing the demand for farm, pasture, and ranch land. In particular, he points out that the design of the land tenure system in Brazil is a significant factor. By its provision for logging as a proof of the land being occupied, it encourages people to settle down on marginal land and engage in agricultural and ranching activities, thus increasing the deforestation.

Binswanger does not try to quantify the relative impact on deforestation of all the distortions that he identifies, but discusses their relative importance as regards their implications for the use of land.

Fiscal and legal provisions

Binswanger identifies and focuses in his study on five sets of fiscal and legal provisions that tend to increase the rate of conversion of forest land into other uses:

(1) Taxes on agricultural income

(2) Rules of land allocation

(3) Land taxes

(4) Regional and sectoral taxes

(5) The system of credit

1) Taxes on agricultural income

Landholders can choose between two tax policies. They can either be taxed on 10 per cent of their gross agricultural revenues, or the cost of modern inputs or investments can be subtracted from gross agricultural income. Furthermore, fixed investments, animals, buildings, machines and vehicles can also be depreciated several times over by using a multiplication factor which ranges from two to six. It has been shown that up to 80 per cent of farm profits can be sheltered because of these provisions. Thus, either of these tax policies makes agricultural income almost exempt from taxation.

Corporate agricultural profits are taxed at a rate of only 6 per cent. Combined with the depreciation provisions, the tax on corporate agricultural profits can be as low as 1.2 per cent.

Binswanger argues that a consequence of this tax treatment is that private and corporate investors may undertake projects in agriculture, even though the projects have a lower economic rate of return than nonagricultural projects. A further implication of the income tax is that it tends to increase the demand for land on the part of higher income individuals (as small farmers and other poor individuals do not pay income tax), as well as providing incentives for the accumulation of large land holdings.

Moreover, as the taxation of corporate profits from other sources than agriculture (which are taxed at a rate between 35 and 45 per cent) differs considerably from the tax treatment of agricultural income, these tax preferences will be capitalized in land prices. Thus, this further affects the poor negatively, increasing the difficulties of the poor people in buying land.

2) Rules of Land Allocation

Land can in many cases be acquired by the right that states that a squatter who lives on unclaimed public land and has used it "effectively" for at least one year and one day has a usufruct right over 100 hectares. If the squatter fulfills the condition of living on and effectively using the land for more than five years, he has the right to acquire a title to land. In some areas the administrative rule applied is that a claimant who lives on the land may obtain a title for land of up to three times the area which he cleared of forest. Thus, the design of the land tenure system by its provision for logging as a proof of the land being occupied encourages deforestation.

Binswanger further points out that the rules of land allocation, though they appear to favour small firms, in reality favour large private and corporate ranches. The reason is the advantage these may have as regards the fact that they may build access roads into the forest to lay claim on land far away, an option that is not open to most small farms.

3) Land Taxes

Though the initial structure of the land tax was progressive (leading to making it less profitable to have land in large holdings), the tax code has come to contain so many exceptions that the prevailing effective tax rates are not progressive in practice. An example of this is that the land tax may be reduced according to the "productivity" of the farm. As forest land is considered unused and, hence, non-productive, this implies that a farm containing forests is taxed at higher rates than one containing pastures or crop land. The impact of this legislation is, therefore, that conversion of forest land into other uses is being encouraged.

4) Regional and Sectoral Taxes
Binswanger identifies no other federal tax regulations (such as commodity or capital gains taxes) apart from the taxes discussed above, that tend to affect deforestation. He identifies, however, several regional and sectoral tax regulations which have a great impact on deforestation through their encouragement of uneconomic livestock production.

The regional and sectoral incentives listed in Binswanger's study and their relative importance as contributing to an increased deforestation are listed below:

- *Income tax holidays* of up to 10 years. This policy seems to be of minor importance as regards the effect on deforestation, the reason being that agriculture and livestock corporations already almost escape the income tax via the general provisions for agriculture.

- *Reinvestment tax credits* that approved enterprises can use for expansion or for modernization investments. For the same reason as in the income tax holiday case this policy is of minor importance for agriculture and livestock corporations. The reinvestment tax credits may, however, induce investments with a negative expected profit for enterprises having taxable profits. If it is the case that forest or agricultural products are utilized, this policy may also have an impact on deforestation.

- *Generalized tax credits* that any corporation in Brazil can use to set up, invest in, or participate in approved enterprises. This policy allows any corporation to use up to 25 per cent of its tax liabilities to invest in approved enterprises or to acquire equity in such corporations. Like the reinvestment tax credits this may create the incentive for corporations to invest in approved enterprises even if the enterprises have negative rates of return to overall invested resources. Due to the fact that an approved enterprise located in the Amazon can finance up to 75 per cent of its planned investments taking advantage of the favourable generalized tax credits, this tax policy creates strong incentives for further investments in the area.

- *Tax credits* for individuals *to invest in stocks* of regional and sectoral investments funds. Binswanger consider this tax policy to be of less importance due to the fact that few investors have taken advantage of the provision.

- *Exemptions from import tariffs, export taxes, and commodity taxes* for imports or exports of approved enterprises. Binswanger does not in his study stress these tax policies as important as regards the conversion of forest land into other uses.

Binswanger concludes that the combined effect of the regional and sectoral incentives programmes is more rapid deforestation in the Amazon and very modest afforestation in areas of old settlement. As regards the cost-effectiveness of the fiscal programme, it is concluded that to the extent that the stated goals of increased livestock production and increased rate of afforestation are achieved, these are met at a very large fiscal cost. This is based on studies of the performance of the system.

5) The System of Credit

The real interest rate on loans for agriculture is lower than in the nonagricultural sector. By this credit policy, in the way it favours agricultural activities, the demand for land tends to increase, leading to a more rapid expansion of crop and pasture land.

The difference of credit terms between sectors furthermore tends to be capitalized into the land price. Hence, this implies that the system of credit reduces the possibility for poor individuals to buy land, leading to an increase in the movement of settlers to frontier areas.

Conclusion

Although Binswanger has not tried to rigorously quantify all the effects from the legal and fiscal policies identified, he concludes that all the distortions appear to work in the same direction, that is, towards an increasing rate of deforestation.

Apart from leading to a more rapid conversion of forest into agricultural uses, other effects from the policies are that these contribute to a more rapid conversion of forest to agricultural uses, land price appreciation, and an increasing concentration of land ownership.

Although Binswanger did not find any tax or subsidy provision that seemed to slow down the conversion of forest land into other uses, it should be pointed out that attempts to stem the rate of deforestation have been made. That is, programmes that aim at encouraging the cultivation of tree crops have to some extent been implemented. In spite of these efforts any afforestation projects are not likely to succeed in the presence of considerable distortions creating perverse incentives. Thus, this highlights the importance of examining the prevailing economic incentives and how these affect peoples' actions concerning the land use. It may be a necessary condition that the distortions are removed first in order to make any environmental programme succeed.

Other Studies

Other studies focusing on the role of economic policy of environmental resource use in developing countries are Barbier (1987), Repetto (1987 and 1988), Repetto and Gillis (1988) and Warford (1987).

7.7.3 Upper Watershed Degradation in Java

Source: Barbier, E., 1989: *Economics, Natural-resource Scarcity and Development - Conventional and Alternative Views*. Earthscan. London.

Introduction

In his study of Java, Barbier focuses on the role of economic policies, incentives and investment strategies in controlling upland erosion. In particular he examines two aspects of the incentive structure; the incentives for the farmers to adopt soil-conservation measures and some more general policies and their effect on farmers' land-use patterns.

Although the study mainly deals with policies pursued by the government in order to improve the environment, the author also identifies other policies which are likely to have a negative impact on the environment. Because of these important observations, Barbier's survey was selected for the present book as a case study illustrating policy failures.

Background

In the densely populated uplands of Java, significant erosion is caused by the inappropriate cropping patterns of small farmers. Erosion is also caused by absentee farm owners who cultivate crops which are highly profitable, but erosion-inducing under the present crop management. A further cause of erosion is the failure to prevent illegal fuelwood collection on state-owned tree plantations.

Incentives for soil conservation

The construction of bench-terraces has been the most widely used technical approach for combatting upper watershed degradation in the area. Subsidies have therefore been provided in order to encourage such construction. These have mainly been in the form of cash wages and/or free agricultural inputs, either directly or on credit. The adoption of improved cropping patterns has also been encouraged through increased information. The programmes that have been implemented in order to reduce the erosion have had varying results. Several experiences may be drawn from these programmes, some of which are listed here.

There is a growing awareness that different approaches to encouraging soil conservation have to be implemented according to geographical area, given the variability in topographic, soil, agroecological and socio-economic conditions across these watersheds.

Another aspect of soil conservation which has not been adequately considered when designing the programmes is the considerable labour time that is required for terracing.

The experience from the programme on Java is that many farmers are far short of the labour time needed in order to construct terraces. To hire labour means additional cash expenditures, and as a consequence only relatively wealthy farmers can afford to construct the terraces required.

Some programmes have also encouraged agroforestry on the slopes. There is, however, a "waiting cost" of three or more years before harvesting can begin. Security of land tenure has in these cases been identified as a crucial factor which determines whether the farmers are willing to bear the cost of waiting.

Economic policies and investment strategies

Agricultural policies in Indonesia have largely been biased towards lowland irrigated agriculture, especially rice cultivation. It has, however, been recognized that a general re-orientation of agricultural policies is needed, especially since slower economic growth calls for a more efficient allocation of resources. It would be too costly, for example, to try to replicate in the uplands the policies pursued in other parts of Indonesia, which were aimed at bringing about rice self-sufficiency. Instead, the highly diversified soil conditions in the uplands are more suitable for mixed cropping patterns. This is particularly due to government investments and subsidy programmes for rice production which have already created rice surpluses in other parts of Indonesia and have resulted in high storage costs and subsidized exports.

Over-use of fertilizers as a result of subsidies is another environmental problem, particularly in the lowland areas. Fertilizer consumption per ha of arable land is much higher in Indonesia than in other Asian countries. The subsidies act as a disincentive to proper land management, since the farmers who apply the relatively cheap fertilizers do not adopt more environmentally sound methods to maintain soil fertility. That is, the fertilizer subsidies discourage farmers from facing the full economic costs of declining soil fertility.

The high level of subsidy for irrigation has also caused problems of over-use, which can lead to water scarcity problems. These subsidies serve as examples of the way in which active policies may result in prices which are far from reflections of the negative environmental impacts resulting from the use of these inputs.

Lack of well-functioning credit markets also create problems. Only 15% of the demand for credit by farmers is met by the formal market. This is recognized as being a major obstacle to adopting of an environmentally sound management approach for the agricultural lands.

Another point Barbier makes is that since crops like coffee, tea and cocoa play a vital role in sustainable upland development, the competitiveness of these export crops should be maintained by an exchange-rate policy that improves their terms of trade. A prerequisite that such a policy would encourage the farmers to grow these crops is that the benefits of the improved terms of trade actually reach the farmers and do not remain in the hands of the traders and other intermediaries, which have considerable market power.

Conclusion

The study emphasizes that it is necessary to understand the economic incentives that determine farmer decisions as regards choice of crops and land management techniques. It is concluded that, in the case of the Indonesian uplands, a major reason for failure of land management programmes is a lack of sufficiently strong incentives. A lesson learned from the study is that isolated soil and water programmes may fail if they are not complemented by pricing and credit policies, as well as investment in infrastructure and other appropriate agricultural development policies.

7.7.4 Tropical Deforestation in Eastern Ecuador.

Source: Southgate, D., Sierra, R., and Brown, L., 1989: *The Causes of Tropical Deforestation in Ecuador: A Statistical Analysis*. LEEC paper 89-09. International Institute for Environment and Development. London.

Introduction

This study of the causes of tropical deforestation in Ecuador differs considerably from the other studies that are presented in this chapter in order to illustrate policy failures. The present study examines a broader geographical area than the others'. It has generated several sets of data, which have allowed for a statistical analysis instead of the more "penetrating" approach utilized in the other studies. The aim of the study is to explore the relationship between land clearing, rural population pressure, local demand for agricultural commodities, infrastructure development and security of tenure.

Background

The model focuses on agricultural colonization and land clearing in eastern Ecuador. The environmental problem examined here is therefore similar to the one presented in section 7.7.1 and 7.7.2, where the tropical deforestation in the Amazon is the issue of concern.

The Model

The authors build a statistical model which consists of two regression equations, and use data from eastern Ecuador's twenty cantons. The first equation deals with agricultural colonization, while the second one deals with actual land clearing. The underlying assumption of the first equation is that settlement in tree-covered lands is stimulated by the prospect of capturing agricultural rents. In the equation the canton's agricultural labour force is the dependent variable, which is regressed upon ("explained by") the canton's urban population, the area covered with soils suitable for crop production and the prevalance of roads in the canton. The dependent variable is assumed to be an indicator of rural population pressure. The first explanatory factor in the regression equation, the canton's urban population, reflects the local demand for agricultural commodities. Strong local demand for agricultural commodities enhances rents in the agricultural sector. The third explanatory factor, the prevalance of roads, is assumed to reflect accessibility to outside markets.

The second equation of the model relates the extent of land clearing to demographic pressure and to tenurial conditions. Demographic pressure is simply expressed by the dependent variable in the first equation. The factor expressing tenurial conditions consists of an index which is constructed so as to indicate differences in formal tenure security among cantons. If the value of the index for any particular canton is greater than

1.00, then that canton's farmers are more likely than others in eastern Ecuador to hold formal tenure in their land.

The Data and the Results

The data used in the regressions were obtained from different sources. Agricultural labour and urban population figures were obtained from the 1982 Ecuador census. The data for the variable expressing the extent of soil were obtained from interpretation of soil maps. Road maps were used to calculate the exact number of kilometres of roads that exist in each canton. The second dependent variable, the extent of tropical deforestation in the area, relied on aerial photographs 1977 - 1985. As regards the security of land holding for the different cantons, this index was calculated from land adjudication records.

The equation system was estimated by ordinary least squares.[4] As regards equation one, the relationship between agricultural colonization and all three explanatory factors were shown to be positive. That is, the presence of roads and urban centers as well as the soil condition seem to attract rural settlement. The second equation, which tried to explain deforestation, showed that the variable expressing population pressure was positively related to deforestation, while the land tenure variable was negatively related to deforestation. That is, land clearing seems to be an increasing function of population pressure and land tenure insecurity.

It should be pointed out that shortcomings of the study are that the sample used is small, and there are reasons to believe that there is a high covariance between the variables "urban population" and "roads" in the canton.

Discussion of the results

All the results obtained in the regressions were consistent with the expectations ex ante. It is interesting that this study provides a further example (compare section 7.7.2) of how institutional issues, like land tenure security, are a cause for concern when dealing with environmental problems. In the case of Ecuador, the formal property law is executed by the Ecuadorian Institute for Agrarian Reform and Colonization, which requires a long period, sometimes years, to adjudicate claims for formal property rights. In view of the impact this may have on the extent of deforestation, it is preferable that the time taken up by such procedures is shortened.

---

4. The ordinary least squares (OLS) technique is one of the most frequently used estimating techniques in regression analysis. The principle is to chose parameters in the model in such a way that the sum of the squared discrepancies between the values obtained from the regression and the actual sample is minimized. See e.g. Pindyck/Rubinfeld, 1984, for a detailed description of the regression technique.

Bibliography

Abelson, P., 1979: *Cost-benefit Analysis and Environmental Problems.* Saxon House, Teakfield Ltd., Westmead, Farnborough, Hants., England.

Adelman, I. and Robinson, S., 1978: *Income Distribution Policy in Developing Countries - A Case Study of Korea.*

Ahluwalia, M.S., and Chenery, H., 1981: *Redistribution and Growth.* Chapter XI.

Ahmad, Y. (ed.), 1981a: *The Economics of Survival. The Role of Cost-benefit Analysis in Environmental Decision-making.* UNEP Studies no. 4.

Ahmad, Y.J., 1982: *Analysing the Options.* United Nations Environmental Programme Studies, 5. Pergamon Press Ltd., Headington Hill Hall, Oxford, England.

Ahmad, Y. (ed.), 1982: *Evaluating the Environment.* UNEP Studies no. 6.

Ahmad, Y.J., Dasgupta, P., and Mäler, K-G.(eds.), 1984: *Environmental Decision-Making.* Volume Two. The United Nations Environmental Programme. Hodder and Stoughton Ltd., Mill Road, Dunton Green, Sevenoaks, Kent, England.

Ahmad, Y.J., El Serafy, S., and Lutz, E. (eds.), 1989: *Environmental Accounting for Sustainable Development.* The World Bank, Washington, D.C.

Åkerman, J., 1987: *Ekonomisk hälsoriskvärdering. En genomgång av teori, metoder och empiriska resultat.* EFI Research Paper 6317. Stockholm School of Economics.

Akroyd, D., 1985: "Policy Priorities for Agricultural Development in Africa with Particular Reference to Agricultural Project Planning", in *Agricultural Administration.* Vol 19. pp. 101-113. Elsevier Appl. Science Publ. Great Britain.

Alfsen, K., Bye, T. and Lorentsen, L., 1987: *Natural Resource Accounting and Analysis.* Statistisk Sentralbyrå, Oslo - Kongsvinger.

Anderson, D., 1987: *The Economics of Afforestation - A Case Study in Africa.* The World Bank Occasional Paper Number 1/New Series. The John Hopkins University Press, Baltimore, Maryland, U.S.A.

Archibugi, F., and Nijkamp, P. (eds.), 1989: *Economy and Ecology: Towards Sustainable Development.* Kluwer Academic Publishers, Dordrecht.

D'Arge, R., Ayres, R., and Kneese, A., 1972: *Economics and the Environment: A Materials Balance Approach.* Baltimore.

Arrow, K.J., 1969: "The Organization of Economic Activity: Issues Pertinent to the Choice of Market Versus Nonmarket Allocation", in *The Analysis and Evaluation of Public Expenditure: The PPB System.* Subcommittee on Economy in Government of the Joint Economic Committee, Congress of the United States. US Government Printing Office. Washington D.C.

Arrow, K.J. and Lind R.C., 1970: "Uncertainty and the Evaluation of Public Investments Decisions", *American Economic Review.* Vol. 60, pp. 364-78.

Barbier, E., 1987: "Natural Resources Policy and Economic Framework", in Tarrant, J. et al (ed.) *Natural Resources and Environmental Management in Indonesia.* USAID. Jakarta.

Barbier, E.B., 1989: *Economics, Natural Resource Scarcity and Development - Conventional and Alternative Views.* Earthscan. London.

Barnett, H.J., and Morse, C., 1963: *Scarcity and Growth: The Economics of Natural Resource Availability.* Johns Hopkins University Press. Baltimore.

Barrett, S., 1990: "The Problem of Global Environmental Protection." *Oxford Review of Economic Policy.* Vol. 6, No. 1.

Baumol, W.J. and Oates W.E., 1975: *The Theory of Environmental Policy. Externalities, Public Outlays and the Quality of Life.* Prentice Hall. Englewood Cliffs, New Jersey.

Bergman, L., 1990: *General Equilibrium Effects of Environmental Policy: A CGE-Modeling Approach.* EFI Research Paper 6415. Stockholm School of Economics.

Berkes, F., 1985: "The Common Property Resource Problem and the Creation of Limited Property Rights". *Human Ecology* 13 (2),(1985).

Binswanger, H.P., 1989. *Brazilian Policies that Encourage Deforestation in the Amazon.* The World Bank. Environment Department Working Paper No. 16.

Birdsall, N., 1988: "Economic Approaches to Population Growth", pp. 477-542 in Chenery, H. and Srinivasan, T.N. (eds.) *Handbook of Development Economics.* Volume I. Elsevier Science Publishers. Amsterdam.

Birgegård, L-E., 1975: *The Project Selection Process in Developing Countries. A Study on the Public Investment Project Selection Process in Kenya, Zambia and Tanzania.* EFI, The Stockholm School of Economics, Stockholm.

Blaikie, P., 1985: *The Political Economy of Soil Erosion in Developing Countries*. Longman. London.

Blomström, M. and Hettne, B., 1984: *Development Theory in Transition. The Dependency Debate and Beyond: Third World Responses*. Zed Books. London.

Bohm, P., 1973: *Social Efficiency: A Concise Introduction to Welfare Economics*. The MacMillan Press Ltd. London.

Bojö, J., with the assistance of Hultkrantz, L.,1985: *Kostnadsnyttoanalys av fjällnära skogar*. Fallet Vålådalen. The Stockholm School of Economics.

Bojö, J., 1989: *Cost-Benefit Analysis of Soil and Water Conservation Projects*. A Review of 20 Empirical Studies. Paper presented to the 6th International Soil Conservation Conference, Kenya and Ethiopia, 6-18 November 1989. Stockholm School of Economics. Stockholm.

Bojö, J., 1990: *Economic Analysis of Agricultural Development Projects. A Case Study from Lesotho*. EFI Research Paper, Stockholm School of Economics. Stockholm.

Bojö, J., 1991: *The Economics of Land Degradation. Theory and Applications to Lesotho*. The Economic Research Institute. Stockholm School of Economics. Stockholm.

Boserup, E., 1981: *Population and Technology*. Basil Blackwell. Oxford.

Brealey, R., and Myers, S., 1984: *Principles of Corporate Finance*. McGraw Hill International Book Company. London.

Brookshire, D.S., d'Arge, R.C., Schultze, W.D., 1979: *Methods Development for Assessing Air Pollution Control Benefits*. Vol. II. EPA. Springfield, Va.

Brookshire, D.S., Eubanks, L.S., Randall, A., 1983: "Estimating Option Prices and Existence Values for Wildlife Resources". *Land Economics* 59 (1): 1-15.

Brown, S.P.A., 1983: "A Note on Environmental Risk and the Rate of Discount", *Journal of Environmental Economics and Management*. Vol. 10, 282-286.

Burmeister, E., and Dobell, A.R., 1970: *Mathematical Theories of Economic Growth*. Collier-MacMillan, New York.

Carlsson, A., 1988: *Estimate of the Costs of Emission Control in the Swedish Energy Sector*. Stockholm School of Economics. Research Report No. 91-7258-273-1. Stockholm. Sweden.

Chambers, R., 1988: *Sustainable Livelihoods, Environment and Development: Putting Poor Rural People First.* Institute of Development Studies. University of Sussex. Mimeo.

Clark, B.D., Chapman, K., Bisset, R. and Wathern, P., 1978: *Environmental Impact Assessment in the USA: A Critical Review.* Department of the Environment, 2 Marsham St. London SW1P 3 EB. 74 pp.

Clawson, M. and Knetsch, J.L., 1966: *Economics of Outdoor Recreation.* The Johns Hopkins Press. Baltimore.

Coase, R. H., 1960: "The Problem of Social Cost." *Journal of Law and Economics.* Vol. 3. No. 1, 1-44.

Coddington, A., Opschoor, H. and Pearce D., 1972:, "Some Limitations of Benefit-cost Analysis in Respect of Programmes with Environmental Consequenses", in *Problems of Environmental Economics*. OECD. Paris.

Cooper, C., 1981: *Economic Evaluation and the Environment.* Hodder and Stoughton. London.

Daly, H. (ed.), 1980: *Economics, Ecology, Ethics.* W.H. Freeman and Company, New York.

Dasgupta, P., Marglin, S. and Sen, A., 1972: *Guidelines for Project Evaluation.* UNIDO. United Nations, New York.

Dasgupta, P. and Heal, G., 1979: *Economic Theory and Exhaustible Resources.* Cambridge University Press. Cambridge.

Dasgupta, P., Hammond, P. and Maskin, E., 1980: "On Imperfect Information and Optimal Pollution Control", *Review of Economic Studies.* Vol 47.

Dasgupta, P., 1982: *The Control of Resources.* Basil Blackwell. Oxford.

Dasgupta, P., 1990: "The Environment as a Commodity." *Oxford Review of Economic Policy.* Vol. 6, No. 1.

Dasgupta, P., and Mäler, K.-G., 1991: *The Environment and Emerging Development Issues.* Proceedings of the World Bank Annual Conference on Development Economics. The World Bank.

Dervis, K., de Melo, J. and Robinson, S., 1982: *General Equilibrium Models for Development Policy.* World Bank Research Publication. Washington D.C.

Desvousges, W.H., Smith, V.K. and McGivney, M.P., 1983: *A Comparison of Alternative Approaches for Estimating Recreation and Related Benefits of Water Quality Improvements*. EPA. Office of Policy Analysis. Washington D.C.

Dixon, J.A. and Hufschmidt, M.M., (eds.), 1986: *Economic Valuation Techniques for the Environment. A Case Study Workbook.* Johns Hopkins. Baltimore.

Dixon, J.A., with the assistance of Bojö, J., 1988: *Economic Analysis and the Environment.* Report to the African Development Bank.

Dixon, J.A., Carpenter, L.A., Fallon, L.A., Sherman, P.B. and Manopimoke, S., 1988: *Economic Analysis of the Environmental Impacts of Development Projects.* Earthscan. London.

Dorfman, R., 1962: "Decision Rules under Uncertainty", in Layard, R., (ed.), 1972: *Cost-Benefit Analysis.* Penguin. Hammondsworth, England.

DSE, Deutsche Stiftung fur Internationale Entwicklung, 1985: *Environmental Impact Assessment (EIA) for Development.* In cooperation with UNEP.

Elzinga, A., 1981: *Evaluating the Evaluation Game: On the Methodology of Project Evaluation, with Special Reference to Development Cooperation.* SAREC Report R1:1981. Stockholm.

FAO, 1982: *Environmental Impact of Forestry. Guidelines for its Assessment in Developing Countries.* FAO Conservation Guide 7. Rome.

Feenberg, D., Mills, E.S., 1980: *Measuring the Benefits of Water Pollution Abatement.* Studies in Urban Economics. Academic Press, Inc., New York, U.S.A.

Feeny, D., et al., 1990: "The Tradegy of the Commons: Twenty-Two Years Later." *Human Ecology.* Vol 18, No. 1.

Finney, C.E., Western, S., 1986: "An Economic Analysis of Environmental Protection and Management: An example from the Philippines". *The Environmentalist.* Vol 6. No 1.

Fisher, A.C., 1973: "Environmental Externalities and the Arrow-Lind Public Investment Theorem", in *American Economic Review.*

Fleming, W.M., 1983: *Phewa Tal Catchment Management Programme: Benefits and Costs of Forestry and Soil Conservation in Nepal*, in: Hamilton, L.S. (ed.), Forest and Watershed Development and Conservation in Asia and the Pacific, Westview Press, Boulder, CO.

Fones-Sundell, M., 1987: *Role of Price Policy in Stimulating Agricultural Production in Africa.* Issue Paper no. 2. Swedish University of Agricultural Sciences. International Rural Development Centre. Uppsala.

Försund, F., 1985: "Input-Output Models, National Economic Models, and the Environment", in Kneese A. and Sweeney, J. (eds.) *Handbook of Natural Resource and Energy Economics.* Vol. I, North Holland. Amsterdam.

Freeman, M., 1979: *The Benefits of Environmental Improvement.* Resources for the Future. Published by Johns Hopkins University Press. Baltimore and London.

Friedman, L.S., 1985: *Microeconomic Policy Analysis.* McGraw-Hill, U.S.A.

Fudenberg, D., and Maskin, E., 1986: The Folk Theorem in Repeated Games with Discounting and Incomplete Information." *Econometrica* 54: 533-554.

Georgescu-Roegen, N., 1971: *The Entropy Law and the Economic Process.* Harvard University Press. Cambridge, Mass.

Gittinger, J.P., 1982: *Economic Analysis of Agricultural Projects.* 2nd ed. Johns Hopkins University Press. Baltimore & London.

Goodland, R. and Ledec, G., 1987: "Neoclassical Economics and Principles of Sustainable Development", *Ecological Modelling.* Vol. 38. Nos. 1/2, September. Elsevier Science Publishers.

Grainger, A., 1982: *Desertification. How People Make Deserts, How People Can Stop and Why They Don't.* An Earthscan Paperback published by the International Institute for Environment and Development. London & Washington D.C.

Graaff, J. de., 1967: *Theoretical Welfare Economics.* Cambridge University Press.

Hannesson, R., 1975: "Fishery dynamics: a North Atlantic Cod Fishery". *Canadian Journal of Economics.* No.2. Canada.

Hardin, G. and Baden, J., 1977: *Managing the Commons.* Freeman & Co. San Francisco. (Contains the original: Hardin, G., 1968: "The Tragedy of the Commons" in Science, Vol. 162, 13 December).

Harrison, P., 1987: *The Greening of Africa.* International Institute for Environment and Development and Earthscan. London.

Hazilla, M., and Kopp, R.J., 1989: *The Social Cost of Environmental Quality Regulations: A General Equilibrium Analysis*. Discussion Paper QE89-11. Resources for the Future. Washington, D.C.

Helmers, F.L.C.H., 1979: *Project Planning and Income Distribution*. Martinus Nijhoff Publishing. Boston, The Hague and London.

Hoekstra, D., 1985: *Choosing the Discount Rate for Analyzing Agroforestry Systems/Technologies from a Private Point of View*. ICRAF, Reprint No. 20. Nairobi.

Hoekstra, D. and van Gelder, A., 1985: *Annotated Bibliography of Economic Analysis of Agroforestry Systems/Technologies*. ICRAF. Nairobi.

Hudson, N., 1986: *Soil Conservation*. Batsford. London.

Hufschmidt, M.M., Hyman, E.L., 1982: *Economic Approaches to Natural Resource and Environmental Quality Analysis*. Tycooly Ltd., Dublin, Ireland.

Hufschmidt, M.M., James, D.E., Meister, A.D., Bower, B.T. and Dixon, J.A., 1983: *Environment, Natural Systems and Development. An Economic Evaluation Guide*. Johns Hopkins. Baltimore and London.

Hydén, G., 1983: *No Shortcuts to Progress*. African Development Management in Perspective. Heinemann. London.

IIED, 1988: *Country Environmental Profiles Natural Resource Assessments and other Report on the State of the Environment. Environmental Planning and Management Project Supported by USAID's Office of Forestry*, Environment and Natural Resources. Mimeo.

Independent Commission on Disarmament and Security Issues under the Chairmanship of Olof Palme, 1982: *Common Security. A Programme for Disarmament*. Pan, World Affairs. London.

Irvin, G., 1978: *Modern Cost-Benefit Methods. An Introduction to Financial, Economic and Social Appraisal of Development Projects*. The Macmillan Press Ltd. London and Basingstoke.

IUCN, 1980: *World Conservation Strategy*. Gland. Switzerland.

James, D., 1985: "Environmental Economics, Industrial Process Models, and Regional-Residuals Management Models", in Kneese A. and Sweeney, J., (eds.), *Handbook of Natural Resource and Energy Economics*. Vol. I, North Holland.

Johansson, P-O., 1987: *The Economic Theory and Measurement of Environmental Benefits*. Cambridge University Press.

Kim, S-H. and Dixon, J.A., 1984: "Economic Evaluation of Environmental Quality Aspects of Upland Agricultural Projects in Korea", in Dixon J.A. and Hufschmidt, M.M., (eds.), 1986, *Economic Valuation Techniques for the Environment*. A Case Study Workbook. Johns Hopkins. Baltimore.

King, B.B., 1981: *What is a SAM? A Layman's Guide to Social Accounting Matrices*. World Bank Staff Working Paper No. 463. Washington D.C.

Kingdom of Lesotho. October, 1988: *National Environmental Action Plan*. Maseru, Lesotho.

Kneese, A.V., and Bower, B.T., 1968: *Managing Water Quality: Economics, Technology, Institutions*. Johns Hopkins, Baltimore.

Kneese, A.V., and Mäler, K-G., 1973: "Bribes and Charges in Pollution Control: An Aspect of the Coase Controversy", *Natural Resources Journal*. 1973 Symposium Issue.

Krutilla, J.V., 1967: "Conservation Reconsidered", *American Economic Review*. Vol. LVII.

Landreth, H. and Colander, D.C., 1989: *History of Economic Theory. Second Edition*. Houghton Mifflin Co. Boston.

Layard, P.R.G. and Walters, A.A., 1976: "The Date of Discounting in Cost-Benefit Studies", pp. 263-266 in *Journal of Transport Economics and Policy*. Volume X. London School of Economics and Political Science. London.

Lichfield, N., Kettle, P., and Whitbread, M., 1975: *Evaluation in the Planning Process*. Pergamon Press. Oxford.

Lind, R.C., 1982: *Discounting for Time and Risk in Energy Policy*. RFF. Johns Hopkins University Press. Baltimore and London.

Lipton, M., 1981: "Why Poor People Stay Poor", in Hariss (ed.), 1982, *Rural Development. Theories of Peasant Economy and Agrarian Change*. Hutchinson University Library. London.

Little, I.M.D. and Mirrlees, J.A., 1974: *Project Appraisal and Planning for Developing Countries*. Heinemann. London.

Lundahl, M., 1979: *Peasants and Poverty: A Study of Haiti*. Croom Helm. London.

Mahar, D., 1989. *Government Policies and Deforestation in Brazil's Amazon Region.* The World Bank. Washington, D.C.

Mäler, K.-G., 1971: "A Method of Estimating Social Benefits from Pollution Control. *The Swedish Journal of Economics.* Vol 73.

Mäler, K.-G., 1974: *Environmental Economics. A Theoretical Inquiry.* Johns Hopkins University Press. Baltimore and London.

Mäler, K.-G. and Wyzga, R.E., 1976: *Economic Measurement of Environmental Damage.* OECD. Paris.

Mäler, K.-G., 1977: "A Note on the Use of Property Values in Estimating Marginal Willingness to Pay for Environmental Quality", *Journal of Environmental Economics and Management.* No. 4.

Mäler, K.-G., Bergman, L., Bojö, J. and Haig, C., 1980: "Nationalekonomisk utvärdering av energisparprogrammet. Slutrapport", in *Energihushållning och Samhällsekonomi* Expertbilaga 1 till SOU 1980:43. Bostadsdepartementet.

Mäler, K.-G., 1985: "Welfare Economics and the Environment", in Kneese, A.V. and Sweeney, J.L. (eds.), *Handbook of Natural Resources and Energy Economics.* Vol. I. Elsevier Science Publishers. Amsterdam.

Mäler, K.-G., 1989: "The Acid Rain Game", in: Folmer, H., and van Ierland, E., (eds.) 1989: *Valuation Methods and Policy Making in Environmental Economics.* Elsevier. Amsterdam.

Mäler, K.-G., 1990a: *National Income Accounts.* Research Paper, Stockholm School of Economics. Stockholm. Sweden.

Mäler, K.-G., 1990b: *Sustainable Development.* Research Paper, Stockholm School of Economics. Stockholm. Sweden.

Mäler, K.-G., 1990c: "International Environmental Problems." *Oxford Review of Economic Policy.* Vol. 6, No. 1.

Mäler, K.-G., and Olsson, C., 1990d: "Cost Efficiency of Sulphur Abatement." *European Journal of Agricultural Economics.*

Mäler, K.-G., 1991: "National Accounts and Environmental Resources." *Environmental and Resource Economics.* Vol. 1., No. 1. Kluwer Academic Publishers. Dordrecht. The Netherlands.

Markandya, A., and Pearce, D., 1988. *Environmental Considerations and the Choice of the Discount Rate in Developing Countries.* The World Band, Policy Planning and Research Staff, Environment Department Working Paper No. 3.

Matsaba, T.G.K., 1985: *A Case for Fuelwood Production in the Kingdom of Lesotho.* Department of Forestry and Wood Science. University College of North Wales. Bangor, Gwynedd. United Kingdom.

Mattsson, B., 1984: *Värderingar av fördelar och kostnader i svenska samhällsekonomiska kalkyler 1970-1983.* Forskningsrapport 1984:2. Högskolan i Karlstad.

McCay, B.M., and Acheson, J.M., (eds), 1987: *The Question of the Commons. The Culture and Ecology of Communal Resources.* The University of Arizona Press. Tucson.

Meister, A.D., 1989. *Overview of Environmental Regulation & Use of Economic Instruments for Environmental Planning and Management.* Workshop on designing a regional training programme for integration of environmental considerations in development planning. Kuwait, 21-25 October, 1989. Massey University Palmerston North. New Zealand.

Mishan, E.J., 1982. *Cost-benefit Analysis.* Third ed. Allen & Unwin. London.

Mitchell, R.C., and Carson, R.T., 1989: *Using Surveys to Value Public Goods. The Contingent Valuation Method.* Resources for the Future. Washington, D.C.

Newcombe, K., 1984: *An Economic Justification for Rural Afforestation: The Case of Ethiopia.* The World Bank Energy Department Paper No. 16. (August 1984).

OECD, 1981: "Atmospheric Corrosion of Materials", in: *The Costs and Benefits of Sulphur Oxide Control.* Paris.

Overseas Development Administration. Evaluation Report EV 392., 1986: *Initial Evaluation of the Social and Environmental Impact of the Victorian Dam Project.* Stag Place, London, England.

Pearce, D., 1976: "The Limits of Cost-Benefit Analysis as a Guide to Environmental Policy", in *Kyklos.* Vol. 29, 97-112.

Pearce, D., 1987: *Natural Resource Management in West Sudan.* A Report by the Government of Sudan and the World Bank. Mimeo.

Pearce, D., 1988: "The Sustainable Use of Natural Resources in Developing Countries" in Turner, R.K. (ed.), *Sustainable Environmental Management. Principles and Practice.* Belhaven Press. London.

Pearce, D. and Nash, C.A., 1981: *The Social Appraisal of Projects. A Text in CBA.* Macmillan.

Peskin, H.M., Seskin, E.P., 1975. *Cost Benefit Analysis and Water Pollution policy.* The Urban Institute. Washington, D.C., U.S.A.

Pigou, A.C., 1920: *The Economics of Welfare.* Macmillan. London.

Price, C., 1973: "To the Future: with Indifference or Concern? - The Social Discount Rate and its Impliatons in Land Use", *Journal of Agricultural Economics.* Vol. XXIV, No. 2. pp. 393-398.

Prince, R., 1985: "A Note on Environmental Risk and the Rate of Discount: Comment", *Journal of Environmental Economics and Management.* Vol. 12, 179-180.

Proposition 1987/88: 100: Utrikesdepartementet. Littera C. *Internationellt utvecklingssamarbete.* Stockholm.

Pyatt, G., and Round, J.I., 1985: *Social Accounting Matrices - A Basis for Planning.* The World Bank. Washington, D.C.

Raiffa, H., 1968. *Decision Analysis.* Random House. New York.

Redclift, M., 1987: *Sustainable Development: Issues and Options.* Methuen. London.

Reiling, S.D. and Anderson, M.W., 1980: *The Relevance of Option Value in Benefit-Cost Analysis. Life Sciences and Agriculture Experiment Station.* University of Maine at Orono. Technical Bulletin 101.

Repetto, R., 1987: "Economic Incentives for Sustainable Production" *The Annals of Regional Science.* Vol XXI, No. 3. pp. 44-59.

Repetto, R, and Gillis, M., (eds.), 1988. *Public Policies and the Misuse of Forest Resources.* Cambridge University Press.

Repetto, R., Magrath, W., Wells, M., Beer, C., and Rossini, F., 1989: *Wasting Assets, Natural Resources in the National Income Accounts.* World Resources Institute. Washington D.C.

Rosen, S., and Thaler, R., 1976: "The Value of Saving a Life: Evidence from the Labor Market", in Terleckyj, N.E. (ed.): *Household Production and Consumption.* Colombia University Press. New York.

Rosenfield, P.L., Bower, B.T., 1978: *Management Strategies for Reducing Adverse Health Impacts of Water Resources Development Projects.* Discussion Paper D-3. Resources for the Future. Washington, D.C.

Samuelson, P.A., 1950: "Evaluation of Real National Income." *O.E.P.*, Vol. 2, No. 1.

Schumacher, E.F., 1973: *Small is Beautiful. A Study of Economics as if People Mattered.* Sphere Books Ltd. London.

SGN, Stockholm Group for Studies on Natural Resources Management, 1988: *Perspectives of Sustainable Development. Some Critical Issues Related to the Brundtland Report.* Stockholm Studies in Natural Resource Management, No. 1.

Shecter, M., Golan, L., and Kim, M., 1987: "Valuation of Morbidity Reduction due to Pollution Abatement: Direct vs. Indirect Measurement." Paper Presented at the Conference on *"Environmental Policy in a Market Economy."* Wageningen. The Netherlands.

SIDA, 1987: *SIDA's Guidelines for Project Support.* Stockholm.

Simon, J. 1981: *The Ultimate Resource.* Martin Robertson. Oxford.

Smith, K.V., 1986: "A Conceptual Overview of the Foundations of Benefit-Cost Analysis", in Bentkover, J.D., Covello, V.T. and Mumpower, J., (eds.) *Benefits Assessment. The State of the Art.* D. Reidel Publishing Co. Dorderecht, The Netherlands.

Smith, K., Desvousges, W.H., 1986: *Measuring Water Quality Benefits.* Kluwer Academic Publ. Group, Dordrecht. The Netherlands.

Söderbaum, P., 1986: "Economics, Ethics and Environmental Problems", *Journal of Interdisciplinary Economics.* A.B. Academic Publishers.

Somerton, D.A., June, J., 1984: "A Cost-Benefit Method for Determining Optimum Closed Fishing Areas to Reduce the Trawl Catch of Prohibited Species". *Canadian Journal of Fisheries & Aquatic Sciences* v 41 (1).

Southgate, D., 1988: *The Economics of Land Degradation in The Third World.* Environment Department Working Paper No. 2. World Bank. Washington D.C.

Southgate, D. and Pearce, D., 1988: *Agricultural Colonization and Environmental Degradation in Frontier Developing Economies.* Environment Department Working Paper No. 9. World Bank. Washington D.C.

Southgate, D., Sierra, R., and Brown, L., 1989: *The Causes of Tropical Deforestation in Ecuador: A Statistical Analysis.* LEEC paper 89-09. International Institute for Environment and Development. London.

Spence, A.M., 1974: "Blue Whales and Applied Control Theory." in Ahmad, Y.J., Dasgupta, P., Mäler, K-G.(eds.), 1984. *Environmental Decision-Making.* Volume II. The United Nations Environmental Programme. Hodder and Stoughton Ltd., Mill Road, Dunton Green, Sevenoaks, Kent, England.

SOU 1987:28: *Bistånd för bättre miljö.* Förslag om ett miljömål i utvecklingsbiståndet. Stockholm.

Spofford, W.O., Russel, C.S. and Kelleyl, R.A., 1976: *Environmental Quality Management.* Resources for the Future. Washington D.C.

Squire, L. and van der Tak, H.G., 1975: *Economic Analysis of Projects.* World Bank and Johns Hopkins University Press. Baltimore and London.

Stevens, J.B., 1966: "Recreation Benefits from Water Pollution Control." *Water Resources Research.* Vol.2.

Stocking, M., 1986: *The Cost of Soil Erosion in Zimbabwe in Terms of the Loss of Three Major Nutrients.* Consultants' Working Paper No. 3. Soil Conservation Programme, Land and Water Development Division, FAO. December.

Stone, R., 1985. *The Accounts of Society.* Nobel Prize Foundation, Stockholm.

Ståhl, I., Bergman, L., and Mäler, K-G., 1988: *An Experimental Game on Marketable Emission Permits for Hydro-Carbons in the Gothenburg Area.* Research Paper 6359. Stockholm School of Economics.

Swaney, J.A., 1987: "Elements of a Neoinstitutional Environmental Economics." *Journal of Economic Issues.* Vol XXI, No 4.

They, J., 1989: "Environmental Accounting in Development Policy: The French Experience", in: Ahmad, Y.J., El Serafy, S., and Lutz, E. (eds.), 1989: *Environmental Accounting for Sustainable Development.* The World Bank.

Thomas, J.F., Bennet, D., 1980: "Planning of Water and Related Land Resources in the Murray River Basin" in Hufschmidt, M.M., Hyman, E.L., 1982: *Economic Approaches to Natural Resource and Envrionmental Quality Analysis*. Tycooly. Dublin. Ireland.

Tietenberg, T., 1984: *The Emmisions Trading Program in Principle and Practice: Regulatory Reform in Air Pollution Control Policy.* Resources for the Future. Washington, D.C.

Tietenberg, T., 1988: *Environmental and Natural Resource Economics.* Scott, Foresman and Company, Boston.

Turner, R.K, (ed.), 1988: *Sustainable Environmental Management.* Principles and Practice. Belhaven Press. London.

Uno, K., 1989: "Economic Growth and Environmental Change in Japan: Net National Welfare and Beyond" in Archibugi, F. and Nijkamp, P. (eds), 1989: *Economy and Ecology: Towards Sustainable Development.* Kluwer Academic Publishers, London.

USAID, 1987: *The Environment.* Special Report. Office of Publications, USAID. Washington D.C. 205 23 USA.

USAID, 1988: *Environment and Natural Resources.* AID Policy Paper. Bureau for Program and Policy Coordination. Washington D.C. 205 23 USA.

Veloz, A., Southgate, D., Hitzhusen, F. and Macgregor, R., 1985: "The Economics of Erosion Control in a Subtropical Watershed: A Dominican Case", in *Land Economics.* Volume 61, No. 2.

Warford, J., 1987: "Natural Resources and Economic Policy in Developing Countries" *The Annals of Regional Science.* Vol XXI, No. 3. pp. 3-17.

WCED, World Commission for Environment and Development, 1987: *Our Common Future.* Oxford University Press. Oxford and New York.

Weisbrod, B.A., 1964: "Collective-consumption Services of Individual-consumption Goods, *Quarterly Journal of Economics.* Vol. LXXVIII, No. 3.

Weiss, D., 1978: *Economic Evaluation of Projects. A Critical Comparison of a New World Bank Methodology with the UNIDO and the Revised OECD Approach.* German Development Institute. Berlin.

Weitzman, M.L., 1974: "Prices vs. Quantities", *Review of Economic Studies.* Vol. 41.

Williams, A., 1973: "Cost-Benefit Analysis: Bastard Science? And/Or Insidious Poison in the Body Politic?", in Wolfe, J.N. (ed.) *Cost-Benefit and Cost Effectiveness*. Allen & Unwin. Oxford.

World Bank, 1981: *Accelerated Development in Sub-Saharan Africa*. The World Bank. Washington D.C.

World Bank, 1984: *World Development Report 1984*. Oxford University Press. New York.

World Bank, 1988: *World Development Report 1988*. Oxford University Press.

World Bank, 1989: *Striking a Balance. The Environmental Challenge of Development*. Washington D.C.

Index

Economy & Environment

1. F. Archibugi and P. Nijkamp (eds.): *Economy and Ecology: Towards Sustainable Development.* 1989 ISBN 0-7923-0477-2
2. J. Bojö, K.-G. Mäler and L. Unemo: *Environment and Development: An Economic Approach.* 1990 ISBN 0-7923-0802-6
3. J. B. Opschoor and D. W. Pearce (eds.): *Persistent Pollutants: Economics and Policy.* 1991 ISBN 0-7923-1168-X
4. D.J. Kraan and R. J. in 't Veld (eds.): *Environmental Protection: Public or Private Choice.* 1991 ISBN 0-7923-1333-X
5. J.J. Krabbe and W.J.M. Heijman (eds.): *National Income and Nature: Externalities, Growth and Steady State.* 1992 ISBN 0-7923-1529-4
6. J. Bojö, K.-G. Mäler and L. Unemo: *Environment and Development: An Economic Approach* (revised edition). 1992 ISBN 0-7923-1878-1

KLUWER ACADEMIC PUBLISHERS – DORDRECHT / BOSTON / LONDON

MIX
Papier aus verantwortungsvollen Quellen
Paper from responsible sources
FSC® C105338
FSC
www.fsc.org

If you have any concerns about our products,
you can contact us on
ProductSafety@springernature.com

In case Publisher is established outside the EU,
the EU authorized representative is:
Springer Nature Customer Service Center GmbH
Europaplatz 3, 69115 Heidelberg, Germany

Printed by Libri Plureos GmbH
in Hamburg, Germany